THE
GREAT
PROGRESSION

★ ★ ★

THE
GREAT
PROGRESSION

HOW HISPANICS
WILL LEAD AMERICA
TO A NEW ERA
OF PROSPERITY

GERALDO
RIVERA

A CELEBRA BOOK

Celebra
Published by New American Library, a division of
Penguin Group (USA) Inc., 375 Hudson Street,
New York, New York 10014, USA
Penguin Group (Canada), 90 Eglinton Avenue East, Suite 700, Toronto,
Ontario M4P 2Y3, Canada (a division of Pearson Penguin Canada Inc.)
Penguin Books Ltd., 80 Strand, London WC2R 0RL, England
Penguin Ireland, 25 St. Stephen's Green, Dublin 2,
Ireland (a division of Penguin Books Ltd.)
Penguin Group (Australia), 250 Camberwell Road, Camberwell, Victoria 3124,
Australia (a division of Pearson Australia Group Pty. Ltd.)
Penguin Books India Pvt. Ltd., 11 Community Centre, Panchsheel Park,
New Delhi - 110 017, India
Penguin Group (NZ), 67 Apollo Drive, Rosedale, North Shore 0632,
New Zealand (a division of Pearson New Zealand Ltd.)
Penguin Books (South Africa) (Pty.) Ltd., 24 Sturdee Avenue,
Rosebank, Johannesburg 2196, South Africa

Penguin Books Ltd., Registered Offices:
80 Strand, London WC2R 0RL, England

First published by Celebra,
a division of Penguin Group (USA) Inc.

First Printing, September 2009
10 9 8 7 6 5 4 3 2 1

LIBRARY OF CONGRESS CATALOGING-IN-PUBLICATION DATA:

Rivera, Geraldo.
  The great progression: how Hispanics will lead America to a new era of prosperity/Geraldo Rivera.
    p.   cm.—(A Celebra book)
  ISBN 978-0-451-22881-9
  1. Hispanic Americans—Economic conditions.   2. Hispanic Americans—Politics and government.   3. United
States—Economic conditions—2001–   4. United States—Politics and government—2001–   I. Title.
  E184.S75R58   2009
  973'.0468—dc22   2009016062

Set in Bembo
Designed by Ginger Legato

Printed in the United States of America

To Erica and the children, my loves

ACKNOWLEDGMENTS

To Dr. Ramón Emeterio Betances and General Juan Rius Rivera, for uncommon valor 141 years ago that helped forge a distinct Puerto Rico identity. To the Young Lords who ignited a young man's passion. To Representatives Luis Gutierrez and Silvestre Reyes, who won't let our consciences rest until there is sensible justice for migrants. For U.S. Army Specialist Israel Candelaria Mejias, twenty-eight, of San Lorenzo, Puerto Rico, at press time the last Boricua hero down in Iraq, killed by an IED. For Governor Luis Fortuño, who is reminding us of our civic duty and personal responsibility. To Judge Sonia to mayor, for being way good enough for the U.S. Supreme Court. And to President Barack Obama, the first brown president and a mutt like me.

CONTENTS

THE
GREAT
PROGRESSION

★ ★ ★

★ ★ ★

PROLOGUE

La Alfombra Roja (The Red Carpet)
"I was actually in the studio and I'm looking up watching TV and the tears come into my eyes and you could just feel this amazing energy—it was palpable. Something was happening; you could feel something positive. I get goose pimples thinking about it now."

—Jennifer Lopez to me,
Latino Inaugural Gala,
Union Station, Washington, D.C. (January 2009)

aving evolved from urban to elegant and from street to salon, the woman still fabulously known as J. Lo surfed the wave of camera flashes and reporter questions as she and husband Marc Anthony glided toward my camera position at the end of the red carpet. Washington's historic Union Station was made over into a ballroom for the occasion and packed shoulder-to-shoulder for the Latino Inaugural Gala celebrating Barack Obama's sweeping election to the presidency.

Despite my high-profile forty-year career in the television news business, this was only my second inauguration, and this gala had a much different vibe from the January 2005 events celebrating George W. Bush's second term. Then, with Iraq going to hell in a handbasket, I hosted the Red, White and Blue Inaugural Ball for wounded veterans from Walter Reed Army Medical Center and elsewhere. Roadside and suicide bombings were escalating, casualties were mounting and there was no end in sight to the war.

Crammed with brass including Donald Rumsfeld, the defense secretary, all the Joint Chiefs and assorted general officers, that event had a somber tone of honoring our GIs and the need to "stay the course." I told the gathered service members that they were American society's new "rock stars," and thanked them for everything they and their families were doing for the country. Everyone applauded, but the mood was grim and gritty and overshadowed by the certain knowledge that there was a lot more sacrifice ahead.

This January 2009 Latino gathering celebrating President Obama's victory could not have been more different. It was joyous, optimistic and self-congratulatory, buoyed by the realization that a Latino rising had made a difference in picking the president—maybe *the* difference. Viewed in retrospect, although not an official inaugural ball, which it should have been, the gala was nevertheless a seminal event for the Latino community. It was a Hispanic version of Truman Capote's 1966 Black and White costume ball at the Plaza Hotel, a defining social moment, in this case heralding an entire community's coming-of-age.

Everyone hip and Hispanic was there. Aside from Jennifer "Jenny from the Block" Lopez, there was her rival, pop queen Shakira of "My Hips Don't Lie" fame, Colombia's most famous ever entertainer. Shakira's bold lyric, "Makes a man want to speak Spanish!" aptly captures her smoldering, sexy, charismatic appeal.

In a nod toward bipartisanship, Puerto Rico's new governor Luis Fortuño, a John McCain supporter, joined one of the nation's highest-ranking Hispanic officials in the brand-new Obama era, former Colorado senator Ken Salazar, President Obama's new Secretary of the Interior, not to mention most of the Congressional Hispanic Caucus; the major Hispanic advocacy organizations, like the National Council of La Raza (NCLR) and the League of United Latin American Citizens (LULAC); along with half of Hollywood's Hispanics, all black-tied or begowned.

Even *American Idol*'s tiny teen David Archuleta showed up to sing the national anthem, telling me how much he regretted not being able to vote for Obama, turning eighteen only after election day. I made a fool of myself calling him "Archie" on live television, only to be corrected by a red-faced public relations guy, which forced me to say, "I knew his name is David; I'm cool." That got a big laugh from anchor Shep Smith back in the FOX studio. David rolled his eyes.

Sporting stiletto heels, her hair piled high, her face literally sparkled, and her mood sparkling, J. Lo wore an electric blue strapless gown, and gorgeously towered over Marc Anthony, her diminutive pop-star husband, father of their ten-month-old twins. Defying rumors of marital strife, overcoming her normal reticence to speak on substantive issues and brushing aside criticism of her failure to endorse Obama during the campaign, the thirty-nine-year-old superstar was ebullient when I asked her about the historic nature of the Obama victory and, more specifically, its relevance to the Latino community.

"There's something great going to happen, like anything is possible. It restored our hope, gave the nation a new future to look to. It was just amazing." J. Lo spoke enthusiastically and sincerely.

And why the huge Hispanic voter turnout for Obama? I asked. But only after first earning major husband brownie points by introducing her to my own gorgeous wife, Erica. I knew that the audience wanted to hear from this extraordinary woman who captures the essence of the Nuyorican spirit better than Maria in *West Side Story*.

"I honestly believe," J. Lo continued, totally focused despite a thousand distractions, "that for the first time I really felt like he [Obama] gave the Latino community a lot of importance that we related to and could share. We have shared experiences in being minorities in this country. And I really felt that he understood what it was to be different. And I think Latinos showed up to vote because they thought, 'Well, somebody's going to be thinking about us.' And I think that was a big part of the Latino community support for Obama."

"He does look kind of Puerto Rican," I added glibly, not sure about the appropriateness of the remark. And I don't want to give short shrift to Jennifer's husband, a Latino Sinatra for many Hispanic women. He later took the stage and got that big house swinging with three hot salsa numbers that fueled the celebratory mood.

Affecting a modern zoot-suit-hipster image, Marc also has a perhaps surprising ability to speak with intelligence and passion. "It's so amazing how addictive the word *possibility* is, right?" he gushed during the gala. "It's almost like you can't get enough of it. You wake up different; you go to sleep different. I think that it was even the possibility of putting someone in the White House who knew what it was to be considered different in the U.S. You understand what I'm saying? That's about as close as any candidate has ever been to representing us."

So as the nation's first president of color assumed office, he did so with the ringing endorsement of America's most prominent and influential Hispanic couple, the Bronx, New York–born, world's most famous Puerto Rican actress, designer, producer and singer and her not-to-be-underestimated Puerto Rican–born husband, who, aside from making some great hit songs like "I Need to Know," was terrifically sleazy in *Man on Fire*, that Denzel Washington little-girl-kidnapped-in-Mexico movie. And while they may not qualify as Beltway pundits, their mutual expressions of joy and hope at the election of Obama was shared by virtually everyone in that crowded, cavernous hall, including the few Republicans.

Luis Fortuño, the freshly elected Puerto Rican governor who was previously the island's representative in Washington, the elected Resident Commissioner, identifies himself as a Reagan Republican. He took the stage at one point to cheer on the notion that the old definitions of individual Latino nationalities were obsolete. "We are no longer just Puerto Ricans or Mexicans or Dominicans; we are all Latinos!"

It was a kind of "We Are the Latino World" moment that was not lost on an audience sensing a hinge in history, the emergence of an important new constituency that was beginning to feel and flex its potential political muscle.

"There's so much talk about Barack Obama being the first African-American president. I think he is the first Latino president," deadpanned comedian George Lopez to me at the inaugural gala. Suckered in, I waited for him to continue with some sage explanation. Instead, George cracked, "Yeah, because he's going to live in a house he doesn't own. And he's going to spend money that's not his, and his mother-in-law's going to be living with 'em and watching the two kids!"

As I burst out laughing on live television, George continued, "I think nothing can speak louder than a Latino. I'm looking for some blue awning on the White House and the pillars to be painted blue." What about a low-rider in that sweeping driveway? I asked. "There'll be a car on blocks out there that'll take eight years to fix," he cracked. Again, a laugh out loud from me live on FOX News.

But then even the mischievous George Lopez, whose show is a hit in syndication on the CW and Nick at Nite, got serious. "I have been a huge supporter of the Latino movement, as you have over the last thirty-plus years. This is the time that everything has pulled together. I was at the Lincoln Memorial today with everybody there and there's a sense of finally having a purpose. It's just like Tiger Woods made golf cool. Barack Obama's made politics very cool."

Fresh off hosting *Saturday Night Live* the weekend before, Rosario Dawson, the lovely actress who started on *Sesame Street* and starred in movies like *Rent* and *Sin City*, put it this way:

"I think what was so amazing when we were doing all the voter registration over the past four years, you know, as of March 2003 Latinos became the largest minority in the country. And we knew that was going to say something, that we were going to start seeing it in the actual numbers in voting. But when the early polls were coming in, the Latinos were being discounted. It was the first time a lot of them were going to be voting. They were using cell phones (invisible to pollsters). It was a lot of the young community that was coming out. They weren't getting polled. People weren't really looking at it. And I think that's why there's surprise at the numbers that came out; that's what's making everyone sort of step back and go, Wow! That's what we're all here to celebrate right now."

Importantly, Rosario noted how even the more affluent and settled Hispanics who in 2004 had increasingly aligned themselves with President Bush had this time around turned against the Republican Party, adding that the turnout also "demystified the idea that Latinos vote as a monolithic voting bloc. They don't. They vote according to the issues and clearly Obama spoke to their issues."

Another old friend, perky, sexy and effervescent Rosie Perez, the Academy Award–nominated actress whose most recent film in January 2009 was *Pineapple Express*, told me three reasons for the surge of Latino voters who went for Barack Obama by 67 percent to 31 percent for John McCain. "One is that Barack Obama really reached out to the Latino community.

He even translated his campaign slogan from 'Yes We Can' to '*Sí, Se Puede*.' And also it's that the Latino community was ready to have America hear their voice. They want political power and they want it now. And I think third, the last administration, the Bush administration, did not address the concerns of the Latino community and they were tired of it. And they wanted change."

Driven by the reasons expressed by Rosie and the other celebrities at the Latino Inaugural Gala, the U.S. Hispanic community played a pivotal role in the election of our forty-fourth president. And if the exit polls are to be believed, aside from the dreadful economy, the single biggest concern of the Latino community was the devastating impact on its sense of belonging and well-being of the acrimonious and hyperbolic immigration debate.

"It is the defining issue among the fastest-growing group of new voters in this country," says Frank Sharry, executive director of America's Voice, an immigration reform group that favors widespread amnesty for undocumented workers. Experiencing a wave of prejudice and persecution unseen since the scary days of the last Great Depression, Hispanic citizens registered and voted for the political party they believed would best protect their economic and social interests. And if the current climate persists, the odds are that the face of American politics has been forever altered.

Put another way, if Latinos continue to vote for Democrats at the rate they voted for Barack Obama, then there may never be another Republican in the White House. It is simply a function of American demographics.

INTRODUCTION

For the first time in modern world history a powerful nation is changing complexion right before the eyes of its citizens. In real time it is possible to watch America become more culturally diverse, its face physically darker. The United States has vastly more Latinos than it did just a relatively few years ago, and their numbers are increasing at an explosive rate, on average almost four thousand per day.

This book is about what that dramatic trend means for the country.

Aided by the vast oceans that separate the United States from the planet's densest population centers, and by America's early instincts toward isolation, for most of the twentieth century our nation managed to exclude most Asians, Africans and Latinos. With passionate vigilance and a largely race-based immigration policy, the country remained overwhelmingly white and Anglo for the first two and a half centuries of its existence.

The relaxation of that restrictive policy in the 1960s civil rights era resulted in a tsunami of Latino migration, which, when coupled with an explosive domestic birth rate, inflated the U.S. Hispanic population to a size almost ten times bigger than it was just fifty years ago, in both absolute and relative terms. In 1950, there were 5 million Latinos. Today, there are more than 46 million. And the recent downturn in illegal immigration due to the lack of good construction jobs in our faltering economy will only marginally slow the pace. During that half century, Asian and African-American populations also increased, but not by nearly as impressive a rate as that of Hispanics.

A library of scary books and an almost infinite galaxy of anti-immigration opinion pieces warn of how the inexorably increasing numbers of Latinos in the United States are or will soon be overwhelming the existing social order and making America a fundamentally different nation from the one contemplated by the fifty-six signatories of the Declaration of Independence, who were all white Anglos (and only one of whom, Charles Carroll of Maryland, was even Catholic, a then still exotic religion in the thirteen original colonies).

By fundamentally different, I mean a nation other than the industrious, God-fearing, ethical, family-valued, disciplined, self-governing and moral New World colossus the Founding Fathers contemplated. Those fears are widespread, and whether you think them justified or overblown, it is undeniable that the phenomenal Latino population surge in the United States since those revolutionary days is stunning and irreversible.

The percentage of Latinos in the United States population stands at 15.4 percent, which in April 2009 amounted to about 46.7 million people, if not yet strong, getting stronger politically, culturally and economically. Despite the dramatic decrease, even reversal, in recent immigration caused by the collapsing U.S. economy, by the time you read this that 46.7 million figure will already be an understatement of a rapidly expanding demographic, which grew more than 3 percent in the single year between July 2006 and July 2007, and more than doubled just since 1990. Hispanics for the first time outnumber non-Hispanic whites in Dallas, Texas. They are 37 percent of the population of Houston and over 28 percent of the population of Chicago, Illinois. Similarly, when the Census Bureau announced in March 2009 that New York City had reached a record 8,363,710 people, the bureau revealed that 28 percent were Hispanic, 2,341,839, up 27,000 between July 2007 and July 2008, and most of them native-born. The Latino populations of New York City (2.3 million) and Los Angeles (1.86 million) both outnumber the entire population of Barcelona, Spain, which has just 1.6 million residents. As Marcelo Suárez-Orozco, a professor of globalization and education at New York University, said when the population of the United States hit the breathtaking 300 million mark on October 17, 2006, that 300 millionth American was probably born in Los Angeles and was probably the daughter of Mexicans. "Probably, her name is Maria. . . . She is the future of America. She is a child of an immigrant. She is a U.S. citizen like you and me."

In political terms, what makes that historic 15.4% statistic even more impressive is that it is comprised mostly of native-born Hispanics, citizens born in the U.S.A., not immigrants either legal or illegal. That is the most potentially profound political development since the silent majority.

As Rosario Dawson reminded us during the inaugural gala, as an ethnic group, Latinos are already second in size behind only non–Hispanic American whites. And the percentage of Hispanics is growing by twice their rate and almost that much faster than American blacks whom they supplanted as the nation's largest minority, far ahead of the date predicted by the social scientists of the 1960s.

The states of Arizona, California, Colorado, Florida, Georgia, Illinois, Massachusetts, Nevada, New Jersey, New Mexico, New York, North Carolina, Pennsylvania, Texas, Virginia and Washington all have at least a half million Hispanic residents.

If current trends hold, 25 percent of the U.S. population will be Hispanic by 2040, and by the end of the twenty-first century, the United States will be a majority-Hispanic country. Put another way, there are people alive today who will be around to watch America take its place as the world's largest Hispanic country by population. Perhaps more surprisingly, it is already number two behind just Mexico, and already ahead of Spain. There was a March 2009 article reprinted in the *Latino Business Review* that referred to America's burgeoning Latino population as Nuevo Hispania. "With more than 46 million people, Nuevo Hispania is the 27th-largest nation on Earth and the fourth largest in the Western Hemisphere," the article by NBC reporters Timothy Sun and Alex Johnson said.

"Even as the rest of the economy contracts in global recession, Nuevo Hispania remains a thriving, even booming, market that's expected to grow by 48 percent in the next four years."

I wouldn't encourage that "Nuevo Hispania" bit. It sounds way too nationalistic. There are already too many hard-core conservative critics who allege that our hidden goal is to separate the Spanish-dominant areas of the nation from the rest of the country. I would rather emphasize our inclusion as part of the American whole.

Lest you think the prospect of a majority-Hispanic America off-putting, the good news is that Latinos, by the most important measures, are pretty much the same as "traditional" Americans. As I said in my first book on this topic, *HisPanic*—which, let me helpfully point out, is now available in paperback—most of us speak English (almost certainly after the first generation). We love our children, our wives, families and friends, our country, our teams, pets, our prides and our prejudices. We certainly have our bad *manzanas* (apples), but in broad strokes, most work hard, go to church, serve in the military (a hundred thousand strong), and now vote, just like most Americans, maybe soon more than most. Almost three in four Latinos surveyed following the 2008 presidential election said they were more interested this time than in the 2004 election, and that their newfound interest in the political scene would continue. The sleeping giant is awake.

And from the point of view of the nation, that is a good thing, because the widely held work ethic among Latinos and the driving ambition so many hold to move their families up the social and economic food chain will help propel America to further greatness and prosperity. Latinos are the secret weapon of the country's economy.

Granted, it might seem counterintuitive that Latinos, of all people, should be identified as the current force to help right America's economic ship of state. For many generations tracking back to the Middle Ages, Hispanics have been identified as virtually synonymous with grifters, gigolos, romancers, rapists, strike breakers, duelists, thieves or, in the New World worst of all, immigrants, especially illegal immigrants, takers from American society, not player-participants.

It is a bad rap made possible partially by the stereotype born of shared antagonistic history. In literature and movies our cultural ancestor Spain's Catholic King Philip II is always portrayed as greasy, dark, tricky and wackily religious. And to many Anglo-Americans, U.S. Hispanics inherited and imported those traits into the United States. Since at least the 1588 defeat of Philip II's Spanish Armada by the navy of Elizabeth, queen of England, and exacerbated by competition between the Spanish and English empires for world dominion, Hispanics have had a swarthy, amoral aspect attributed by the prevailing culture to our national/ethnic/racial roots, something vaguely sinister, voluptuous and lazy. Think belly-scratching siestas or Captain Hook, mustache-twirling predator.

Like Japanese-Americans during World War II, we have been the victims of a smear job of historic proportions. The deeply negative effect of the reckless anti-Hispanic immigrant propaganda campaign, especially during the early stages of the 2007–2008 presidential election cycle, cannot be overstated from the point of view of most Hispanics in America, regardless of their party affiliation, economic heritage or racial self-image. There is almost no one—rich, poor, black, white, brown, peasant, *jíbaro*, *caballero* or *caudillo*—who is not still more or less offended by the harsh tone of the debate over Hispanic immigration.

The hard-right social conservatives shrieked about the Mexican swarm and made profoundly negative icons of young Latinos climbing the wall near Juárez or wading across the Rio Grande near Laredo, rafting ashore in south Florida, hiking across the Arizona desert at Nogales or beating the U.S. Customs and Immigration line at Tijuana. Meantime, real-world Hispanic-American citizen voters looked around and realized how insulting the conversation had become.

In November 2008, Latinos made the Republican Party pay, and the price was steep: control of Congress and the White House. In record numbers Hispanics voted and in the end made a major, if not the decisive difference in the elections. By several sober analyses, including my own, there but for almost 12 million Hispanic voters John McCain would be president. But "I told you so" is not what this is about. The surge of Latino voters happened and, in a larger societal sense, is happening, and this book is about what that means.

My late, great ex-father-in-law Kurt Vonnegut once told me that when you talk to people, their primary concern is what your topic has to do with them. He also told me they were interested in how they could get your job, but that's another story. Let me hasten to say that every conscientious American should root for the success of U.S. Hispanics, because they will be doing a hefty portion of our stressed nation's economic heavy lifting going forward.

Like every group of immigrant newcomers that has come before, Latinos are filling vital and expanding roles in the U.S. economy. There is an entire class of strivers whose shops and bodegas do the commerce of the barrio, and that entrepreneurial spirit is matched by an intense and widespread work ethic among the legions who occupy the nation's lower tiers of employment. "Latinos enter the labor force relatively early and do so robustly; Hispanic men in particular have the highest labor force participation rate of any subgroup (80.5%)," says the NCLR, quoting the U.S. Labor Department. That means more Latinos work, percentage-wise, than any other ethnic group.

I've been saying for most of my public life that in much of the United States there is scarcely a lawn mowed, a fruit picked or a baby cared for, but by a Hispanic. Citizen or not, millions toil in jobs that mainstream white and black cultures have moved away from, like fruit picking, poultry processing and meatpacking. "Those are Mexican jobs," is an increasingly popular refrain in urban America. While many consider those dirty jobs as Gunga Din-class labor and see them as demeaning drudgery, Latinos, particularly the newer arrivals, have seized the opportunities that exist at or near the bottom of our still relatively affluent society, so down-low it is only minimally affected even in these times of widespread economic travail, turmoil and stress. You can still find plenty of jobs cleaning toilets, scrubbing pots, plucking chickens and cutting off cow heads in August in Iowa.

None of the furloughed Big Three automakers nor the financial wizards exiled by Citigroup or Merrill nor most of the newly unemployed white-collar middle-class are going to take those grinding, chain gang-like jobs picking blueberries in Michigan, avocados in California, doing minimum-wage, cold-weather, semiskilled construction jobs in Jersey (good luck if they can even find them) or sewing cheap shirts in south Florida. Put a different way, if mainstream workers feel the need to compete for those jobs at the very bottom, the nation really is up the creek without a paddle.

And those young, hardworking Hispanic go-getters play a role beyond today. Because we have been inundated by unending, seldom varying cable news and talk radio reports and commentaries alleging the strain and drain Hispanics put on the economy, it is another perhaps counterintuitive fact that these largely entry-level workers are the secret weapon in the battle to keep the U.S. elderly solvent.

As American society gets older, economists are united in their fear that the Social Security trust fund will be bankrupted by the explosive number of boomer retirees in proportion to the dwindling number, relatively speaking, of their children, those still producing and contributing to the system. But the grim prognosis does not adequately figure in the exceptional Latino population explosion that is filling the depleted ranks of the U.S. working class.

The median age of the white U.S. population is well over forty years old. For Hispanic Americans it is 27.6. In other words, the U.S. Hispanic population is on average more than twelve years younger than whites. You do the math when it comes to who will be working and paying into the Social Security trust fund.

Now, the nation, with President Obama at the wheel, is driving through a tough patch, maybe one of the toughest ever. Among Latinos, aside from worrying about their economic future, there is also concern that the tremendous gains made in integrating into larger American society will be eroded, that anti-immigrant sentiment is being further stoked by financial uncertainty, that an already difficult situation is being aggravated by hard times. This book attempts to explain why it is in America's best interests to cheer on and encourage the legitimate aspirations of the group destined unalterably to play a gigantic role in our nation's future. Like the Irish, Asian, African, German, Italian, Greek, Northern and Eastern Europeans, we are proud, eager, able travelers on our country's Great Progression.

★ 1 ★

THE FIRST BROWN PRESIDENT

> "Years ago, in the middle of the Whitewater investigation, one heard the first murmurs: white skin notwithstanding, this is our first black President. Blacker than any actual black person who could ever be elected in our children's lifetime. After all, Clinton displays almost every trope of blackness: single-parent household, born poor, working-class, saxophone-playing, McDonald's-and-junk-food-loving boy from Arkansas."
>
> —Toni Morrison, *The New Yorker*, October 1998

Seventy-year-old author and editor Toni Morrison certainly had most of the world for company when in 1998 she lowballed the chance that an "actual black person" could be elected to the nation's highest office anytime soon. So the Nobel Laureate in Literature anointed embattled President Bill Clinton with the honor of being "our first black President," and for almost a decade the honorific stuck. The more the Clintons were attacked by partisan critics for real or conjured malfeasance, the more blacks coalesced behind them.

In January 1999, Whoopi Goldberg sat in the VIP gallery of the U.S. Senate when Clinton's impeachment trial began, a symbol of the near-universal support the beleaguered president commanded among black Americans.

The former president and his wife were the objects of such widespread affection among African-Americans, there was an assumption that Hillary Clinton could count on the community's enduring support in her own race for the White House. "This was not and is not and will not become a race-based decision for me," said the Reverend Dr. Calvin Butts in importantly endorsing her. I was there that Sunday in January 2008 when Hillary came to Harlem's historic Abyssinian Baptist Church on West 138th Street, just a half mile from her beloved husband's office on 125th, Uptown's main drag.

"I respect Senator Obama. I applaud him, and I love him as my brother," Butts explained, "but a vote for Hillary is not a vote against Barack Obama or any community. . . . A vote for Hillary Clinton is a vote to elect someone who has proven through time to me and to this community and this country that she has the experience to make things happen and the vision to return us to a place of prosperity."

Despite some ominous booing from a pro-Obama crowd across the street, which I noted at the time boded ill for Senator Clinton and indicated the African-American grass roots going one way and New York's community leaders going another, Hillary did fairly well among blacks early on, scoring other important endorsements from black congressional leaders like Sheila Jackson Lee of Texas and the powerful head of the House Ways and Means Committee, New York's Charlie Rangel.

But beginning with Oprah's monumental May 2007 endorsement of Obama, a move by the world's most influential woman that was later said to have been worth a million votes, and later, the Illinois senator's crucial victory in the first-in-the-nation Iowa caucuses, Hillary was on the ropes in the 'hood. Her decline rapidly accelerated after Bill Clinton's gaffe in South Carolina, which attempted to discount Obama's victory in the primary there as strictly race based, and it was soon over as far as the black vote. From that point on, most African-Americans considered an Obama endorsement as mandatory, and those persistently reluctant to do the right thing, like my longtime friend author and PBS/NPR commentator Tavis Smiley, were scandalously marginalized as Uncle Toms.

Black support and the community's historic turnout and one-sided vote in the bitter primary battles between January and June 2008 therefore were essential to Obama's nomination victory over Clinton. When push came to shove, those voters convincingly chose the real black man over the wife of the honorary one.

That overwhelming surge toward Obama led to an increased and even more intensely loyal turnout by blacks in the general election, African-Americans voting by at least 95 percent for the Democrat in November

2008. The tears of joy from Oprah and the Reverend Jesse Jackson Jr. in packed Grant Park in Chicago that magical election night, the sincere pride declared by former secretary of state Condoleezza Rice later in Washington, and Colin Powell's joyous exultation, "Look what we did!" came to define world reaction to the historic event.

While I was in Washington for the historic inauguration, two chance encounters among many stand out. The first was in the crowd on the slope near the Washington Monument in the moments before Obama was sworn in by Chief Justice John G. Roberts, who lamely neglected to memorize the oath of office. An elderly black lady grabbed me and said, "Now I can tell my grandchildren I was here. I only wish my grandparents could see me now." And another, younger African-American woman who got into the elevator with Erica and me in the Hamilton Crowne Plaza on K Street, where we were staying for the festivities, spontaneously hugged me, crying about how happy she was to see this moment.

But despite the righteous and long overdue joy in the black community, sober analysis shows that black support is not the reason Barack Obama is president. Hispanic-Americans have a better claim to that honor.

Elections in this country always have race as a subtext, white versus black. An argument can be made that the two parties are essentially defined by it, suburban versus urban, South versus North. However race is defined, it is certain that most non-Hispanic whites vote for the GOP, while virtually all blacks vote for the Democrats. It is an enduring fact of American political life that the Civil War didn't end our racialist tendencies; they are still part of our essential fabric, although not often directly addressed in polite society. The Democrat's 2004 candidate, windsurfing, Frenchy effete John Kerry, is one of the whitest senators imaginable, yet he got 88 percent of the black vote, which always favors the Democrat. Only slightly cooler, stylistically speaking, also-stiff Al Gore—a white man who can't jump—got 90 percent of the black vote back in 2000 in his epic tie with George W. Bush.

Just as reliably, since the Dixiecrats went GOP after the George Wallace "Segregation Now, Segregation Forever" era, and particularly after the thirty-sixth president, Lyndon B. Johnson, signed the Civil Rights Act of

1964, whites, even those who are not particularly well-off, have favored the Republican presidential candidate. Fifty-four percent of them voted for Bush over Gore in 2000, and even though he ran against the black guy, McCain got about the same percentage of the white vote, 55 percent in 2008.

In assessing his candidate's loss in the days immediately following the 2008 election, McCain pollster Bill McInturff said, "There are any number of states that McCain just lost that he got the same percent of the white vote that Bush did in 2004." In a November 2008 *Politico* piece titled "GOP back to square one with Hispanics," McInturff added, "The percent of the white electorate is dropping every election cycle, and when you look ahead at America, black and Hispanic, by age bracket, there is a demographic trend that is obvious—our country is becoming more diverse."

Bluntly stated, Latinos are the reason Barack Obama is president, their votes roughly equivalent to Mr. Obama's margin of victory in the popular vote and in key swing states. As Bill Clinton became the first "black" president, Obama was enthusiastically adopted by Hispanics. After their original favorite Hillary dropped out, they raced to embrace Obama, driven from even considering the GOP standard by that party's raw and blatantly anti-Hispanic rhetoric on the issue of immigration. In doing so, they forever put to rest the old canard that Latinos would never vote for a black candidate and made Obama a major beneficiary of the browning of America.

Nationally, Obama trounced McCain by more than thirty-five points among Hispanics. The 7.35 million who voted for Obama represent almost his entire 8.6 million margin of victory nationally. But the importance of the Latino vote is more clearly seen on a state-by-state basis. Florida's Latino vote gave the White House to George W. Bush in 2000, and helped him keep it in 2004. In 2008 those Latino voters swung the Sunshine State to Barack Obama. According to a survey done by the *Florida Sun-Sentinel*, Hispanics went 57 percent to 42 percent for the Democrat, about the opposite of their 2004 preference for the Republican. To understand why Hispanic votes were so crucial to Obama, they made up almost 8 percent of his total Florida vote; since he only won the state by 4 percent, it is clear the Hispanic swing put him over the top.

Latinos also helped turn New Mexico, Nevada, North Carolina, Virginia and Colorado from red (Republican) states to blue (Democrat). Arizona and Texas will be the next political dominoes to fall in the Democratic camp unless the GOP understands the extent to which the party has alienated this rapidly expanding and righteously angry constituency.

Without belaboring the point, during the Bush years the pragmatists in the GOP understood that Latinos, particularly after the first generation, are much like any other Americans. Those who prosper become interested in lower taxes, safe streets and better schools. "They're Republicans," Ronald Reagan said sagely, "they just don't know it yet."

George W. Bush recognized that simple fact, for example, when he addressed the Hispanic Chamber of Commerce in Washington in March 2001. "A lot of times in the rhetoric, people forget the facts. And the facts are that thousands of small businesses—Hispanically owned or otherwise— pay taxes at the highest marginal rate."

While his syntax was unique, his vision was clear. Latinos are up for grabs, politically speaking. Or at least they were. And that is particularly true when you add in the millions who, though not well-off, regard themselves as socially conservative, antiabortion, anti–gay marriage, churchgoing and patriotic. They are the Latino equivalent of what used to be called Reagan Democrats.

As a border state senator and a reasonable man, John McCain also understood the significance of the emerging constituency. In 1988 he was honored by the civil rights group La Raza for opposing a proposition calling for English to be adopted as Arizona's official language.

"Why would we want to pass some kind of initiative that a significant portion of our population considers an assault on their heritage?" McCain asked with dignity and passionate reason, attacking Proposition 106 more than twenty years ago. "Our nation and the English language have done quite well with Chinese spoken in California, German in Pennsylvania, Italian in New York, Swedish in Minnesota, and Spanish throughout the

Southwest. I fail to see the cause for alarm now." Bravo, McCain, circa 1988 to 2007.

During an early May 2007 GOP presidential debate at the Reagan Library in Simi Valley, when the fate of the immigration reform legislation he coauthored still hung in the balance, McCain said reasonably, "We've been working very hard for a couple of months with Democrats and Republicans, led by the president and his Cabinet, to come up with a comprehensive solution and resolution of this terrible problem of illegal immigration. One thing we would all agree on, the status quo is not acceptable. We have to secure our borders. But we also need a temporary worker program, and we have to dispose of the issue of 12 million people who are in this country illegally. This issue needs to be addressed comprehensively."

But after being booed by anti-immigration activists in Iowa and Michigan, and with his campaign threatening to unwind under the pressure, the war hero reversed course. In a CNN-sponsored January 2008 presidential debate he said spectacularly that he would not even vote for his own reform legislation.

I remember when this noble man I so admired was asked by Janet Hook of the *Los Angeles Times*, "Your original immigration proposal back in 2006 was much broader and included a pathway to citizenship for illegal immigrants who are already here. At this point, if your original proposal came to a vote on the Senate floor, would you vote for it?"

Then John McCain broke our hearts, answering, "No, I would not, because we know what the situation is today. We will secure the borders first when I am president of the United States. I know how to do that. I come from a border state, where we know about building walls, and vehicle barriers, and sensors, and all of the things necessary."

I felt a sense of sadness hearing him running scared and reduced to obvious political pandering. He was doomed by basic miscalculation. McCain tilted right on the issue of immigration. He should have stayed in the middle. He tried to solidify the Ann Coulter/Sean Hannity/Rush Limbaugh vote. He already had them. There was no way conservatives were going to vote for a Democrat, especially a black guy named Barack Hussein Obama. Who would have thought that someone middle-named Hussein could ever win an election anyway, especially one only five years after Saddam Hussein was our archest of archenemies?

The vote McCain should have aimed for was mine and other moderate Hispanics'. But when he backed off on immigration reform, Latinos deserted him. In the months leading up to the election a survey by the Pew Hispanic Center found that what had been a twenty-one-point edge among eligible Latino voters for the Democratic Party (49–28) in July 2006 had ballooned into a thirty-four-point advantage (57–23) by midsummer 2008.

"This U-turn in Hispanic partisan allegiance trends comes at a time when the issue of illegal immigration has become an intense focus of national attention and debate on the presidential campaign trail; in the corridors of federal, state and local governments, and on cable television and talk radio," wrote the authors of the Pew report, Paul Taylor and Richard Fry.

Despite McCain's history of supporting Latinos on issues of vital concern, because of his flip-flop on immigration and his party's tarnished brand, the Hispanic community rejected him and his party, which had chosen demonizing over discourse. Confronted on a nightly basis by insulting rhetoric and stereotyped images on cable news; troubled by the escalation of workplace raids and escalating deportations; annoyed and harassed by the anti-immigrant activities of local police who disturbed Hispanic citizens and immigrants alike, the GOP paid the price. And they can't say they didn't see it coming.

President Bush's former speechwriter Michael Gerson told the *Washington Post* in September 2007, fourteen months before the election, that, "I have never seen an issue where the short-term interests of Republican presidential candidates in the primaries were more starkly at odds with the long-term interests of the party itself. At least five swing states that Bush carried in 2004 are rich in Hispanic voters—Arizona, New Mexico, Nevada, Colorado and Florida. Bush won Nevada by just over 20,000 votes. A substantial shift of Hispanic voters toward the Democrats in these states could make the national political map unwinnable for Republicans. . . . Some in the party seem pleased. They should be terrified."

Even the usually reliably red state of Indiana turned blue, when Latino voters helped tilt it into Obama's column, crushing any hope McCain had of a late surge. Hispanic Hoosiers, who would have figured?

Gerson's remarks were prophetic. The GOP should have been terrified. Instead, driven to distraction by anti-immigrant firebrands like Lou Dobbs, about whom I've written before in *HisPanic,* an improbably reenergized Rush Limbaugh, Dick "I'm On Your Side" Morris, my pals Sean "You Know He's Right" Hannity and Ann "the Conservative Carnivore" Coulter and crew, the Republican Party cut off its nose to spite its face.

"The harsh Republican line on immigration is usually depicted as motivated by concern about jobs, national security, drugs or terrorism. But that tune has a persistent undercurrent of fretfulness about race, culture and ethnicity," said a February 2009 *New York Times* editorial titled "The Nativists are Restless."

Because public displays of dissatisfaction are scorned, many did not appreciate the smoldering depth of Latino voter discontent and how profoundly "they were turned off by the discourse, offended by the way Hispanics were demonized," according to Frank Guerra, Hispanic media adviser for the McCain campaign.

My longtime go-to Hispanic GOP expert, San Antonio, Texas–based public relations guru Lionel Sosa, a Republican stalwart dating back to the Reagan years, speaks of how "Hispanic dismay over the tone of the immigration debate in the Republican primaries over immigration policies drove Hispanics from the party."

"If Senator McCain wants what's best for our families . . . he would not have flip-flopped on his own legislation to firmly and fairly reform our broken immigration system," said Representative Xavier Becerra, Democrat of California, in what became a familiar refrain and the prevailing Latino wisdom during the campaign. "But he did [flip-flop]."

A December 2008 in-depth analysis of the Hispanic vote by the pro-immigration group America's Voice titled "Republicans: Fenced in by Immigration" proves how the attempt by the GOP to use immigration as a social wedge issue failed miserably.

"Candidates and the [Republican] Party spent millions of dollars and ran hundreds of ads in scores of races across the nation, charging Democrats with supporting amnesty and opposing immigration enforcement . . . the GOP immigration strategy went down in flames, and the party was handed another major setback at the ballot box, from Congress to the Presidency."

The study probes twenty-two competitive House and Senate races in 2008 where the Republican candidate tried to use illegal immigration as a wedge issue against a Democratic challenger. These were swing districts that the Cook Political Report considered "in play" two months before the election.

"Based on our review, 20 of 22 winners advocated immigration policies beyond enforcement-only. This includes 5 of 5 Senate races (in Colorado, North Carolina, New Hampshire, New Mexico and Oregon) and 15 of 17 House races listed as 'toss up' or 'leans' one way or another according to the Cook Political Report."

Among the congressional anti-immigration casualties was Republican Party stalwart Senator Elizabeth Dole of North Carolina, who reached for the illegal immigration wedge issue to attack Democratic challenger Kay Hagan when her candidacy began to falter. In May 2008 Dole released a TV ad touting her role in helping North Carolina sheriffs crack down on illegal immigrants.

Her opponent, Kay Hagan, took a more reasoned and conciliatory approach, supporting a "practical solution that is fair to taxpayers and addresses the problem at its roots: by strengthening the borders, enforcing and upgrading laws that crack down on employers who knowingly hire illegal workers, and eliminating the shadow economy that drives down wages and working conditions." But candidate Hagan's more progressive campaign went on to say that, "if North Carolina's farmers and seasonal businesses are having trouble finding the help they need, Kay would support the reform of guest-worker programs to ensure farmers and businesses are able to meet their needs legally and stay competitive while protecting American workers' jobs."

To understand why the difference between the campaigns and the need for inexpensive guest workers resonated in North Carolina, you must know that the prevailing business sentiment there is that jobs, particularly in the all-important textile and furniture industries, went from white workers to black to brown to gone—that is, exported to nations like China. Absent Hispanic workers, those North Carolina–based industries cannot compete.

"Immigration played a very important role in getting them to reject the Republican Party and to begin the movement toward the Democratic Party by voting first for Hillary Clinton and then later for Obama in the final vote," said noted pollster Sergio Bendixen of Hispanic voters after the election. His associate Fernand Amandi told HispanicBusiness.com in even stronger words that, "The Republican Party embraced an almost suicidal posture when it came to the immigration issue. I think it will cause long-lasting damage to their brand in the minds of Hispanic voters." He added that for the GOP to survive in a post-Hispanic pluralistic America they have to be part of the process of resolving the immigration issue "in a way that does not alienate Hispanics who are here and who are voting. . . . If they don't turn that sentiment around, they will continue to get this kind of low margin in the vote," Amandi told the Web site.

Noting that Hispanics turned out in record numbers in the November 2008 elections, Clarissa Martinez of the National Council of La Raza, the Hispanic civil rights organization, said, "What is clear after three election cycles of using this tactic is that it is not working with the mainstream elec-torate, but what it is doing is alienating Latinos," lamenting the existence of a "climate of hostility toward all Hispanics, no matter their immigration status or how long their forebears have been in the country."

"Anti-immigrant rhetoric and votes in favor of walling off the southern border did not win votes for Republicans," wrote reliably conservative, old-school antitax Republican Grover Norquist, author of *Leave Us Alone: Getting the Government's Hands Off Our Money, Our Guns, Our Lives.*

"We can't afford to do to the Hispanics what we did to the Roman

Catholics in the late 19th Century," Norquist continues, "tell them we don't like them and lose their vote for a hundred years."

Norquist joins Karl Rove and other bluntly pragmatic Republican philosophers in lamenting how their party's nativist wing, prodded by hard-right media, wrecked their hopes for the 2008 election and beyond. I interviewed Rove in the early January 2009 days leading up to President Obama's inauguration. Without oversentimentalizing his statement, and remembering his bare-knuckle brand of cutthroat partisan politics, I still thought he seemed genuinely moved by the history Obama's victory created.

"It's a great thing about America, isn't it? After he takes the oath of office, he's going to go down and sit in that reviewing booth and see the parade, and then he and his wife are going to walk into the White House, where they're going to live for the next four years. They're going to live in a house which slaves helped build. That says something about the trajectory of the American story, the arc of America. And it really is something we all ought to be enormously proud of. It really is a remarkable testament to what this country is."

For the Machiavellian devil incarnate, Rove has some remarkably moderate, practical, even noble ideas. I asked about Latinos and the GOP.

"Are you fearful that the Republican Party in the post-Bush era will abandon the kind of pluralism that he symbolized? And I'm thinking specifically about Hispanics, because I don't think that the GOP will ever return to power unless they can bring the Latinos back."

"It's a vital element of the Republican recovery," he answered without hesitation. "I'm increasingly confident that people get it, that the answer to it is to make our arguments fervently and passionately in the Latino community, and to find Latinos whom we can run for office and enthusiastically back, even in districts that are not dominated by Latinos.

"And I'm feeling increasingly comfortable, but you put your finger on it. There are two or three challenges. One is, we have to do better among Latinos."

Rove was more forlorn in a January 2009 *Newsweek* column titled "A Way Out of the Wilderness," where he noted, "An anti-Hispanic attitude is suicidal."

Rove also said that the GOP should even attempt reaching out to blacks, a sentiment that helped our FOX News colleague Michael Steele, the African-American former lieutenant governor of Maryland, become chairman of the Republican National Committee in January 2009, the RNC's first-ever black chairman.

By the way, when I asked Rove, the edgy man once famously called "Bush's Brain," whether he thought he'd be remembered primarily as the evil manipulating genius of the forty-third president's administration, he replied by comparing himself to Grendel in *Beowulf*, saying, "I'm often talked about but rarely seen," and promised to debunk the prevailing "myths" in his own tell-all book.

In another January 2009 interview, President Bush, who had been notoriously reluctant to second-guess himself, engaged in some Monday-morning quarterbacking and identified his failure to push through immigration reform as perhaps his biggest mistake. "I probably, in retrospect, should have pushed immigration reform right after the 2004 election and not Social Security reform," the outgoing president told syndicated columnist Cal Thomas, a terrific colleague and one of the first of the real uncrazy conservatives.

"If I had to do it again," Bush continued, "I probably would have run the immigration policy first, as part of a border security/guest worker/compassionate campaign.

"See," said Bush plaintively, "I happen to believe a system that is so broken that humans become contraband is a system that really needs to be re-examined, seriously. I know there's a lot of concern about our borders, and there should be. And we've done something about that.

"On the other hand," he continued, "I don't see how you can have a comprehensive border security without a program that recognizes that there will be people doing jobs Americans aren't willing to do, and therefore there ought to be a way for them to temporarily come here on a verifiable basis in a way that would cause them not to have to sneak here or pay for a coyote or get stuffed into an 18-wheeler, or try to walk across the desert and die."

It is a waste of time to wonder what would have been, if only George

W. Bush had had the courage to push for reform against the screamers in his own party at a time when it would have made a difference. That was 2004. A resolution then would have deprived the hatemongers of four years of material. What would they have talked about? In the avalanche of dreadful choices Mr. Bush made, it would have stood as a historic accomplishment.

Additionally, his feelings of regret at not passing compassionate reform seem casual and cruel when weighed against the draconian crackdown launched by his own Department of Homeland Security in the wake of the reform bill's defeat. Either he was willfully unaware of what his DHS was doing or he was like a spoiled child kicking his dog because his parents didn't give him his way. We Latinos were the dog. The disruption caused by the crackdown that followed the bill's defeat cannot be minimized. Entire Midwestern communities were shattered, including some that had been models of immigrant enterprise and assimilation for decades.

Is there any wonder that the Latino community responded at the ballot box? The beneficiary is the forty-fourth president, who was swept into office by the extraordinary turnout of Latino voters.

"You showed how powerful you are on November 4th," the new president wrote to a group of advocates, civil rights activists and legislators who convened in January 2009 for the second annual Latino State of the Union at a Capitol Hill hotel, his remarks read by Tina Tchen, the White House director of public liaison. There to prioritize their "wish list" for the new administration, the group understandably put immigration reform at the top of the list.

"We have to take immigration away from the border and present it as an issue of national interest defined by cooperation, rather than confrontation, with Mexico and Latin America," said John Trasviña, president of the Mexican American Legal Defense and Education Fund (MALDEF), which hosted the event.

"It is a question of fostering acceptance of Latinos, who have been victimized by hate, in the hands of perpetrators who attack them because of their ethnicity, and overzealousness, in the hands of local police officers who have been deputized to act as immigration enforcers in communities nationwide," Mr. Trasviña said, according to Fernanda Santos in *The New York Times*.

Mr. Obama pointed to his appointments of Ken Salazar as Secretary of the Interior and Hilda Solis as Labor Secretary as "a measure of my commitment" to run a government that reflects the nation's diversity.

One fringe benefit was that the Latino surge for Obama also swept away the self-fulfilling stereotype of animosity between blacks and Latinos, an old rub dating back to the days of competition for federal urban aid dollars during the "poverty pimp" era of President Johnson's 1965 Great Society. That tension between people of color had recently been aggravated in places like Los Angeles, where traditionally African-American neighborhoods on the south side have been transformed into Hispanic enclaves. Bad feelings also surfaced during the immigration debate, when some blacks expressed the feeling that the jobs the undocumented workers were taking would have otherwise gone to them. With those reservations blown away by the embrace of shared aspirations and the strong perception that the Republican Party was a mutual enemy, blacks and browns stood solidly shoulder-to-shoulder in November 2008 for the first time since the civil rights era.

More than 10 million Hispanics voted in the presidential election. That is almost three times as many as voted in 1992. And they voted overwhelmingly for the Democrat. Now Obama's party has to step up to the plate. Understanding that there are legitimate concerns, the president is pledging to continue the effort to secure the borders, particularly in the face of escalating drug violence and civil disorder on the Mexican side of the line. But he also understands that he must eventually advocate for a legal path to citizenship by naturalizing the people already here and, in the interim, granting labor rights for all who are law-abiding.

Interestingly, Latinos may not be able to rely on John McCain to enthusiastically support future reform. At a March 11, 2009, meeting with Hispanic business leaders brokered by Republican senators seeking to heal the rift with the Latino community, McCain was said to rebuke Hispanic voters. Said to be stung over the voting bloc's two-to-one support of Obama, "the senator says to look to the new president for immigration leadership," reported the *National Journal.* "He was angry," the *Journal* quotes one business leader who attended the parlay. "He was over the top. In some cases, he rolled his eyes a lot. There were portions of the meeting where he was just staring at the ceiling, and he wasn't even listening to us. We came out of the meeting really upset. He threw out [the words] '*You people*—you people made your choice. You made your choice during the election.'"

Early indications are that "you people" are optimistic about the new administration. In February 2009, a poll showed 72 percent believed that Barack Obama would have a successful first term, a number that exceeded even the young president's sky-high popularity among all Americans, who gave him a whopping 67 percent approval rating even as the economy tanked and congressional critics screamed about his stimulus package. That sense of optimism was especially pervasive among young Latinos; according to a survey done by the Pew Hispanic Center, 81 percent of Latinos ages eighteen to twenty-nine expected the forty-fourth president to succeed.

Ironically, the community also appears ready to cut the new president some slack in terms of the speed with which he specifically addresses immigration reform. There seems a tacit, mostly unspoken agreement, even among barn burners like La Raza and the Congressional Hispanic Caucus (and me) to let the issue come off the front burner for right now out of respect to the victims of the nation's troubled economy. It is a feeling that all Americans are taking this journey into economic uncertainty together.

In mid-February 2009 President Obama affirmed in an interview on Spanish-language radio that he hadn't forgotten his Latino supporters. He told Eddie "Piolín" Sotelo, the influential radio host and former illegal immigrant who was one of the architects of the massive pro-immigration rallies that blanketed the nation in May 2005 and 2006, that "we've got to have comprehensive immigration reform."

But then the president cautioned Piolín and his audience that "It's going to take some time to move that forward, but I'm very committed to making it happen." And right now, that is good enough for most Latinos. Although more than half of those over the age of eighteen are first-generation immigrants, by far their biggest priorities in early 2009 were the economy (57 percent) and education (51 percent).

That hefty majority of Latinos wants President Obama to get America back on an even keel, creating jobs and educational opportunities for the distressed communities already here and feeling the squeeze of the Great Recession. In success, the feeling seems to be that Obama can do the right thing vis-à-vis the newer arrivals and on a host of issues we share in common with blacks and other disadvantaged Americans.

Aside from needing each other, the black/brown partnership of convenience shared goals and values that reemerged in the 2008 election, and promises to be an impressive coalition for foreseeable election cycles. If Democrats can continue appealing to people of color, along with the young and the college educated, then there seems scant hope that Republicans will soon prevail again nationally.

Therefore, the Latino vote is now too important to be ignored. That fact will foster the federal government's gradual evolution toward pragmatic compassion on immigration reform as the nation comes to grips with the impossibility of effectively walling off Latin America even if the physical border fence is completed, which now appears likely. Simon Rosenberg of the New Democratic Network, a pro-immigration think tank, points to the 2010 Census and the congressional redistricting that will follow. "I anticipate a dramatic shift in power toward heavily Latino parts of the United States" following the redistricting, Rosenberg told the *Times*'s Fernanda Santos. "Remember: in redistricting, we count people, not citizens."

Remember when Vermont Republican Senator Judd Gregg belatedly declined Obama's offered job as Commerce Secretary? Gregg withdrew his name from consideration only when he heard he would not have control of the Census, with its all-important impact on redistricting. It is impossible to think the events were unrelated, although Judd hasn't said. He's moved into the role of the Senate Republicans' fiscal watchdog, and now the White House is in control of the 2010 Census, which every ten years determines federal funding and apportionment of seats in the U.S. House of Representatives.

With the Democrats' traditional tilt toward immigrant inclusion, everybody is going to be counted. The implications are vast for the flow of money and power to states and cities that have significant populations of undocumented immigrants. It is an historic opportunity that can only be sabotaged by those too lazy, frightened or misguided to participate.

In that regard, in a deeply troubling development, in late April 2009 a group called The National Coalition of Latino Clergy and Christian Leaders began urging undocumented immigrants not to fill out Census forms unless Congress first passes "genuine immigration reform." How bogus! Clearly, this group, which purports to represent 20,000 evangelical churches in 34 states, doesn't understand that in a democracy, the ability to effect change and make a difference comes from participation not boycott.

"Our job is to count every single person," Census spokesman Raul Cisneros told *USA Today*. "We are disappointed that any organization would urge anyone not to participate in their 2010 Census."

The only people a Census boycott would make happy are those opposed to immigrants' rights. I'm sure Lou Dobbs and his pals in the Minutemen and the other virulently anti-immigrant organizations are cheering NCLCCL on. As the November 2008 elections demonstrated conclusively, we are re-shaping America's political landscape. We have the potential to change what ails us. Like Latino citizens, the undocumented must also assume personal responsibility for effecting their own political destiny. Running and hiding never fixes anything. It only empowers the opposition.

If this NCLCCL edict is ignored, as it must be, the implications of an accurate Census are awesome. Given that perennially undercounted Hispanics will now presumably be counted, the regions where they are residing will be strengthened politically. Cities like Chicago, New York, Denver, and Los Angeles which expend billions for immigrant education and health care would be fairly reimbursed. Something more akin to fair and balanced government will be emplaced; then those districts will decide on leaders and legislation that suits them. Will they stay with the Democrats? Will the citizens among them keep voting at the same or a greater rate in the future? No one knows for sure, but most will stay with this president; of that I have no doubt. Unless Republicans come up with someone shockingly different, Obama's our guy now.

If President Clinton can be said to be the nation's first black president, a stronger case can be made for Barack Obama as our first brown one. Add to his other impressive and historic accomplishments that he reforged an old and formidable coalition. Picture a scene that never happened: Martin Luther King Jr. marching shoulder-to-shoulder with César Chávez, surrounded by students, traditional middle-class and upscale liberals and newly unionized workers. It may be the enduring image of America's dominant political force for the foreseeable future. Dramatic progress started with Obama, but as the following chapter demonstrates, while certain, the road to enlightenment will be neither quick nor easy.

2

HAWKEYE STATE SOMALIS
The Illogic of Recent Immigration Policies

"*¡La Migra! ¡Salvese él que pueda!*" ("Immigration! Save yourself if you can!")

—Scattering immigrant workers at the Postville, Iowa, meatpacking plant that was the scene of the biggest single-site immigration raid ever, May 2008

t wasn't as enduringly miserable as the war in Iraq or as ruinous as the collapse of the banks or the housing market would soon become. Nevertheless, it was the exact moment the Republicans lost the swing Latino voters who were critical to their 2008 bid for the White House. This was the day John McCain lost the presidency by losing a crucial constituency that in normal times might have been his.

At precisely ten a.m. on Monday, May 12, the armed might of the United States was unleashed in a picturesque northeastern Iowa town on a pitiful group of exploited Latino workers, men, women and children who threatened no one. The ensuing outrage convinced many Hispanic-American citizens that President Bush and his party had changed sides in the cause he once championed—rational, humane immigration reform.

Instead, heeding the hard-line "enforcement only" advocates within the GOP, those whose idea of immigration reform consists of jailing undocumented working people, the chief of the swollen Department of Homeland Security ordered his Immigration and Customs Enforcement (ICE), an agency on steroids since the terror attacks of 2001, to redirect its most elite force at heartland towns like Postville, Iowa. And we knew it was coming. In July 2007, after the Senate failed to pass "comprehensive immigration reform," DHS Secretary Michael Chertoff said ominously that the increase of arrests of undocumented immigrants was "going to get ugly," by which he obviously meant otherwise innocent working families were about to be targeted.

I mean no disrespect to the undoubtedly patriotic agents who carried out what was at the time the largest U.S. workplace raid ever (that dubious distinction now falls to a later, but equally melancholy August 2008 raid on a Laurel, Mississippi, factory, Howard Industries, which makes electrical equipment. 595 undocumented workers from Peru, Mexico, El Salvador, Guatemala, Panama, Honduras, and Brazil were rounded up, interviewed, fingerprinted and processed for deportation in that one). And I specifically reject Democratic congressional critics like Representative Luis Gutierrez of Illinois, who subsequently referred to ICE as "jackbooted thugs," but even the agents involved must have shaken their heads at the humble, harmless nature of their designated targets in the Iowa plant, the grossly exaggerated actions taken, and the draconian punishment subsequently inflicted.

Though ICE was created to battle the terrorists and criminal aliens who threaten American life, liberty and the pursuit of happiness, on this spring day soldiers for the agency waged war on innocent civilians who were barely making minimum wage doing difficult, dirty, distasteful jobs that, as you will see, no traditional Americans want.

With two powerful helicopters hovering overhead and military-style vehicles roaring all around, approximately nine hundred heavily armed federal ICE agents carried out what was their largest, cruelest workplace raid in history on the sprawling meatpacking plant run by Agriprocessors, the nation's biggest kosher slaughterhouse employing 968 workers, hundreds of them here illegally, most from Guatemala, some from Mexico.

Picture the chaos as the shouting, armed and armored agents explode on the plant with coordinated quasi-military-style tactics and arms to match. Too bad it isn't Osama bin Laden inside this factory, because these warriors are ready for any enemy, however formidable. But this day they should be carrying butterfly nets instead of machine guns, because what they find aren't enemies of the state, but rather hundreds of panic-stricken male butchers and female chicken processors, the ladies whose humble job is to salt the poultry, all trying to escape. The men and women are scattering through the plant or collapsing in tears at the terrifying sight of these roaring, helmeted giants, men who tower over these tiny, mostly Mayan-Indian-descended, undocumented or, more commonly, falsely documented workers who have dreaded this exact moment in their every nightmare.

Some workers manage to slip through the iron wall of law enforcement surrounding and spreading through the plant; most don't. The escapees bring word to the Hispanic reaches of Postville surrounding the plant, and panic spreads through the tamale restaurants and El Vaquero clothing store sitting side by side in the three-block-long downtown area. Frantic mothers gather their children from school and head to the sanctuary of St. Bridget's Catholic Church. Stores are shuttered, and a sense of community is destroyed by the biggest display of domestic "shock and awe" ever. Never had the nation witnessed so huge and competent a force turned loose on so modest a target.

St. Bridget's becomes sanctuary to nearly four hundred frantic relatives of the arrested workers, mostly mothers and their children, many of the latter of whom are U.S. citizens by birth. It is the Monday after Mother's Day.

Federal officers later boast how the raid on the huge, filthy, child-abusing, worker-exploiting Postville plant is "the largest single-site operation of its kind in American history."

Rather like the Laurel, Mississippi, raid that followed, it was an ill-advised, misdirected exercise in executive banality and judicial abuse of power. It punished the victims of employer exploitation by making felons out of honest, hardworking people who worked in harsh conditions to make six or seven dollars an hour so they could take care of their loved ones and maybe send a couple of dollars back home to poor family members in the slums or countryside around Guatemala City or Oaxaca, Mexico.

In August, three months after the raid, then less than three months before the November elections, Monica Rhor of the Associated Press interviewed the mayor about his traumatized town. "We've got a lot of people here who need help. We can't just throw them out on the street.

They're our family. They've made their homes here, had jobs here, raised families here."

In one of the worst political calculations of the twenty-first century, Bush administration immigration officials did something most Hispanic voters would neither forgive nor forget on November fourth. In taking this and similar actions, ICE abandoned the mission it had sworn before Congress in 2003: to use its massive and muscular post–9/11/01 power to round up the nation's most threatening unlawful immigrants, those who were convicted criminals or terrorism suspects. A secret January 31, 2006, memo started the slide away from that noble national security goal by drastically raising immigration arrest quotas to quiet hard-right critics demanding that the federal government do more now to mitigate the scourge of illegal aliens.

To meet those expanded quotas, agents were soon allowed to count the arrests of nonfugitive, nonterrorist, noncriminal, otherwise law-abiding immigrants as fulfilling the enhanced target goals set for the national security program. People like the Postville workers.

From coast to coast, armed ICE agents who should have been chasing drug cartel bandits and their street-gang arms and drug smuggling associates, instead were assigned to overwhelm entire communities, using awesome power to raid private homes without warrants, separate children from their parents, arrest working people, terrorize their families, including the citizens among them, and, in the case of Postville, to shatter the long-established fabric of the town.

More egregiously, to dispose of detainees following the Postville raid, they effectively rigged the judicial system with prearranged plea deals the detainees could not refuse. The result was to ensure a severely damaging legal outcome for the workingmen and -women they herded onto the fast track to federal prison and felony records.

Florida International University professor Erik Camayd-Freixas was one of the twenty-six federally certified court interpreters who, as the hitherto secret Postville raid was unfolding, had been simultaneously sneaked into the neighboring town of Waterloo, Iowa, with no idea why they had been hired. Many subsequently expressed their disgust at having been misled. Camayd-Freixas and the other interpreters were taken to the National Cattle Congress's sixty-acre fairground, which had been converted into what the professor describes as a "concentration camp or detention center."

"Fenced in behind the ballroom/courtroom were 23 trailers from federal authorities, including two set up as sentencing courts; various Homeland Security buses and an 'incident response' truck; scores of ICE agents and U.S. Marshals . . . prosecutors had established a command center; and a gymnasium filled with tight rows of cots where some 300 male detainees were kept, the women being housed in county jails."

There Professor Camayd-Freixas describes seeing the "saddest procession" he had ever witnessed, and which the public would never see because cameras were not allowed. " . . . Driven single-file in groups of 10, shackled at the wrists, waist and ankles, chains dragging as they shuffled through, the slaughterhouse workers were brought in for arraignment. They sat and listened through headsets to the interpreted initial appearance, before marching out again to be bused to different county jails, only to make room for the next row of 10."

They were mostly "illiterate Guatemalan peasants with Mayan last names. . . . Some were in tears; others had faces of worry, fear, and embarrassment." Tiny, almost aboriginal-seeming brown-skinned people, they stood "in stark racial contrast to the rest of us as they started their slow penguin march across the makeshift court."

Camayd-Freixas's graphic insider account describes the typical man being torn from his workplace, charged, convicted, sentenced and incarcerated pending deportation. They went destined to be thrown out of the country, but that only after five months behind bars as convicted federal felons who can never legally return to the United States, even to retrieve their wives and children. The professor tells of interviewing a Guatemalan who spent the interview weeping in fear for the fate of his family, before telling the story of how he had come to be in Postville. "I walked for a month and ten days until I crossed the [Rio Grande] river." Forming a bond with other recent arrivals he hitched a ride to Dallas, then to the promise of a job in Postville, where he had worked only two months before the immigration raid heard 'round the world.

"I just wanted to work a year or two, save, and then go back to my family, but it was not to be."

The story gets worse. Remember the setting, rustic Postville, Iowa (population 2,273), and the makeshift courts in the cattle field in nearby Waterloo, where by prearrangement that gave scant warning to hastily court-appointed defense attorneys, all 389 workers arrested, "waived their right to be indicted . . . hoping to be quickly deported since they had families to support back home."

Under ordinary circumstances—that is, a less hysterical historic period than this one—the typical disposition of an immigration case would have been probation followed by immediate deportation. Two hundred and seventy of the Postville 389 (or 390 by some accounts) were coerced instead into accepting a felony conviction and a prearranged five-month prison sentence, only then followed by deportation. They walked into a legal ambush in which they were "criminally charged with 'aggravated identity theft' and 'Social Security fraud'—charges they did not understand," said Camayd-Freixas.

As they were used following the pathetic Postville Raid, these charges are among the most bogus on the books today. Think of it this way: these men are now felons and therefore barred forever from seeking legal status in the United States because they paid money into our Social Security trust fund in the form of payroll taxes that they have no hope of ever redeeming. It is their gift to America. And most of the workers had no idea they were even committing a crime. According to testimony, they were simply using identity cards given to them by their employer as a condition of working in the plant. In fact, the U.S. Supreme Court in *Flores-Figueroa v. United States*, a unanimous 9-0 decision in May 2009, overturned the law the government had used to pressure the workers into pleading guilty.

Now, just using a fake Social Security card is not enough to support conviction under the law. The government has to prove illegal workers intentionally stole legitimate cards, which actually belong to another person. Although the decision led to calls for dismissal of their guilty pleas, it came too late to help the Postville 389 because most had already served their time and had been deported. And who were they exactly?

Analyzing the cases of these hapless working people arrested by an agency designed to combat criminals or terrorists, of the 389 arrested, seventy-six were women; fifty-six of them were mothers with unattended children in Postville who were released on humanitarian grounds pending court dates. Twelve were juveniles also released conditionally. Most of the parolees were forced to wear electronic ankle monitors or be directly turned over for deportation.

As of this writing, eleven months after the noxious raid, and 100 days into the Obama presidency, the women, who are known as "*las mujeres con brazaletes*" (the women with the electronic bracelets), are still daily reminders of the iron hurricane that swept through Postville and through the lives of so many families.

Importantly, only five had the previously required criminal record, which was supposed to be ICE's priority—five of 389. The other 384 were the sitting ducks whose lives are ruined, even as their families were terrorized and remain bereft, their mothers feeding them with food and supplies from the local volunteer food bank created by townspeople, various faith-based groups and outside supporters moved by the families' plight.

When the abusive conditions of their employment at the slaughterhouse were later revealed by testimony, the outrage over the arrest and hustled justice was renewed. Why were the workers targeted for such harsh treatment? Why them and not their employer, the Rubashkin family, which had restored the town's defunct meatpacking plant in the late 1990s and built it into the nation's largest kosher processor?

Various post-raid investigations revealed that management had systematically given these poor immigrant employees their false identification, underpaid them on the pretext of defraying immigration fees, refused restroom use during ten-hour shifts, failed to pay overtime, and had routinely used underage workers and physically abused them.

All the while, a small community of fellow Hasidic rabbis of the

Lubavitcher sect had been working to ensure that the plant processes complied with strict kosher dietary laws. The rabbis certified the plant was kosher, but apparently did nothing to alleviate the suffering of the workers or even the animals. But the grim conditions did not escape notice entirely by members of the Jewish community. Following an exposé of the animal suffering in the plant by PETA and other activists, on May 26, 2006, the *Jewish Daily Forward* newspaper published in an editorial:

"The company's workers tell a grim tale of long hours, low pay, humiliating treatment by capricious supervisors, dangerous conditions and insufficient safety measures. The workers, many of them undocumented immigrants, spoke to the *Forward* on condition of anonymity, fearing dismissal or deportation if they were identified."

The disturbing probability that the rabbis involved knew of and condoned the abusive work conditions sent shock waves of regret and embarrassment through the U.S. Jewish community in the aftermath of the May 2008 raid. Speaking about the outrageous situation in Iowa with the congregation of Temple Tifereth, Erica's family synagogue in Shaker Heights, near Cleveland, several months later, I had a lively discussion with a compassionate, deeply concerned audience on Judaism's ethical requirements, which everyone present acknowledged was as important as the technical requirements of keeping kosher.

Agriprocessors' original management was criminally charged under various labor and immigration laws, but only after protestors demanded it. Two officials pleaded not guilty to federal charges alleging visa fraud and harboring illegal aliens. Rabbi Sholom Rubashkin, the former CEO for Agriprocessors' Postville plant, and operations manager Brent Beebe pleaded not guilty to all charges. Another Agriprocessors employee charged in the indictment, human resources worker Laura Althouse, pleaded guilty in October 2008 to helping illegal workers use false documents to work at the plant. Karina Pilar Freund pleaded guilty to similar charges in December 2008, when the company was also fined $10 million by Iowa regulators, but all of those penalties are subject to review given the U.S. Supreme Court's may 2009 ruling.

Aside from becoming the flashpoint in the immigration debate and the gift that kept giving voters to Barack Obama's presidential campaign, helping rally Hispanics to the Democrats' banner, pathetic Postville has a postscript that would be funny if it weren't so preposterous.

Those 389 jobs vacated by the draconian raid were not filled by strapping young white farm boys or the Midwest's urban poor or laid-off factory workers from other hard-hit areas of recession-era America.

When Agriprocessors reopened, those Guatemalan and Mexican workers arrested were replaced by 150 immigrants from Somalia. In the United States legally as political refugees, the young Muslim men were brought into Postville, a town where, bizarrely, the families of the arrested Latino workers still live. It is a common sight to see a turbaned Somali walking alongside a Guatemalan woman and her children and a felt-hat-wearing Hasidic rabbi. This is just one of the unintended consequences of this bogus action. And this trend of importing Somalis is happening in post-ICE raid towns throughout the Midwest. In one case the Somalis made headlines when they staged a protest about their employer's alleged failure to provide them their requisite prayer time.

In Postville, the new workers are being paid thirteen dollars an hour, twice what their arrested Latino predecessors received under far more onerous circumstances. I do not begrudge the Somalis either their jobs or their salaries. I have seen close-up the anarchy and savage violence in Mogadishu, Somalia. The only growth industry in that wretched and dangerous place is the high-seas piracy that has spread terror to ships and crews transiting the Horn of Africa.

In fact, the closely knit Somali community in Minneapolis from which the workers were drawn made headlines in early 2009, when the Senate Committee on Homeland Security and Governmental Affairs held hearings about the disappearance of twelve to twenty young Somali-Americans who are believed to be affiliated with al-Shabab, a militant group linked to al-Qaeda. The fear is that because they are here legally and can move freely, the missing youth are establishing sleeper terrorist cells in the United States.

The fears were born in October 2008, when suicide bomber Shirwa

Ahmed, a naturalized American, took part in a series of coordinated attacks in Somalia. Ahmed's suicide attack followed an American air strike in Somalia in which the leader of al-Shabab was killed. The group then announced "that from that point, it would target all U.S., Western, and U.N. personnel and interests," Davidson College political science professor Kenneth Menkhaus told the *L.A. Times*.

Like I said, I don't begrudge any honest person a job, but is it not a little strange for ICE to stage this massive military-style Postville raid using our most elite antiterrorist-immigrant task force at the cost of enormous time, energy and taxpayer expense, including the mobilization of dozens of assistant U.S. attorneys taken off their real job of prosecuting real criminals, and put everybody through all these painful contortions, just to transfer jobs from Latino peasants who have been coming for decades and have deep roots in the community to Africans imported from far farther afield? Somalis in Iowa; weren't any Eskimos available? What exactly was the point of the Postville raid? Making America safer? Law and order? Please.

On Sunday, July 27, 2008, a thousand protestors, including those Latino immigrant family members not too fearful of being arrested if they showed their faces in public, descended on downtown Postville to demand changes in U.S. immigration policy, which makes criminals of people who have come to the United States just to make a living. Many of the demonstrators were from organizations like the Chicago-based Jewish Council on Urban Affairs and the Minneapolis-based Jewish Community Action, who joined local Christian leaders in a citywide march calling for an end to workplace raids that inflict so much pain and disrupt so many lives.

The Migration Policy Institute, a nonpartisan Washington think tank, armed with documents obtained via the Freedom of Information Act, later confirmed in February 2009 that the Immigration and Customs Enforcement program under which the otherwise innocent workers had been arrested had originally been pledged to target the most dangerous immigration fugitives. Furthermore, the report found that the Postville raid was just one example of a distressing pattern.

"In spite of the fact that the program supposedly prioritized its targets based on their dangerousness, the program primarily arrested the easiest targets," Margot Mendelson, coauthor of the MPI report, told Susan Carroll of the *Houston Chronicle*.

"While ICE prioritizes our efforts by targeting fugitives who have demonstrated a threat to national security or public safety, we have a clear mandate to pursue all immigration fugitives—even those with no documented criminal history in the United States," ICE spokesman Greg Palmore told Carroll lamely.

Again, I don't question either the patriotism or professionalism of the ICE personnel involved in workplace raids like Postville, or even those who kick in the doors of suspected illegal immigrants in the dark of night without a warrant. They are following orders and doing their jobs. I do, however, accuse their bosses of engineering an enormous bait and switch. And I have high hopes for the new Homeland Security secretary, former Arizona governor Janet Napolitano. As a border state governor, she has the experience necessary to protect our borders, but to do so in a compassionate, reasoned, humane way that her predecessor forsook in the hubris of political calculation.

Specifically I blame Julie L. Myers, whose nomination as assistant secretary of Homeland Security for U.S. Immigration and Customs Enforcement got out of committee on a strict majority-Republican, party-line vote. Myers, who did not have the experience required by statute, received what is called a "recess appointment" in January 2006, just in time to amp up the effort against innocent immigrants. The full Senate never voted on her disastrous selection.

It was during Ms. Myers's tenure that ICE was polluted by anti-immigration activist politics. She is perhaps the Republican most responsible for the excesses that sank John McCain's chances of winning the Hispanic vote. McCain wasn't perfect, but he deserved better than this political hack who got the job because, at the time of her appointment, her husband was Homeland Security secretary Michael Chertoff's chief of staff and her uncle was chairman of the Joint Chiefs of Staff.

It is perhaps unsurprising that Ms. Myers formerly worked for Kenneth Starr, the special prosecutor who hounded Bill Clinton to impeachment for getting that Oval Office blow job and then lying about it to his wife—the way men always lie when they get caught getting blow jobs at work.

Myers was also Starr's lead prosecutor in the Independent Counsel's notoriously failed case against Clinton friend Susan McDougal, one of the true heroes of the wretched Whitewater era, who refused to conjure evidence against the forty-second president to save her own behind.

Myers's rocky tenure at ICE was marked by an infamous Halloween costume party she hosted for ICE employees, of which she was the judge, awarding first prize to a white ICE agent who came dressed in blackface as an escaped Jamaican prisoner. She is also alleged to have been the source of the illegal leaking of the news that Barack Obama's Kenyan aunt was in the United States illegally, a charge she denies. Unsurprisingly, Myers resigned the day after Obama's historic election, which is reason enough to applaud his victory.

By playing up the agency's abilities to deal with any domestic law enforcement contingency, ICE was given lavish post-9/11 funding, $625 million over five years to hunt terrorists and criminal immigrants. Instead, to satisfy the talk radio crowd they went lazily and ideologically for the "low-hanging fruit," the otherwise innocent immigrant workers who, mixing metaphors, were sitting ducks. And they did it because they were ordered to do it by the Bush administration's Ms. Myers, who effectively altered the nation's immigration enforcement policy without the inconvenience of getting a congressional vote.

"It looks like what happened here is that the law enforcement strategy was hijacked by the political agenda of the [Bush] administration," Peter L. Markowitz, who teaches immigration law at the Cardozo School of Law and worked on the MPI report, told Nina Bernstein of the *New York Times*.

One result of that distortion of federal policy is the dramatic altering of the ethnic composition of offenders sentenced in federal courts. In 2007, Latinos accounted for 40 percent of all sentenced federal offenders, more than triple their share of the total U.S. adult population. And most of those were convicted for the mere crime of being in this country illegally.

"Fully 75 percent of Latino offenders sentenced for immigration crimes in 2007 were convicted of entering the U.S. unlawfully or residing in the country without authorization, and 19 percent were sentenced for smuggling, transporting or harboring an unlawful alien," says Mark Hugo Lopez, associate director, Pew Hispanic Center. In other words, the taxpayers are paying approximately three hundred dollars per person per day to imprison the thirty-four thousand otherwise noncriminal immigrants arrested in fiscal 2008 by the National Fugitive Operations Program, including the 389 arrested in Postville, Iowa; $10,200,000. Per day.

"Here's my beef," I said during an exclusive interview with former Pennsylvania governor Tom Ridge, the granite-jawed first Homeland Security secretary, who left the agency in 2004, before its descent into political hackery. "After you left, something bad happened. Because of political pressure, I believe they decided to go for the big numbers. They decided to unleash ICE, this elite police force, on ordinary working immigrants. Not the criminals or the terrorists that you were seeking."

"Well, there was a lot of pressure, Geraldo. I think your instincts are pretty good on this, to the extent that there was a lot of pressure to enforce the law. And in enforcing the employment laws, they went in and took people out of businesses where they were going to work, paying taxes, and while they may have been here illegally, they were trying to live lawfully.

"And ICE is probably still understaffed," Ridge continued. "I'm sure they could use more agents to go after the drug dealers, the predators within that illegal community. So I don't know whether there was a shift of emphasis, but there was sure a lot more publicity about shutting down employers who did have unlawful employees who were actually trying to do some good, adding some value and raising families, when we know we got a lot of other illegal aliens, unlawful immigrants who are part of our crime culture. And we ought to be focusing on that culture first."

I added, "Them and the gangs, the street gangs that are now acting in concert with these Mexican drug cartels."

Mr. Ridge agreed: "Yeah, we've got a lot of illegal immigrants in this country. But they're trying to do the right thing by their families and their employers. And we have a smaller group of criminals. But this is the group, I think, we ought to be targeting. They're very much a part of the criminal culture. And we ought to be spending most of our time trying to rid them from our midst."

The ICE professionals left behind after the election did their best in February 2009 to counter the damning MPI report, which "seems to suggest that law enforcement should not arrest any immigration fugitive who does not have a prior criminal conviction, even though they have ignored a judge's order to leave the country," Ivan Ortiz-Delgado, an agency spokesman, told the Associated Press. "We disagree."

The ICE bureaucrats in Washington disagreed. Worse, in a stunning display of independence or arrogance, just a month into his presidency they ordered their first work-site raid since Barack Obama took office, and they did it without bothering to inform their new boss, the newly confirmed Homeland Security Secretary, Janet Napolitano.

In the early morning hours of February 24, 2009, ICE agents swept into the Yamato Engine Specialists factory in Bellingham, Washington, a company that specializes in rebuilding Japanese car engines and transmissions, rounding up twenty-five men and three women, all Mexicans except for a Honduran, a Salvadoran and a Guatemalan. Two were deported immediately, two released for health reasons and the three women paroled to care for their children.

"The lure of jobs in the United States continues to be one of the primary factors fueling illegal immigration," ICE spokesperson Leigh Winchell told the *Seattle Times* shortly after the arrests. Then, after pointing out that these twenty-eight jobs would soon be filled by citizens, she added, "ICE remains committed to investigating cases where the evidence shows employment laws are being violated." More than three hundred thousand people were trying to find a job in Washington State at the time of the raid. Unemployment in the city of Bellingham had soared above 8 percent, more than twice the rate a year earlier. FOX News and other media outlets eagerly pointed out the lines of presumably citizen job applicants at Yamato in the days following the unauthorized raid.

Clearly, ICE officials believed the local economy's travails would provide them cover to carry on doing what they had been doing across the country: using massive police power to disrupt businesses using undocumented workers. But they miscalculated the resolve of the Obama administration to change the way ICE's business is done. "I want to get to the bottom of this as well," a blindsided, outraged Secretary Napolitano told mostly sympathetic lawmakers during a hearing in Washington, promising a review of a punitive action that clearly flew in the face of the new administration's promise to emphasize employer sanctions over workplace raids.

"We urge President Obama to deliver on his promise of change by stopping the raids, and signing just and humane immigration reform into law," a deeply disappointed Marissa Graciosa of FIRM, the Fair Immigration Reform Movement, told the Associated Press in the wake of the Bellingham raid.

But whether the raids stop or not—and, aside from Yamato, early indications are that they are being stopped by the Obama administration because they cause far more disruption than justice—there is no denying that our nation's current economic plight will only add to tensions over immigration.

If things continue to get worse, and domestic citizen unemployment continues to deteriorate, so will the shrill tone of the debate over reform. The point is felt even more deeply at times of widespread financial distress like our country currently suffers. It is much more challenging to be in favor of increasing the labor pool when you're the one out of work and looking for a job.

Fortunately not too many citizens have been pushed into the hard-core menial labor most often performed by immigrants. You still don't see many laid-off factory workers or financiers cleaning toilets at O'Hare airport or picking apples in upstate New York, not yet anyway. In spring 2009, with the stubbornly spreading recession, however, there have been increasing, though still isolated examples of competitive friction for jobs.

When the huge ICE raid on Howard Industries, the manufacturer of electrical distribution equipment in Laurel, Mississippi, resulted in the arrest of nearly six hundred suspected illegal immigrants in late August 2008, the *L.A. Times* reported that many black and white residents in the town applauded the crackdown. "They need to go and do this in every little town." *Times* reporters Miguel Bustillo and Richard Fausset got that distressing reaction from resident Tonya Jackson.

"Jackson, who is black, said that over the years she had applied numerous times for a job at the locally owned manufacturer, which employs about 4,000 workers. Jackson, 30, said she never received a callback. The raid, she said, was a welcome purge of illegal Latino laborers who had taken jobs they didn't deserve," write the reporters in the *L.A. Times*.

As unpleasant as that sounds, the tension Ms. Jackson's comments reveal remains almost nonexistent. Still, advocates of immigration reform must recognize the tight spot the new president is in right now and find a measured way forward toward a compassionate, reasoned and practical solution. There is a natural instinct, particularly in hard times, to want to purge foreigners, restrict trade and protect domestic industry. But as President Obama said to great effect during the G20 summit in London in April 2009, the benefits of protectionism are short-lived. Immigration opponents must be gently lobbied to see current events in the broad tapestry of American history. In order for Hispanics to make the contribution I believe they will to the future of this country, we must stop treating them like the enemy. Far from dreaming of destroying the U.S.A., these workers are just the latest in our grand tradition. As you're about to see, ICE has much more dangerous fish to fry.

3

THE STORM ALONG THE BORDER

"We're in the eye of the storm. If it doesn't stop here, if we're not able to fix it here and get it turned around, it will go across the nation."

—Phoenix Police Chief Andy Anderson to ABC News
after ruthless Mexican drug cartels made his city
America's kidnapping capital, February 2009

"*Plata o Plomo*." (Silver or Lead)

—A standing cartel threat to Mexican police or
soldiers to take bribe money or get shot

"We need the fence, and we need it yesterday."

—*Free Republic* blog, February 2009

Despite the critical role the Hispanic community played in electing Barack Obama president and thereby helping change the face, character and immediate future of American politics, most of the national media focus on Latinos in the first half of 2009 remained negative and still framed around the persistently abrasive issue of illegal immigration.

Worse, a putrid fog of fear and resentment still lies heavily over the entire Hispanic community, citizen and immigrant alike. There seems to be a bad vibe, a defensiveness among many in mainstream society— certainly in the media—about the surging Latino population stealing jobs and public services, committing crimes and plotting to take America to a place the nation has never been.

In terms of a historic comparison, it is not unlike the early World War II period when populist, media-driven movements sprang up in cities around the country to physically isolate Japanese-Americans and to ban spoken Italian. The language that at the time was the nation's second most popular became the target of a "don't speak the enemy's language" campaign, because

Italy had sided with Germany in the war. Almost overnight, in once vibrant Little Italys, spoken Italian became suspect, withered away and died for a generation. Virtually none of my Italian-American friends of my generation speak their parents' native tongue. Their children are studying Italian in school as families try to resurrect the hometown connection, but the impact of that wartime hysteria lasted for decades.

The scars of Japanese-American internment likewise are only being alleviated by the passage of two-thirds of a century of smoldering bitterness. In both cases, historic wrongs are being soothed by the salve of time, as both Italians and Japanese assume their rightful place in America's Great Progression, but in both cases, years were lost, and my fear is that the same is happening now to Hispanic-Americans, whose language is being assailed, and an entire community slandered, in the context and under the cover of the divisive debate over immigration.

The discussion has been aggravated by our terrible economy. As vocal and energetic as anti-immigration and, by extension, anti-Latino sentiment has been in the United States, remember, this was during the boom times. Domestic unemployment was under 5 percent and there were labor shortages everywhere. Now unemployment is twice that rate—double digits loom; in fact, by the spring of 2009 they had already arrived in Michigan, South Carolina, Oregon, North Carolina, Rhode Island, California and Nevada and everywhere else among minorities.

During these hard times, the position of advocates of a more restrictive policy toward outsiders is naturally strengthened because more Americans are out of work. It is easier to blame the immigrant (a.k.a. "them") for what ails the citizen (a.k.a. "us"), including increased crime, public health care costs, drug addiction and job stealing. As you will see, the same people who have campaigned so aggressively against illegal immigration are now blaming those hapless foreigners for the subprime mortgage fiasco and the collapse of the housing market. Apparently, UFOs were not available.

More urgently, our nation's economic distress coincides with a deteriorating security situation south of the border. Mexico is at war with itself, a real, bloody, shooting war between the nation's military and heavily armed militias fielded by the Mexican drug cartels. The violence is so widespread it is stoking an unhelpful new angle, which weighs heavily on the public's sense and sensibility about Hispanic assimilation and our rightful place in American society: The new rage is the danger posed to our national security by anarchy in Mexico.

"While drug war violence has dominated the recent news about the possible irreversible status as a society beyond remediation, the topic of immigration has been either marginalized or used to further promote fears that the conflict may spread to the United States. Drugs, national security, and economic recession have replaced immigration reform on the United States' policy agenda," reports the authoritative, nonpartisan Council on Hemispheric Affairs (COHA).

Cable news and talk radio audiences are again being told on a daily basis by commentators like Michelle Malkin and Glenn Beck, the latter my newest colleague at FOX News, that Mexican civil disorder is pouring over our borders, and that we stand on the precipice of cross-border invasion by marauding cutthroats bent on rape and rapine.

One night in February 2009, Mr. Beck became so emotional on the air while interviewing the stepfather of a young woman who disappeared in Mexico in 2004 that he actually began weeping. Because I had reported the disappearance of Yvette Martinez and interviewed her stepfather, William Slemaker, years earlier, I found Beck's passion a curious, delayed reaction. Even Mr. Slemaker seemed uneasy about Beck's flowing tears. Put in the best possible light, those tears were more a frustrated lament on America's failure to understand the current danger posed by Mexican organized criminals than they were sorrow for this one young lady gone missing in Mexico five years before.

In fact, I thought Beck was nuts, wildly exaggerating an admittedly serious situation along the border to make a cheap political point. The next morning on *FOX & Friends*, I criticized his segment, and said more generally that Beck's consistently apocryphal, gloom and doom, on-air, antigovernment rants did not speak for me. But it pains me to admit that, in this case his main point was correct: The story of spreading border anarchy was underreported at the time of his Slemaker interview. Ideological hyperbole is infuriating, but on this subject it was not hype.

Some of the bloodiest battles in Mexico were being fought in two cities I know well: Ciudad Juárez across the Rio Grande River from El Paso, Texas, and Tijuana, adjacent to San Diego right along the California/ Baja border. Both big cities on the Mexican side of the line have until recently been frequent haunts of millions of tourists, especially kids in college or the military on the naughty hunt for cheap liquor, authentic cuisine, suntans, sex, drugs or mariachi music. I discovered them while a student at the University of Arizona in Tucson just sixty miles—an hour's drive—from the border city of Nogales.

Tellingly, the U of A issued a warning to all students to avoid even traveling to Mexico, which was specifically off-limits for the 2009 edition of spring break. Worse for that troubled nation's economy, the State Department issued a travel alert to potential tourists that bystanders were being injured or killed in the drug-related violence and gun battles.

"Some recent Mexican army and police confrontations with drug cartels have resembled small-unit combat," said the alert, dated March 2009. "Large firefights have taken place in many towns and cities across Mexico, but most recently in northern Mexico, including Tijuana, Chihuahua City and Ciudad Juárez."

The border metropolises where most of the Mexican violence is being meted out are living examples of the schizoid nature of our neighbor's national life. This vast and dramatic land is as close to America as skin, and as far away as the other side of the world. At its best Mexico is dynamic, creative, ageless, exciting and gorgeous, both people and place. At its worst the nation is a volcano of wild emotion that drives this crazy violence that I swear to God is more about pride and machismo than it is about rival drug gangs fighting to control the trade. It's about whose dick is bigger.

Aside from truckers working the cross-border trade, which has also been severely curtailed by politics and violence, these days only the hard-core traveler goes to Juárez. Tijuana is officially off-limits to U.S. military personnel and virtually off-limits to U.S. civilians following a rash of tourist-related incidents that are connected to the malignant climate of drug crime that has distorted these familiar places and made them foreign and unfamiliar in the extreme.

These border cities combine Mexico—the modern, sophisticated democracy of skyscraper businesses, traffic and taxis—with Mexico—the last refuge of Wild West gunfighters and desperados. Deadly street shootings, decapitations and other murders have made Juárez Mexico's murder capital, with eleven homicides on a single Sunday in January 2009, seven on that Monday, six on Tuesday and nine on Wednesday. "And on Thursday [January 22nd], at least six men had been killed by the evening, including an unidentified man found tied up and stabbed to death not far from the new U.S. Consulate," Chihuahua state police told the *El Paso Times*.

February was worse in Juárez. Consider the following news wire service headlines. February 9: "Mexico Arrests Police Chief over General's Murder." (The chief was suspected of orchestrating the military officer's assassination after receiving payment from a drug cartel.) February 10: "Drug Gang Clash with Army Kills 21 in Mexico." The thirteenth: "Texans Getting Caught in the Crossfire of Mexican Drug Violence," and that same day, "Mexican Army Repels Drug Gang Attack, Killing Three." The fifteenth: "Gunmen Shoot 12 in Mexico Including Children," and "Top Mexican Drug Cop Charged with Working for Cartel." Advocating comprehensive immigration reform or expanding public educational benefits for the children of immigrants under the circumstances of these grisly current events a stone's throw from the United States became very difficult.

I returned to Juárez/El Paso in March 2009 to see the situation firsthand. It was heartbreaking. With a brave local reporter, Edgar Román of Juárez's Canal 44, we drove all through the embattled city, where an average of about five people a day had been murdered since January 2008. "They've broken every unwritten rule. Now they're killing wives and children. They kidnapped eight little girls in a single day. They even killed an evangelical preacher during a sermon, to send a message to his parish that prayers won't make the cartel go away," Román told me.

I stood on a pedestrian bridge over the culvert containing the trickle of water otherwise known as the Rio Grande, a dusty wind filtering the southwestern sun. As I reported, "It is really a tale of two cities. On the Mexican side, Ciudad Juárez, with about two thousand murders just since January

2008; on the other side of the line, El Paso, with fewer than twenty homicides during that same period. And because these are twin cities about the same size with members of the same families living on both sides of the line, the obvious worry is that sooner or later, what's happening over there in Mexico will be happening over here in the United States."

Hispanic legislators are concerned even for the fate of Mexico's elected government. "The only thing I want to say is that the situation is very serious and very critical," U.S. Representative Silvestre Reyes, Texas Democrat and chairman of the House Permanent Select Committee on Intelligence, told the *El Paso Times*. "It is a danger because the cartels are fighting among each other, and the Calderón administration has decided to take on this issue of the cartels and criminal gangs."

It is another lamentable fact that since brave president Felipe Calderón deployed his army in 2006 to dismantle the drug gangs that had assumed a perverse sovereignty over much of Mexico's border region, "over 8,000 casualties have been violently claimed in cartel hot spots across Mexico," according to COHA, which points out that "Early in 2009 the violent trend set in motion during the two previous years has shown no sign of slackening." By press time's final reckoning more than ten thousand Mexicans had died in gang warfare across the country since 2006, which caused some to question whether Mexico itself would unravel.

David Blair, diplomatic editor of the U.K.'s *Daily Telegraph*, first reported on the existence of a U.S. Army "Joint Operating Environment" study pointing to two potential national catastrophes. "Two large and important states bear consideration for rapid and sudden collapse: Pakistan and Mexico." Blair quoted the report, whose existence has subsequently been confirmed by the Pentagon: "The Mexican possibility may seem less likely, but the government, its politicians, police and judicial infrastructure are all under sustained assault and pressure by criminal gangs and drug cartels. . . . Any descent by Mexico into chaos would demand an American response based on the serious implications for homeland security alone," says the report, which set off a firestorm of commentary about the possibility that good old Mexico next door might become as incendiary and as explosively fragile as Pakistan.

While Mexican officials reacted with horror at the comparison, without a doubt the increasingly violent struggle along the border resulted in a yearlong eruption of deadly ambushes, street shootings, home invasions, assassinations, kidnappings and decapitations, and brought anarchy to Mexican border towns and deep apprehension to American cities near the line. "Where in the world are you most likely to be beheaded?" wrote the *Huffington Post's* Johann Hari. "Where are hand grenades being tossed into crowds to intimidate the public into shutting up? Which country was just named by the U.S. Joint Chiefs of Staff as the most likely after Pakistan to suffer a 'rapid and sudden collapse'? The answer is Mexico."

According to the United States' National Gang Intelligence Center, aside from the cartels' own drug smugglers, Texas-based prison gangs like the Aztecas and transnational Hispanic street gangs, including MS-13 and the 18th Street gang, "have close associations with Mexico-based drug trafficking organizations and contract to smuggle drugs and illegal immigrants from the Mexican smugglers engaged in these activities."

The situation is real enough to have caught the attention of neighboring California's attorney general, Jerry Brown, who soberly voiced concern that the U.S. government is too focused on "traditional" terrorists like al-Qaeda, and must remember the terrorizing criminals closer to home. "Those, for the average Californian or the average American, may be a more immediate threat to their well-being," Brown told ABC News.

On the March 2009 Saturday I broadcast live from the Mexican border, the situation was deemed so serious that President Barack Obama was briefed that morning by Admiral Mike Mullen, the new chairman of the Joint Chiefs of Staff, on how U.S. security forces might help the Mexican government in its fight against brazen organized armies that had gone beyond mere criminal activity and were acting more like the Taliban. "Not only are they acting like al-Qaeda, with these beheadings and so forth, these gangs are trying to replace the government, to become the government. We must be concerned for the security of our southern flank," terror expert Walid Phares told me, expressing a spreading, if still overstated concern. It is bad, don't get me wrong, but Mexican militias aren't about to charge over the border wearing suicide belts or planting roadside mines.

As the U.S. government contemplated an enhanced American role in battling the savage gangs, some sources even spoke of the politically explosive possibility that our police or even military forces might be deployed on the Mexican side of the border. That is a contingency that the Mexican government, not to mention a majority of the Mexican people, has long resisted, at least since the Texas War of Independence in 1835–36 and the Mexican-American War of 1846–48 resulted in a loss of half of Mexico's national territory to the United States. But hard times make strange bedfellows, and for our southern neighbor, these are the hardest of times.

"The government, its politicians, police and judicial infrastructure are all under sustained assault and pressure by criminal gangs and drug cartels. How that internal conflict turns out over the next several years will have a major impact on the stability of the Mexican state," reported COHA, and then, more alarmingly on March 5th, 2009: "The Mexican economy and many of its national institutional structures may be on the brink of collapse."

From the point of view of the U.S. Hispanic community, most of which is of Mexican origin, until this border anarchy has run its course, many American families, particularly border-state Latinos in cities like San Diego, Brownsville, Laredo and El Paso, will pay a price in terms of severely restricted cross-border life. "That is why we are hoping that the Mexican president will be successful, because we do miss the environment that we had here prior to the killings escalating to the point where they are now," El Paso County sheriff Richard Wiles told me during a border interview. An incredible 80 percent of the sheriff's department and the El Paso city police have family members living on the Juárez side of the line. "We were one community where people could cross back and forth and enjoy the culture of both cities. But clearly that is not happening anymore."

President Felipe Calderón, who won the presidency by a tiny margin of a fraction of 1 percent, called on his nation to "stand behind our army's fight against this common enemy." He vowed "to continue fighting organized crime, without pause or mercy," adding that seventy-eight soldiers have been killed in the past two years in battles against the drug cartels. "Mexico faces a historic challenge in converting itself into a safe country, a country of true law and order." Calderón made that statement even as drug bandits killed their second Juárez city councilwoman of the week. Both Patricia Avila and Cristina Aranda were shot in the head at close range as they sat in their cars. The police chief quit when the cartel said it would kill a cop a day until he left town. After two cops died, the chief split.

I asked the Mexican ambassador to the U.S., Arturo Sarukhan, an elegant man and longtime Calderón ally, about the reports of American military assistance. "We are asking for enhanced cooperation," he answered firmly, determined to speak frankly, but to quell talk of Mexico as a failed state. "I will in no way try to minimize the level of violence that the drug traffickers have unleashed. I will not minimize the challenge that we face as we strike out against them. I will certainly not minimize the fact that this is going to be a long, protracted fight. It is not going to be over tomorrow. There is no silver bullet that will solve the problem."

And the violence isn't staying south of the border. According to federal and state authorities, a dangerous and deadly epidemic of kidnapping-for-ransom cases has hit Phoenix, over 350 in 2008 alone, making the Arizona capital second only to Mexico City as the kidnapping capital of the world. In cases throughout central Arizona's Valley of the Sun, both the victim and the perpetrators are criminal aliens connected to the Mexican drug trade.

Working with Phoenix police, ace reporter Brian Ross and his ABC News team uncovered horrific cases of hands, legs and even heads cut off if the victim's family or criminal associates didn't pay the demanded ransom fast enough. But this crime wave was largely under the media radar screen, because the vicious over-the-top violence was almost exclusively contained within the criminal community itself. So far, it has scarcely affected law-abiding Americans on the U.S. side of the line.

"Since the violence started, we have treated every incident as a potential border violence incident," Luna County, New Mexico, sheriff Raymond Cobos told reporters along the border in January 2009. "But so far, nothing has spilled over."

Indeed, law enforcement experts are unanimous in believing that the last thing Mexican drug lords want is direct conflict with the United States military, law enforcement or border security forces.

"We all pretty much feel like the violence is going to be contained in Mexico," said El Paso, Texas, police chief Greg Allen, refusing to become overly alarmist in the face of crisis. "Our concern is minimal."

There is an infamous scene in Al Pacino's classic 1983 movie *Scarface* that accurately encapsulates both the operatic horror of the current gory violence, and the relative nonimpact on ordinary Americans. The film is set in Miami during the height of the cocaine violence there. Remember when Tony Montana's friend Angel is cut up with a chain saw by a rival criminal trying to convince Tony to divulge inside information about the drug trade? Similarly, these banditos are carving one another up on a medieval scale, but are not yet a public health or safety menace in the United States. One of the few U.S. citizens killed was a San Diego pizza shop owner named Jorge Norman Harrison, an ex-con drug dealer who, after being kidnapped, was later found chopped up outside Tijuana despite the fact his family had paid out a twenty-thousand-dollar ransom to the cartel. He must have done something criminal to the criminals.

Because the dead or kidnapped and tortured crooks elicit little sympathy, what is worse long-term is that the widespread and horrifying nature of their intramural violence is reinvigorating critics of Hispanic immigration, like Texas Republican Senator John Cornyn and Lone Star State governor Rick Perry, who, in March 2009, were asking that the border barrier, already formidable, be further fortified with federal troops, which is about the dumbest idea around. What is the 101st Airborne Division (Air Assault) going to do in Texas? Stare at sand dunes?

Tellingly, Governor Perry joined the lunatic fringe when he suggested a month later during the Tea-Party demonstrations on Tax Day 2009 that because Texans were so fed up with Obama's fiscal policies they might secede from the Union. Hey Governor, what happens if Texans vote to leave the United States? Does that mean when the state has an Hispanic majority it can vote to re-join Mexico? Give me a break.

Cheap-shot political polemics aside, the Border Patrol and local, county and state law enforcement are more than adequate to protect the southern line. It's the transnational cartel-based gangster activity inside the United States that needs attention now. We have to go after these criminal syndicates using wiretaps, informants and RICO statutes, the way we went after the Mafia. Using the military against Mexican drug gangsters is like using the military against American-Italians to fight traditional organized crime.

You saw the *Godfather* movies. Can you imagine Humvees and tanks being deployed to quell the violence of the five families in the five boroughs? How about sending the New York–based 10th Mountain Division to Coney Island to battle the Russian mob? Or, closer to this border reality, sending the California National Guard to take control of overwhelmingly Hispanic and gang-riddled East Los Angeles? Trust me, the U.S. military could not be more ill-suited for this mission; no patriot could do that to the world's best military, maybe the greatest armed force ever fielded. Would you make the ultimate defenders of the United States Constitution beat cops in their own country? That is wasteful, ill-advised and dangerous.

Help by all means with surveillance, maybe provide the Mexican military with drones and helicopters and eavesdropping equipment, mount joint intelligence and coordinated police activity, but don't pretend a photo-op deployment of GIs along the border will make a drop of difference.

As chapter two relates, the biggest law enforcement scandal in modern U.S. history is how our most elite antiterror, antigangster immigrant police force was hijacked by political ideologues. Americans have to know that, for the last several years, ICE—Immigration and Customs Enforcement—has been used almost exclusively to sweep up poultry processors and meat packers instead of killers and kidnappers.

Fortunately, the new boss in the White House is on this issue a more sober, reasonable leader. "I'm not interested in militarizing the border," President Obama said with his customary preternatural calm. Then he praised President Calderón, "who I believe is really working hard and taking some extraordinary risks under extraordinary pressure to deal with the drug cartels and the corresponding violence that's erupted along the borders."

As far as the fence is concerned, the controversial 1,951-mile-long security fence being built at a cost of nearly $4 million per mile, according to the Government Accountability Office (GAO), had been under fire from critics calling for a mandatory review of its impact on commerce, animal habitat and migration, the environment and cross-border life.

The fence was President George W. Bush and the late Republican Congress's parting gift to the Minutemen and similar anti-immigration activists. With them both gone, a nonpartisan immigration policy group called the Migration Policy Institute (MPI) joined others in a scathing assessment of the wasteful spending involved in the massive project. The MPI report alleged that the border fence does far more to endanger the lives of ordinary migrants and wildlife than it does to stop murderers, kidnappers and drug traffickers.

Still, with the appalling specter of runaway Mexican violence spilling into the United States, few are advocating that the fence project be abandoned right now; not with the infamous Zetas, the bloody band of drug cartel enforcers, at work on both sides of the line. They are heartless thugs armed with high-powered rifles and even rocket-propelled grenades (RPGs) purchased in the United States, and their savage violence has all the theatrical red-splash gore of a graphic comic book. Example, the Associated Press, April 4, 2009:

"Eleven people were found shot to death around Mexico on Saturday, some bearing signs of torture and left with threatening messages emblematic of drug violence. Four of the victims were found in a car in the western city of Apatzingan, along with a message threatening the Zetas, a group of hit men for the Gulf cartel. The message was signed La Familia, a drug gang battling for territory in western Michoacan state. . . . Four other bodies were found around the southern Pacific coast state of Guerrero, including two men left in the trunk of a car in the resort town of Zihuatanejo. The two were blindfolded and had their hands tied behind their backs, according to a police report."

So while it hurts to admit that the extreme allegations of Mexican murder and mayhem are true, the reports are accurate enough to justify real concern: Magnificent Mexico teeters on the brink of social chaos and extreme dislocation, especially in the troubled border cities. Specifically, throughout the first quarter of 2009, their national army was heavily engaged in battles more violent than our contemporaneous fighting in Iraq and Afghanistan. During the first three months of 2009, Juárez and Tijuana were more dangerous than Baghdad and Kabul.

The most profoundly unnerving aspect of this crisis is the uncertainty of the outcome. In a sea of potent corruption the Mexican Army has remained the nation's only consistently trustworthy, competent, successful and patriotic institution. Yet it cannot do everything, meaning keep the civil peace, interdict the drug traffic and govern democratically. The cartels have billions. They are ruthless. "Here is a hundred thousand U.S. dollars; we're going to use your property for a drug deal, don't be home tonight. If you are and if you say anything then I'll kill your wife and rape your children and their children until the end of time."

These guys are no joke. It will take a major effort to beat them. If that international—i.e., American-assisted—effort is not energetically made, then it is possible that the Mexican government will lose, or more likely not win, and effectively, if informally, relinquish jurisdiction of much of the Mexican borderlands to the gangsters, like Pakistan did in temporarily ceding its Swat Valley to the Taliban or, closer to the point, Colombia did with the Switzerland-size chunk of territory it yielded for a time to the narco-terrorists who I saw up close in August 2001 in the Amazon basin inside 'FARC-Landia' in the full-flush of their sovereign arrogance.

"We really need to help Mexico much more than we have up until now," Congressman Silvestre Reyes told me during an interview on the border. The no-nonsense House intelligence chief is also the tough former head of the Border Patrol, and he knows what he's talking about.

"Mexico is under such stress and turmoil that the administration of President Calderón has asked us to help them. This is an opportunity that frankly is in our best interests, because we are dealing not just with their national security, but ours as well."

When I asked Ambassador Sarukhan if he was confident his nation can win this war, he said, "I'm confident that the Mexican state, the Mexican government, the administration of President Calderón is doing everything we can to cut them down and roll them back." But then the ambassador added something most Americans don't want to hear: "And President Obama's administration fully understands the challenge and the need for the United States to step in and shut down the flow of weapons and bulk cash which are crossing from the United States into Mexico and feeding the drug syndicates operating on both sides of the border."

"Can the bums win and beat the government?" I asked Congressman Reyes.

"Not if we engage and get involved in the response to help . . . If we help Mexico, it is not only helping them, but helping ourselves."

Aside from decreasing our incredible appetite for the illicit drugs coming from Mexico, a multibillion-dollar habit so huge that just one cartel king-pin, Joaquin "El Chapo" Guzman, who escaped from a Mexican prison in 2001 in a laundry cart, is 701st on the 2009 Forbes list of the World's Billionaires, with a billion-dollar fortune described as "self-made."

The alternative to the unlikely curbing of U.S. demand is to legalize drugs in the United States. They could then be taxed, proponents of the sea change in policy suggest, helping the United States out of our Great Recession. They further point out our twentieth-century alcohol prohibition was ended only by the economics of the Great Depression: The 1933-era state governments desperately needed the revenue liquor taxes would provide. I interviewed the former governor of Minnesota, Navy SEAL and professional wrestler, Jesse Ventura, on the subject in May 2009. Now a resident of Baja California in Mexico, he was characteristically blunt about how to solve the problem of drug violence.

"You either get away from or you repeat history," the still flamboyant, still physically imposing Jesse told me. "This is the same with the prohibition of alcohol. The minute alcohol was prohibited you had Tijuana, and other Mexican cities that have all of the current trouble, booming because all of the U.S. people that wanted to drink ran across the border and drank in Mexico. That brought the prostitution; it brought the other behavioral problems. When you prohibit something it doesn't mean it's going away. It just means it's going to be run by criminals now. Well, the criminals get so wealthy they become more powerful than the government, which is a great deal of what's happening in Mexico right now. They have more guns, which they get in the U.S. because it's illegal to own a gun in Mexico. They have guns, they have the power and they have the money. By decriminalizing they [the criminals] are about out of business. They have to find something new. It's not rocket science. It takes politicians with courage. Politicians who aren't afraid."

While state-by-state changes in marijuana laws are certainly probable, particularly here in California, where I write this, a wholesale national policy shift in drug policy seems unlikely, even under President Obama, who admits he inhaled. America is too wedded to the failed model of the trillion-dollar War on Drugs we've been fruitlessly waging since President Nixon deputized drug-addled Elvis in December 1970.

The other way to help Mexico is to cut down on the massive amount of heavy weapons being sold to the drug cartels by U.S. gun stores and wholesalers who have the generally unrestricted ability to buy and resell all the iron they want, as long as they don't specifically know the weapons are going to be used for nefarious purposes. Bravo, NRA! Despite strict Mexican controls on guns and licensing, there is a deadly market for weapons that in many ways is the mirror image of the dope trade. Tons of drugs flow north; tens of thousands of guns and billions in American cash go south.

Conservative commentators who blithely claim the cartels are largely armed by weapons stolen from corrupt Latin American military officials are talking crap. In 2007, the federal Bureau of Alcohol, Tobacco, Firearms and Explosives traced a total of twenty-four hundred weapons seized in Mexico back to dealers in the U.S., eighteen hundred from dealers operating in the border states of Texas, California, Arizona and New Mexico. Because gun laws in the United States allow the sale of multiple military-style rifles to American citizens without reporting the sales to the government, we really have only a limited appreciation of the scale of the problem. When heavy-weapons availability is combined with the fact that American and Mexican authorities search a relative handful of cars going south, then it is clear how the well-established cross-border weapons or weapons-for-drugs trade is now a billion-dollar business.

The U.S. side of the Tex-Mex line is a Second Amendment lover's dream. There are hundreds of gun shops, and they are not there to service the few lone cowpokes or target shooters who happen to come around. Wouldn't it be refreshing to hear Senator Cornyn or Governor Perry publicly lament this aspect of the current border problems? If they are so intent on using the National Guard, why not deploy them along U.S. highways heading toward Mexico so they can search vehicles carrying contraband weapons and cash?

One of the suspect gun marts, X-Caliber Guns in Phoenix, the country's kidnapping capital, was linked to a May 2008 shoot-out in which eight Mexican special agents were killed. The feds allege that the owner, George Iknadosian, sold hundreds of heavy assault weapons to smugglers, knowing they were en route to a drug cartel in the Mexican state of Sinaloa. The ATF spokesman told *The New York Times* that "over the two years leading up to his arrest last May, he sold more than 700 weapons of the kind currently sought by drug dealers in Mexico, including 515 AK-47 rifles and one .50 caliber rifle that can penetrate an engine block or bulletproof glass."

The U.S. government's efforts to suppress our weapons contribution to Mexico's drug violence suffered a setback in March 2009, when Maricopa County (Arizona) Superior Court judge Robert Gottsfield concluded that because the shady characters who bought the heavy weapons by the truck-load from Iknadosian were legally eligible to buy them now that the U.S. ban on assault weapons has been lifted, the prosecutors could not prove that Iknadosian knew the weapons were heading down to Mexico, so he dismissed all charges. The case never even got to trial. This judge was either a willful dumb-ass or he wanted to send a message critical of exceedingly lax U.S. gun laws.

Those laws or the lack of them were near the top of the agenda when President Obama traveled to Mexico City in April 2009, the first visit by a U.S. president to the capital since a Bill Clinton stop in 1997. At a joint press conference at Los Pinos (The Pines), the Mexican presidential compound, after President Calderón complained how drug violence has soared since the U.S. ban on assault weapons was allowed to expire in 2004, President Obama expressed his sympathy, but added how difficult gun control has become in the United States, saying, "I continue to believe that we can respect and honor the Second Amendment in our Constitution, the rights of sportsmen and hunters and homeowners who want to keep their families safe to lawfully bear arms, while dealing with assault weapons that, as we know, here in Mexico, are helping fuel extraordinary violence. Now having said that, I think none of us are under the illusion that reinstating that ban would be easy."

Border-city Mexico reminds me of the South Bronx in 1985–90. Both are what the cops used to call "self-cleaning ovens." The gangsters are killing so many other gangsters, at some point the killing may stop from a temporary shortage of gangsters or sheer exhaustion, like in World War I. There were small signs of that exhaustion in December 2008, when representatives of several major drug cartels met at a seafood restaurant in the traditional drug czar parleying capital, Culiacán in Sinaloa state, reported the *Rio Doce*, a brave Sinaloa weekly newspaper. The purpose of the meeting was "to form a truce because the fighting is interfering with the regular business of narco-trafficking," reported the *El Paso Times*.

The *Rio Doce* weekly stated that the gathering "included representatives of reputed billionaire drug lords Joaquin 'El Chapo' Guzmán [the *Forbes* billionaire], Ismael 'El Mayo' Zambada, the Beltran Leyva brothers [who as I write this have suffered some stinging arrests of key lieutenants, including one colorfully called 'El Primo Rivera,' no relation], Vicente Carrillo Fuentes of the Juárez cartel and the [notorious, fugitive] Arellano family of Tijuana." How's that for reporting specifics? And how about the celebrity of these drug lords? Picture that meeting, all proud, scarred roosters, their heavily armed, deeply suspicious entourages in tow, and all more concerned about pride, face and appearance before their rivals than about the activities of the Mexican armed forces arrayed against them.

But the cartel bosses should have been less arrogant. After they killed 250 in Juárez during the month of February 2009, the gloves came off in Mexico City. During the time I was in Juárez, Mexican president Calderón's army was everywhere, on every major intersection, customs checkpoint and police station, and had totally taken control from the notoriously corrupt local cops who long ago sold their souls to this generous and savage devil. They had such sweet and sour choices. *Plata o Plomo*, silver or lead, take the money or take the bullet. There are many brave, honest dead in Mexico, like the police chief of Piedras Negras just across the border from Eagle Pass, Texas. Vowing to purge corruption in the department, retired Mexican army Colonel Arturo Navarro took over as police chief on April 7, 2009. Soon after, Chief Navarro fired three high-ranking officers as part of a departmental purge. On April 21, seventy of his officers walked off the job to demand Navarro's resignation. According to the Associated Press, the officers "complained that his leadership left them fearful of reprisal attacks from gangs." On April 25, Navarro was killed when assassins wielding AK-47's and American-made AR-15's bushwhacked him as he drove home from work. Six police officers were being questioned in the attack, according to the AP.

Embattled President Calderón and his nation are in a fight for their sovereignty, dignity, economic well-being and, most important to those proud Latinos, their national reputation. The dopers are dishonoring Mexico, which is also having to cope with deflated oil prices, a wretched economy and even a deadly epidemic of swine flu. The nation under Calderón is stirring. They totally dig their army. It is their silver bullet. In committing its last, best chance, Mexico is invested in victory against the cartels, which at incalculable cost will result in a cataclysmic reordering of the drug trade—which really only means maybe moving it to some other intermediary country, the way the 1980–1990 south Florida crackdowns moved the traffic to Mexico in the first place. Junkies will have their dope, after all.

More pragmatically, the bad news is drying up tourism, even in super secure areas like Cancún, Cabo and Acapulco, far removed but no longer unaffected by the border violence. It is exacerbating Mexico's stressed economy, separating families and causing widespread heartache and inconvenience. With the economy already in severe recession, the peso devalued by 50 percent, and a swine flu epidemic, it could not come at a worse time.

The good news is the positive impact the deployment of the Mexican Army has had on law and order along the border. They are kicking butt and taking names in Juárez and Tijuana. The army has called out the bad guys, and if the bad guys keep rising to the bait they will keep getting their asses kicked. Come on, you mothers, come get chopped up by a real army. The further good news is that there is no existential threat to the United States or to any aspect of our national security emanating from our southern border. There hasn't been a Mexican invasion of the United States since Pancho Villa raided Columbus, New Mexico, in March 1916. We must have a measured response that doesn't cater to the anti-immigrant mob. The border per se is not the problem. No fence on earth will stop a skilled criminal. They will tunnel under, fly over or sail around it.

The far more relevant story when it comes to the United States is that the vast majority of America's Hispanics, including immigrants, are hardworking, law-abiding and as worried as the next guy about the struggle between darkness and light south of the border.

★ 4 ★

THE HISPANIC CONSUMER
The New Engine of American Commerce

"¡G-r-r-riquísimos!" ("They're g-r-reat!")
—*Tony el Tigre* (Tony the Tiger). Packaging on a box of Frosted Flakes
(known in Mexico as *Zucaritas*) aimed at the Hispanic market

"Para español toca el numero dos." ("For Spanish hit number two.")
—Bilingual telephone directory information available almost everywhere

lthough less vivid than the turmoil along the southern border, a story of far greater long-term significance to the state of our union is the emerging and expanding financial clout of the Hispanic community, including recent immigrants. By any objective measure Latinos are making a massive contribution to the troubled economy of the United States, propping up otherwise failing towns, businesses, beefing up the Gross Domestic Product (GDP), reinvigorating entire areas of the country, and holding the potential of being a kind of economic Viagra for our aging population.

By 2030, one in five Americans will be Hispanic, according to U.S. Census Bureau projections. If you are talking American teenagers, then as of 2009 one in five teens is Hispanic already. And despite the current recession's sharp cut, the buying power of U.S. Hispanics, teen and parent alike, is projected to continue experiencing significant growth. And the recent track record is impressive by any measure.

Hispanic buying power quadrupled between 1990 and 2007, from $212 billion to $863.1 billion annually, according to *Businessweek.com* and other sources. The Selig Center for Economic Growth at the University of Georgia's Terry College of Business estimates that the buying power of the Hispanic market will swell to $1.3 trillion by 2013. "That's more than 450 percent growth from 1990 to 2011. Non-Hispanic buying power is growing closer to a rate of 176 percent over the same period," said the center's director, Jeff Humphreys, pointing out that Hispanic buying power surpassed black buying power in 2007.

That was the same year the Hispanic consumer market in the United States alone drew even with the nation of Mexico's entire economy in terms of GDP. It is now larger than all of Mexico, despite today's bitter economy. Most estimates put total domestic Latino commerce at around 11 percent of our country's consumer economy. Put another way, about eleven cents of every dollar spent in the United States today is being spent by a Latino, according to various business media sources. "Latinos are twice as likely to eat at home, spending proportionately more on groceries than other groups," according to a Labor Department report; further, "Latinos also spend more than other groups on clothing, telephone services, automobiles, and home furnishings."

"Latinos will change the profile of American society over the next four decades. The Hispanic population will grow much quicker than other population segments, and Hispanic consumers will represent an increasing percentage of the American consumer base," said Tatjana Meerman, of market researchers Packaged Facts in a February 2009 report titled "Hispanics Emerge as Influential Force in U.S. Consumer Economy."

Whereas many in politics and opinion media are deeply hesitant about the growing presence and political clout of Hispanics, American business exhibits no such ambivalence. When Erica (my child bride) and I celebrated her thirty-fourth birthday at Sofrito on West 57th Street, the waiters spontaneously broke into "¡Feliz cumpleaños a ti!" not "Happy Birthday to You." The Chase and Bank of America outlets in our small Hudson River, New Jersey, neighborhood effortlessly offer customers the choice of doing business in either English or Spanish. So do the functionally trilingual Korean-owned businesses that predominate the shops along Main Street in nearby Fort Lee, New Jersey. Spanish people own both my local bagel shops. When I get my regular cream cheese and olives on a bagel and a tall container of regular coffee, I speak only Spanish with the servers, most of whom hail from Mexico, with the occasional Central American thrown into the mix.

"When you look at the demographics of New Jersey, you see that the Hispanic community represents a very significant and growing part of the state's economy," local utility executive Arthur S. Guida told the annual Convention Expo & Career Fair of New Jersey's Hispanic Chamber of Commerce.

"Verizon's future is directly tied to the economic development and prosperity of the Hispanic community," telecom executive Dennis M. Bone told the same gathering.

The barmaid at the corner joint, the guys at the car wash, the teachers in the local public school and the cops on the beat all get the new linguistic reality: that a little Spanish goes a long way. In Passaic County, New Jersey, not far from where I live, you see towns that could be in south Texas, so prevalent are the sturdily built, brown-skinned-cowboy, construction-worker immigrants who would be at home riding the range outside Oaxaca or Culiacán.

Along Bergenline Avenue, the main drag that runs through Hudson County, a bare minimum of every other shopper and shopkeeper is Latino. They are a blend of Caribbean islanders, mostly from Cuba, the Dominican Republic and a scattering from Puerto Rico, and Hispanics from Mexico and Central America, who have come in more recent years and who are easily distinguishable physically, and in terms of customs and culture. The nearby cities of Passaic and Paterson were shabby, nearly abandoned, post-industrial wrecks before the newbies began arriving and urban renewing in the late 1980s.

I drive through, shop, eat or drink in Spanish Harlem and the equally Spanish Manhattan neighborhoods of Inwood and Washington Heights, directly across the big river from my house, almost weekly. I'm looking across the chilly, dark waters of the Hudson at "the Heights" right now (I move around a lot). There is scarcely a small business in either neighborhood that is not run by a Latino or, perhaps more impressively, by a

Pashto-, Creole-, Greek-, or Arabic-speaking immigrant from Asia or Europe conversant in Spanish, this newly important language of better, bigger business. It is like the 1950s, when the *paisans* who own Little Italy learned Mandarin to do business in Chinatown as it swelled next door when Chinese immigration exploded after the Communists took over mainland China.

The Latino market is now an integral part of the larger national market. And every transaction in the lives of those Hispanics, whether citizen, legal resident or otherwise, is taxed, just as similar transactions are taxed in the lives of other Americans. Every time a Latino buys a phone card, or eggs for breakfast, or a pair of shoes, or a gallon of gas, they pay the same tax as the rest of us, which should help belie the notion that immigrants don't pay their fair share. They pay all sales and many other taxes, often including Social Security, they get no deductions, and usually have no hope of either refund or redemptions. And, citizen or not, can these people shop.

According to the U.S. Hispanic Chamber of Commerce, of all ethnic groups, Hispanics frequent the mall the most (10.1 times per every three weeks) and stay the longest (91.5 minutes). To mention a few items, sales of mainstream Mexican and authentic Hispanic convenience foods doubled between 1995 and 2004. Items once considered exotic foreign food, like tacos, burritos and nachos, have become as American as Super Bowl Sunday. New Mexico in general and the small town of Hatch in particular call themselves "the Chile Capital of the World." Salsa outsells ketchup, and tortillas outsell Wonder bread. According to some radical estimates, tacos outsell hot dogs.

Hot and savory cuisine, Latino music, Spanish television programs, and automatic banking services in Spanish are only a handful of the examples of ethnic becoming mainstream. The February 2009 United States–Mexico World Cup–qualifying soccer match, which the U.S. won 2–0, was seen by an estimated 1.2 million viewers on English-language ESPN2. Univision, the Spanish-language network broadcast of the same game, was seen by 10.7 million U.S. viewers, more people than any other sporting event in the history of U.S./Spanish-language television, according to *The NewYork Times*. Margaritas are the most popular cocktail in the country. Mexican beers are 40 percent of all imports, while Mexican brandies and coffee liqueurs rule liquor store shelves.

Spanish-language or -themed magazines like *People en Español* and *Selecciónes* or *Maxim* (also published *en español*, if you care about the articles) have become a whole new market for the distressed publishing business, not to mention that the toy and hobby business is booming in Hispanic areas, with spending in 2006 already approaching $2 billion annually.

Sometimes it takes a while to notice even the five-hundred-pound gorilla. In terms of recognizing the enormous potential in the Latino market in the post-slavery, post–Spanish Colonial sugarcane-and-coffee era, baseball did it first. Major-league scouts understood early in the evolution of the nation's pastime that a spirited blaze of talent lay just below America's southern horizon.

I'll deal with baseball from Roberto "the Natural" Clemente to Alex "the Not-so-Natural" Rodriguez later; the focus here is the impressive awakening of other businesses to the broad and deep possibilities presented by the Hispanic market and the newcomers to the United States who are supplying first workers, but also—and at an accelerating pace—customers and franchisees/owners. By the end of 2007, one out of every ten small businesses in America was owned by a Hispanic. Banks (sometimes with awful effect), business services and government development programs, including some in the 2009 stimulus package, are catering to Hispanics, whose immigrant experience is both similar to and yet unique from previous arrivals.

Those Hispanic consumers who are least assimilated, either because of the diminishing but still potent reason of discrimination or their unresolved immigration status, with its chronic fear of deportation, usually live in a parallel universe. They self-segregate within the geographic confines of a Spanish-dominant community. Usually, they patronize only institutions designed to serve them, specifically those that recognize their *familismo, dignidad* and perhaps even machismo.

Those enterprises range from clothing stores to fast-food restaurants, used-car lots to beauty shops, lawyers' offices, doctors, healers, convenience stores, supermarkets, fortune-tellers and party planners specializing in *quinceañeras*, those sometimes lavish, bat mitzvah–like affairs celebrating a young Latina's fifteenth birthday.

"For companies to grow in the coming years, it is critical to understand how to reach and connect with these consumers," Reinaldo Padua, assistant vice president for Hispanic marketing for Coca-Cola North America, told the *Latino Business Review*.

The dexterity of a company like Pizza Patrón should be an inspiration to American entrepreneurs, a way forward into the new world of free-market *Latinismo*. The company is now known as "Pizza Patrón, *Más Pizza. Menos Dinero*" ("More Pizza, Less Money"), and it was its early policy of accepting pesos, the currency of many border-state Mexican immigrants, that was the multimillion-dollar inspiration that earned broad brand loyalty from its huge and growing clientele.

Antonio Swad, the Lebanese-Italian son of immigrants who is Pizza Patrón's founder, opened his first store in the Pleasant Grove section of Dallas in 1986. "I discovered just after a few days that most of our customers did not speak English, maybe as much as 80 percent of them, despite being a diverse neighborhood. So the first thing I did was hire somebody who could answer the phone and take orders in Spanish."

As his chain spread throughout the Southwest, he expanded to include a Texas-based chain of takeout-only pizza shops based in high-density Hispanic neighborhoods that feature the "Lista" drive-through window (*lista* meaning "ready"). Swad also started an airport and minimall version called the Pizza Patrón Rapidito. Continuing with his Spanglish theme, Swad's restaurants feature items like BreadStix, QuesoStix and, introduced last year, the already famous ChurroStix dessert.

"I'm not saying we don't service other consumer-demographic groups, but we are investing our future in the Hispanic market," Swad told *Restaurant News*.

With over seventy stores in five states and dozens more under development, Swad's Pizza Patrón specializes in large, family-style, fifteen-inch pies that cost just five to seven dollars. Its top-of-the-line offering is an eight-story giant called *La Patrona*, which translates as "boss lady."

"We are about making Pizza Patrón a nationally recognized Latin brand. Domino's can outspend us all they want going after the Hispanic dollars, but they'll never be considered a Latin brand. Everything we do, the people we hire, the in-store marketing, is geared to serve one kind of customer," said Swad.

And if the fast-food industry remake of the quintessential Italian and Italian-American pizza into a Hispanic delight is impressive, imagine what they did with chicken. Spanish people love chicken. *Arroz con pollo* (chicken and rice) is one of the signature dishes on every Puerto Rican table. And the typical Latino family is a tailor-made consumer: big, not rich, and they love chicken hot or cold.

Dallas, Texas-based Pollo Golden brags that it supplements its chicken staples with "such Mexican favorites as charro beans, creamed corn, re-fried beans, tortillas, tacos and rice," in menus printed in English and Spanish.

The Guatemalan-based company called Pollo Campero goes even farther. Customers are greeted by banners reading, "*¡Tierno! ¡Jugoso! ¡Y Crujiente!*" ("Tender! Juicy! And crunchy!") and "*¡Orgullosamente Guatemalteca!*" ("Proudly Guatemalan"). When you step up to the counter, the cashier welcomes everyone with a "*Buenas tardes, le puedo tomar su orden?*" ("Good afternoon, can I take your order?") And if you order in English, that's fine too.

Pollo Campero has begun opening stores in the New York City area, catering its deep-fried chicken to the region's large concentration of immigrants from Colombia, El Salvador, Costa Rica, Nicaragua, Guatemala and other Latin America nations where the two-hundred-plus store chain has outlets. According to Milford Prewitt of the *Restaurant News*, the launch of Pollo Campero's first branch in Los Angeles several years ago was so successful management had to close early to prepare ingredients for the following day. "That outlet topped $1 million in volume in just its first seven weeks."

Thirty-four percent of all U.S. Hispanics are age eighteen or younger.

They are a fast-food marketer's dream. Other chains mining those hungry young Latinos are IHOP, one in three of whose new stores are in heavily Hispanic neighborhoods, and Pro's Ranch Market, "which offers a broadrange of freshly prepared meals-to-go," including "fresh tortillas [that] immediately make first-time shoppers dedicated patrons in new markets," according to its Web site. Still another is Golden Chick. Founded in 1967 it is a southwest regional chain of nearly 100 restaurants, mostly in small-town Texas and Oklahoma, featuring deep-fried and roasted chicken.

Walk through any mall in America near a concentration of Latino consumers and you can see how business is far more welcoming than, say, immigration officials or radio talk show hosts. Pollo Campero sells wristbands with its name on one side and the name of one of the various countries where it does business on the other, so the home sick single guy from Guatemala can wear the name of his nation and favorite fast food as a kind of memento or talisman from home. It's also brilliant marketing, reminding the guy that if he's hungry, it must be for that famous crunchy chicken. It's like eating one for the home team.

A fast-growing chain called Melrose, selling young women's apparel, is aimed specifically at Latina teenagers. "Hispanic teens and young women are very much our target demographic," Koyt Everhart, the company's director of real estate, told the *Latino Business Review*. The San Antonio, Texas–based discount fashion retailer opened its first store in McAllen, Texas, in 1976. It now has eighty-seven stores spread through Texas, New Mexico, Arizona and California. The latest to open in February 2009 was located in an Albuquerque, New Mexico, shopping plaza owned by Pro's Ranch Market, which has its own giant outlet there. Designed to create a kind of one-stop shopping for Hispanics by offering stores catering to their every need, the plaza and others like it are bucking U.S. retail's recent downward spiral.

"As the natural demographics continue to grow in Hispanic and Mexican retail markets, merchants are repositioning to take advantage of that growth," commercial real estate broker Michael Armijo Butler told the

Review, adding, "And the young miss Latina market is exploding in Albuquerque. Melrose will do very well here."

At the International Home and Housewares Show at Chicago's McCormick Place in March 2008, entire lines were devoted to the recognition that the growing Hispanic population needs specific tools to prepare authentic cultural cuisines, like the *molinillo*, a whisk mixer; the *chocolatera*, an aluminum pitcher used to make hot chocolate; and the *caldero*, a large pot used for the rice-and-bean specialties that are to die for.

Bearing in mind that this generation of immigrants is learning English at the fastest rate ever and that English dominance is the rule by the third generation, the extent of Hispanic business bilingualism is nevertheless breathtaking.

In 2005 *Business Week* interviewed Felipe Korzenny, professor and founding director of the Center for the Study of Hispanic Marketing Communications at Florida State University, who called bilingual marketing, "The way of the future . . . more and more Hispanics are spending a lot of time with both English and Spanish media. And there are families where the kids are bilingual; they speak English, and their mother speaks mostly Spanish . . . and the grandparents are completely Spanish dominant, and extended-family members vary in their linguistic ability. So being bilingual is more effective and it is a way to emphasize culture."

Mi Tienda goes even farther. Its gigantic grocery store in Pasadena, near Houston, Texas, began life as a traditional general grocery, but soon shut down for lack of business before totally embracing the emerging Hispanic market. Now the store interior seems like it's located in another country.

"We built this as though you were going to different villages in Mexico," company spokesman Juan Alonso told Vicente Arenas of Houston's 11 News. And the gamble paid off. At a time when many Houston-area businesses are struggling, "Mi Tienda continues to increase its profits every month," according to Arenas, who notes that Wal-Mart and Sam's Club are building a giant outlet targeting Latinos on Houston's north side. Sam's will be known as Más Club to better compete with established rivals like Fiesta.

"Companies are being much smarter about who their customer is and finding their true niche in finding how to cater to this marketplace," ad man Randy Stockdale told Arenas.

Aside from importing specialty lines and stocking items with bilingual packaging, hiring bilingual employees, posting bilingual signs and distributing bilingual coupons, retail businesses have also figured out that shopping for Spanish people is often a family affair. Experts call it "event shopping." Hispanic families shop en masse. Whether it is just an outing to the supermarket, a.k.a. *el supermercado*, or to the local Target or Wal-Mart, it is common to see three generations of shoppers from the same family on a carefully planned expedition built around advertised discounts.

There is Mom and sometimes Dad, the kids and almost inevitably Grandma shuffling behind the younger core group, herding the children and cluck-clucking in a barely audible croak at the various purchase options. Seemingly ancient, often withered by decades of hard labor, clutching her inexpensive oversize purse, which is stuffed with everything from snacks for the children to various medicines, tissues and other go-to supplies, the venerated elder is revered, and woe to the salesperson who disrespects or ignores her.

"Hispanics are driving what little growth there is in supermarket shopping," according to Libbey Paul, a Nielsen senior vice president.

"They tend to be larger households, have more kids and a higher growth rate," said Paul to *HispanicBusiness.com*. "You can understand why Kellogg's would care, why Coke would care." You can also understand how the manufacturers of products like toothpaste, diapers, clothes, shoes, beer and electronics are becoming increasingly adept at marketing specifically to this emerging community.

Understanding the social aspects of Latino immigrant shopping, many retailers provide sitting places for the old-timers. With due deference to non-Hispanics, I believe we are among the best respecters of parents and grandparents, the respect soaring to reverence as they get older. We ask for their blessing, *bendición*, and, since they are holders of a powerful spirit, we feel fortified when we hear their response: "*Dios te bendiga*"—"God bless you."

Over the years I have frequently enjoyed those incongruous occasions when some big, scary, tattooed lug of a Latino who could take on the world has been humbled and chastised in public for a real or perceived offense by a grandmother one-third his size. Nobody messes with *Abuela*.

We are also broadly nostalgic about staying in touch. Whether they are dominant in English or Spanish, Latinos cannot stay off the phone. They are 95 percent more likely than the average consumer to have spent $100 on long distance, and 18 percent more likely to have rung up a phone bill of $150 or more during the last month, according to Nielsen. You don't have to be the geniuses who run AT&T or Verizon to figure out that there's money to be made in them there bills. Why else do you think there is scarcely a bank in a big city that doesn't offer Spanish-friendly ATM machines, deposit slips and instructions? And the money those Latino consumers are depositing and spending is what is powering the assimilation of Hispanics into mainstream American culture—far more effectively than any more remedial legislation.

It is harder to resent or seek to exclude or diminish someone when your livelihood depends on them. Money talks. In fact, money is multilingual, and in any language a $1.3 trillion annual contribution to the nation's economy is a ton and a third of fiscal integration.

In recognition of Hispanics' burgeoning importance to the nation's economy, President Bush appointed courtly, careful Carlos Gutierrez as Commerce Secretary. The fifty-five-year-old, Cuban-born former chairman of the board and CEO of the Kellogg Company became Bush's most enduring Hispanic cabinet pick, serving for his entire second term.

Called "a visionary executive" by the forty-third president at the press conference announcing his selection in November 2004, he's a quality person, a terrific businessman and a wonderful example of that in-between generation: the young children of the first wave of anti-Castro refugees, the educated business class and property owners who understood Fidel's essential Communism long before the *Washington Post* or *The New York Times* did.

Gutierrez was the six-year-old son of a pineapple plantation owner whose holdings faced expropriation at the time he fled the island with his family in 1960. There is a famous story he tells reporters about how he learned English from the "bellhops of a Miami Beach hotel," where the undocumented Gutierrez family lived for a time after landing on the shores of Florida in a small boat, after escaping from Castro's Cuba.

They moved for a time to New York before settling in Mexico, where Gutierrez began his legendary climb from driving a Kellogg's truck selling *Zucaritas* (Frosted Flakes) to general manager of the cereal maker's operations in Mexico to the company headquarters in Battle Creek, Michigan, where he worked his way up the corporate ladder until he was named CEO in April 1999. He's now also remembered as "the father of Special K" and other health-marketed cereals.

"We never imagined that this country would give me this great opportunity," he said when humbly accepting President Bush's 2004 nomination to head the Commerce Department, walking away from a $7.4 million salary, plus bonuses and incentive payments from his firm.

Having met, interviewed and shared the podium with him on several occasions, I like this man. He's not the type to light up the room when he walks in, and he is curiously dispassionate for a Latino, at least in public. But he is extremely competent, reasonable, nonideological, reliable and patriotic.

Not only did he perform creditably at the Commerce Department, he also had the political courage and character to become a staunch defender of a pragmatic, solution-oriented approach to immigration reform that recognized the contribution these hardy newcomers make to the U.S. economy. But he also required the immigrants to step up to the plate, saying, "They'll need to pay taxes. They'll need to pay fines. They'll need to learn English. . . . And so they'll have to make a real commitment to earn legalization and a real commitment to this country. They have to decide that they are going to make this their country and stick it out and earn their legalization."

I couldn't have said it better; if only his fellow Republicans in Congress at the time of the 2007 debate had listened. It would have been better for the country and for the GOP. Look how well his sage advice worked for Frosted Flakes: The brand continues to dominate the Latino market for sugared cereals. They're still "¡*G-r-r-riquísimos!*"

★ 5 ★

HOW BROWN IS MY VALLEY
How Hispanics Will Save Social Security

"The numbers leave nothing to doubt about the financial condition
of the Social Security system. The report underscores the fact that we
need to do something."

—John Snow, Secretary of the Treasury and Social Security
trustee, reporting the projected 2041 insolvency
of the system, March 2005

"No damn politician can ever scrap my social security program."

—Franklin Delano Roosevelt, June 1941

I n short strokes, the crisis America faces in terms of our national retirement account is that there are too many old folks looking to cash out,
and not enough active workers paying into the trust fund to ensure
long-term financial viability. The specter of system insolvency followed
by old-age poverty haunts the generation with living memory of the
Great Depression and malignant fear that another one is around the corner. It preoccupied the domestic policy of the early second term of the
George W. Bush presidency, and it was put on the back burner only by
wars in Iraq and Afghanistan and by the far more immediate economic
crisis that nearly wiped out financial markets and witnessed the evapora-
tion of trillions of dollars in wealth in 2008.

But the long-term Social Security shortfall still looms. In 1950, the
Ozzie and Harriet year my family left Brooklyn for West Babylon, New
York, the ratio was sixteen active workers for every retiree. In 1994, the
ratio was down to 3.3 to one. By 2025, it will be two to one and so on to
insolvency.

The possible antidote to the retirement-era ruination of the aging baby boomer and subsequent generations is already in place. But it is reported far less frequently than the pending system shortfall, or it is spun negatively to scare people about Mexicans. Relatively youthful immigrants and the new wave of U.S.-born Hispanics are increasing the size of the working population relative to the retired population. Therefore, they represent the potential salvation of the system. I don't mean to be willfully naive; systematic reform is inevitable, but these youngsters have the attainable ability to redo the calendar. They can postpone the inevitable.

The statistics are impossible to spin. Half the nation's resident Hispanic population is under age twenty-five; more than 80 percent are under age forty-five. In fiscal year 2007–2008 they accounted for a whopping and unavoidably large 41.7 percent of the total increase in America's working-age population, according to Pew. Since Latinos are on average twelve years younger than white Americans, it is inevitable that as time goes by the working population paying into the national retirement account will be browner and subsequently younger than it is today.

In the words of a 2005 Pew report titled "Hispanics and the Social Security Debate" and published during the big failed President Bush push to privatize the system, "The role that Hispanics play as contributors to Social Security will increase substantially in the next several decades. While the white labor force is projected to fall from 100 million in 2005 to about 94 million in 2050, the Hispanic labor force is projected to more than double, increasing from 19 million in 2005 to about 46 million in 2050. While fewer white workers will be contributing, many more Hispanics will be paying Social Security taxes by the middle of the century."

So the good news is the existence in the United States of this vital, vibrant new population from which to draw vigor into the fabric of life, the economy and, more pragmatically, the Social Security system. Unlike, say, Russia or the other nations of Central and Eastern Europe, which suffer from aging and therefore dwindling populations, in Russia's case the percentage over sixty has doubled in recent decades, America is blessed with a youthful wave of newcomers, citizen and immigrant, legal and illegal, who are pulling down the average age of Americans. How important is that? Well, again, look at Russia, whose population is projected to fall from its current 141 million to just 116 million by 2050, according to the United Nations. The problem of an aging population has led that country to institute an international recruiting drive to repatriate ethnic Russians living abroad, costing $300 million over the last couple years. Moscow is trying to repopulate vast areas of the nation's far east, where population has been drastically reduced.

Absent Hispanics, the United States would face a similar problem. Pew estimated that U.S. population over sixty-five (I was going to say "the elderly population" but realized that I would thus be describing myself) will rise from 37 million in 2005 to 81 million in 2050. And those senior citizens will be disproportionately white. According to the U.S. Census in 2006, the most recent statistics I could get, almost 25 percent of whites were already fifty-five or older, while just 11.1 percent of Hispanics had reached that milestone.

We need these brown people. "Without sufficient newcomers, there won't be enough U.S. workers to sustain the economy," said Dowell Myers, a professor at the University of Southern California.

What about their paying their fair share of the cost of our incredibly compassionate nation's largesse—our public schools, our roads and public services? Even those here illegally pay sales tax, excise tax, gas tax, cigarette tax and every other point-of-purchase tax. Those who commit the additional crime of obtaining false federal identification are ironically doing even more good for the United States than those workers who just wing it with no documentation at all. Those fake-ID holders may be said to be the "Great Brown Hope" to save Social Security.

Here's one of the ways it works, this sub-rosa silver lining to the nation's immigration debate. To appease potential employers and provide them cover from criminal liability, most undocumented workers get fake documentation. In East Los Angeles I documented the relative ease with which documents ranging from green cards to Social Security cards are available. In 2002, my FOX News team and I chronicled the barely disguised, widespread street businesses that provide the complete package, green card and Social Security number, for several hundred dollars. You pay the printer's agent half up front and come back several days later to pick up the documents you need to provide your potential employer with plausible deniability. "How was I supposed to know the documents were fakes? They look real."

According to the Government Accountability Office (GAO), "the Department of Homeland Security requires employers to visually inspect new workers' identity and work authorization documents, but employers do not have to verify these documents, and they can be easily counterfeited." Under the Republicans, the deck was even further stacked against the workers, who were being routinely rounded up, prosecuted and deported, and in favor of the employers, who were scarcely, if ever, investigated. For example, again according to the professionals at the Government Accountability Office, the otherwise dreaded IRS could care less about whether an employee is paying into a nonexistent account. Quoting the GAO, (GAO-05-154), "IRS regulations are minimal; IRS has no record of assessing a penalty for filing inaccurate earnings reports." All the tax man cares about is that somebody is paying the payroll and Medicare taxes. If Al Capone had just remembered that simple lesson he might have died a free man, syphilis and all, and those failed Obama cabinet nominees would have been confirmed.

So unless and until the federal government can prove beyond a reasonable doubt that a particular company knew for a fact that its workers were using fake documentation or that an employer was paying workers "off the books," and thus not paying his own share of the payroll tax, an employer has little to fear. The U.S. Chamber of Commerce has successfully battled all attempts to require even federal contractors and subcontractors to use the Department of Homeland Security's heavily promoted Internet-based E-Verify system to verify their employees' eligibility to work in the United States. Its implementation was suspended at least through spring 2009, ensuring that even government contractors can hire anyone who shows up with identification documents, however flimsy. As I said to a Washington conference, the reason we oppose E-Verify is that it works.

For the worker, however, this shadow system is enormously risky. As I wrote in previous chapters, it makes otherwise law-abiding workingmen and -women vulnerable to enhanced federal prosecution for identity theft or worse. That was particularly true during the last two years of the Bush administration, when ideologically motivated appointees unleashed the full power of the federal government on employees who used phony ID.

Still, obtaining fake Social Security cards is a widespread phenomenon. The numbers on the fake cards are either conjured out of thin air or belong to a real person, alive or dead. There are cases of a single Social Security number being used by as many as a hundred or more undocumented immigrants. I don't know of any case in which a retiree was shocked to learn his or her retirement account was stuffed with an unaccounted fortune, since their maximum payout would still be the same.

The real beneficiary is the Social Security trust fund itself. The seminal article on the topic is still an endlessly quoted 2005 story by *New York Times* reporter Eduardo Porter, who wrote that every year this slush fund was "generating $6 billion to $7 billion in Social Security tax revenue and about $1.5 billion in Medicare taxes."

And how much of that money comes from illegal immigration? "Our assumption is that about three-quarters of other-than-legal immigrants pay payroll taxes," Stephen C. Goss, then Social Security chief actuary, told Porter, using the agency's term for illegal immigration.

Porter wrote how one typical illegal worker who crossed into the United States in 1999, and who had since found hard work harvesting asparagus and pruning grapevines earning up to ten bucks an hour, paid about $2,000 toward Social Security annually and another $450 for Medicare, with no expectation of either a public pension or free health care outside the emergency room when he reached the age of sixty-five.

As with legitimate workers, a contribution from the falsely documented employee and the negligent or willfully blind employer amounting to 15.1 percent of salary is paid as payroll tax into the Social Security trust fund, worker and employer each putting in half. The worker's share is deducted automatically from each paycheck. But if the account is phony then the money is being paid into a false or nonexistent account, with little hope that it will ever be paid out to the worker.

According to the Government Accountability Office, during the 1990s the Social Security Administration (SSA) began holding money received from obviously bogus W-2 payroll statements in what is called the Earnings Suspense File (ESF). "Each year, the Social Security Administration receives millions of employer-submitted earnings reports (Form W-2s) that it is unable to place in an individual Social Security record. If the Social Security number and name on the W-2 do not match the SSA's records, the W-2 is retained in the Earnings Suspense File," wrote the GAO in 2005.

There is a key that unlocks the secret of what the Earnings Suspense File really is: that is, a tacitly acknowledged tax paid by millions of improperly documented workers with the quiet approval of Washington, D.C. Most of those suspense files are concentrated in only three of eighty-three broad industrial categories: 17 percent of the fake accounts came from restaurants, 10 percent from the construction trades and 7 percent from farm operations, the big three employers when it comes to immigrant workers.

During the 1990s, $189 billion was collected in these suspense accounts, and that amount is swelling in the current decade. In 2002, according to reporter Porter, nine million W-2 accounts with false or incorrect numbers amounted to 1.5 percent of total earnings for the entire nation. Put another way, according to several sources, improperly or fraudulently documented immigrant workers, most of them Latino, are subsidizing your Social Security trust fund.

And remember, in virtually every case, the worker paying those taxes has little hope of ever taking a dime out, although in recent years workers who subsequently legitimize their immigration status have had some measured success in receiving "reinstatements" for earnings in years prior to receiving valid Social Security numbers. It should be noted that most anti-immigration groups vehemently oppose the notion of reinstatements, however fair they may seem to the rest of us.

When that $7 billion windfall is added to the increasing amounts being paid in by the expanding number of legal Latino workers, the picture emerges more clearly of how the nation's retirement trust fund may not be as bad off as many doomsayers maintain. According to the Brookings Institution report, "The Census Projects Minority Surge" (2008), "Clearly the aging out of boomers from the labor force years, and their displace-ment by Hispanics and other minorities, bring both opportunities and challenges for incorporating new more ethnically diverse generations into a growing 21st-century labor force." Undoubtedly the biggest challenge is to make Latinos more successful overall.

That's the bad news. Because those mostly eager-to-work young His-panics, particularly the recent arrivals, earn substantially less on average than the rest of the American people, their contributions to the fund do not match their awesome potential. As of right now, they just aren't paying in as much as other groups per capita. Since they contribute less per capita right now, the big-picture possibility that Latinos will lead the way to long-term Social Security viability does not impress critics of immigration reform. Their disdain of new arrivals is now fortified by legitimate con-cern about America's short-term dire economic straits. Why import pov-erty? they ask.

According to the National Committee to Preserve Social Security and Medicare, "Latinos compared to other Americans are more likely to be employed for most if not all of their lives in low-wage jobs without pri-vate pension benefits, making them rely heavily on Social Security for a safe and secure retirement." Another report, this one by the American Center for Progress claims that, "Less than one-third of Hispanics partici-pated in an employer-sponsored retirement plan in 2007, compared to over half of whites." The ACP's "Update on the State of Minorities" (2008) adds that ". . . in 2007, the percentage of Hispanics who partici-pated in an employer-sponsored retirement plan remained considerably lower than that of whites, falling to 30.6 percent, well below the 57.6 percent of whites who participated." And more grimly, according to

NCPSSM, "Without Social Security benefits the poverty rate for Latinos would increase from 19 percent to 55 percent."

The statistics are in constant flux and understate the rapid deterioration in late 2008 and early 2009 of conditions caused by the current economic collapse. But clearly, despite impressive gains over the last fifteen years, the wage and benefits gap is not closing. "Hispanics' usual median weekly earnings were a troubling $192.80 less than those of whites in the second quarter of 2008. Hispanics' usual median weekly earnings stood at just $515.10 (in 2007 dollars) in the second quarter of 2008, while whites' were $707.90," according to the CAP report authored by Amanda Logan and Tim Westrich using data from the U.S. Department of Labor, Bureau of Labor Statistics.

Since college-educated, native-born Hispanics earn almost as much as their white counterparts, most of the current gap is a function of our community's lousy educational attainment and poor job skills, particularly among the most recent arrivals. The last ones into the country are the ones who are least connected, speak the least English, have the least formal education and command the lowest salaries. But the implications for the rest of the nation are dramatic. Using the Labor Department statistics cited above, on average in the first quarter of 2008, whites were earning $36,810.80 per year, while Hispanics made $26,785.20, a difference of $10,026. Assuming a payroll tax of 15.1 percent, whites paid $1,513.86 more per average person than Hispanics. That may not seem like much, but it adds up to a tax gap of more than $1.5 billion per million workers per year.

Put another way, if the projections are correct and there really will be 46 million Hispanics in the American workforce by 2050, then assuming nothing changes, the relative lack of success among Latinos will amount to a potential annual loss to the national retirement account of almost $70 billion.

Even in this era of multibillion-dollar bailouts, $70 billion lost each year due to Hispanic underachievement is a vast amount. Still, you have to be a real pessimist to believe this dynamic population will remain satisfied with life at the bottom of the barrel. According to the Pew Hispanic Center, "studies show that all, or nearly all, of the wage gap between white and Hispanic workers can be explained by gaps in English skills and education. For Hispanic and non-Hispanic workers with similar skills, there is virtually no wage gap." And as their situation is turned around by education and enhanced job skills, Hispanics will increasingly contribute to Social Security's fiscal health.

"The native-born Latino labor force is increasing more rapidly than the labor force for any other group, 4.8 percent compared with only 0.7 percent growth in the U.S. labor force. Thus, as workers retire or leave employment for other reasons, they are increasingly likely to be replaced by native-born Hispanics," reports the Pew Hispanic Center. "Latinos are an important source of workers to the U.S. economy. . . . In contrast to the recent past, however, the vast majority of the increase in the Latino working-age population . . . was native-born."

These potential citizen saviors of the Social Security system will be increasingly middle-class. According to an August 2007 analysis by the Tomás Rivera Policy Institute at the University of Southern California, "there are about 3.7 million affluent Hispanics nationwide. U.S. Census Bureau data for 2002 shows that 36 percent of Hispanic households had middle-class wealth" and "the ranks of the Hispanic middle class will almost certainly continue to grow in coming decades." By that 2002 Census, 20 percent of Hispanic households were already headed by someone with a bachelor's or other advanced degree.

They are doctors, lawyers, teachers and overwhelmingly entrepreneurial, one in eight being self-employed. Four years later, "a 2006 study conducted by J.D. Power and Associates indicates 31 percent of Hispanic households earn over $50,000 annually; 13 percent earn over $75,000 annually; and 6 percent earn over $100,000. . . . Although the average Hispanic household income is lower than the general market, studies denote the wealth of affluent Hispanics is growing faster than the general population," said a report by Cohn Marketing, a research firm.

Cheer those ambitious Latinos on; the enduring viability of the Social Security trust fund depends substantially on their sustained success.

★ 6 ★

REVERSE MIGRATION
When the Building Stopped

"New home construction fell to its lowest level on record in January as builders virtually closed up shop amid a plunge in demand, tightened credit markets and a flood of foreclosure properties."

—The Associated Press, February 2009

"Construction paid me $32 an hour, and with this I could pay my house, bills and invest in my children. Do you think, working at McDonald's, I could do the same?"

—Javier Amurrio,
38, unemployed Argentine immigrant,
to the *Washington Post*, June 2008

It is ironic that all the king's horses and all the king's men could not stem the flow of Latino immigration when there were jobs to be had in the United States, yet that most American of forces, the marketplace, has not only stemmed the flow, it has caused a rising wave of exodus. Across the country tens of thousands of Hispanic immigrants frustrated in their search for work in the struggling U.S. economy are calling it quits and returning to an uncertain future in their own depressed home countries. I saw them in Juárez, Mexico, during March 2009. Scores of undocumented workers carrying all their worldly possessions were trudging south across the Bridge of the Americas from El Paso, Texas. Burdened, dust-covered young men wearing banged-up straw cowboy hats, who had risked everything to go north to find work, were recrossing the Rio Grande. They were going home defeated, arriving in a nation where prospects were even grimmer and disorder widespread.

The trend of reverse migration is apparent from Brownsville, Texas, on the Gulf of Mexico to San Diego, California, on the Pacific coast. In places where migrants once flowed unceasingly into the United States from Mexico, Border Patrol arrests have plummeted to levels unseen since the 1970s. Surely part of the reason is the daunting force and the imposing fence that followed the unprecedented political pressure on Homeland Security to stop the flow; but every experienced observer will tell you that the principle reason fewer migrants are being arrested is that fewer are trying the border. The word is out that the old jobs just aren't there anymore.

The numbers of arrests, which began dropping several years ago, are therefore a solid indicator of the decline in migration. "We were in shock," Border Patrol spokesman Ben Vik told the *Times* about the two days in December 2008 when no apprehensions were reported in the entire 126-mile sector of the border centered on Yuma, Arizona. From October 2008 through February 2009, the *Times* reports that the Border Patrol arrested 195,399 illegal immigrants, a 24 percent decrease from the same period the year before.

"A lot of people who would have come here illegally and stayed illegally are not bothering to come to the U.S. The information that they are getting basically says there are no opportunities here," Demetrios Papademetriou of the Migration Policy Institute told the *L.A. Times*.

Steven Camarota, whose Center for Immigration Studies advocates strict immigration controls, happily estimates that more than 1 million illegal immigrants left the United States in 2008, four out of five of them Latino, a wave that began swelling even before the current recession became truly severe—a function no doubt of the early collapse of the construction trades.

"The current recession is having an especially severe impact on employment prospects for immigrant Hispanics," according to an analysis of the latest Census Bureau data, reports the Pew Hispanic Center. "They are overrepresented in certain industries such as construction. . . . Changes in unemployment during the recession reveal a rapidly worsening situation for foreign-born Hispanics."

In February 2009, noted immigration researchers Thelma Gutierrez and Wayne Drash reported numerous cases like that of Pedro Pablo, an undocumented immigrant from Guatemala who came to the United States to support his wife and five children back home. The researchers watched as Pablo folded up his American flag blanket and stuffed it into his duffel bag, then boarded a bus with a one-way ticket home, paid for by the Guatemalan consulate in Los Angeles. "I left my family and lost four years with them," the construction worker told Gutierrez and Drash. "I will ask them to forgive me. I can't make it here. If I have to suffer, it's better to suffer in Guatemala with my family."

"Things are very dire, and I think it's impacting those at the very bottom even more so," UCLA professor Abel Valenzuela, who has spent years studying day laborers, told the researchers, noting how many of the fruit-picking, meatpacking and domestic jobs they came to fill have since evaporated. "Day laborers are being really, really impacted. All of them are competing for the few jobs being dispatched."

Geronimo Salguero, the director of a day labor site in Los Angeles, told Drash and Gutierrez that employment for day laborers has dropped 75 percent over 2008. "They are completely desperate," said Salguero. "Each day, I have workers coming into the office and say 'Geronimo, help me. I want to go back to my country.'"

The current economic tornado is slamming unevenly into Hispanic America, which consists roughly of two big parts. The larger, say 70 to 75 percent, consists of the native-born and long-term immigrants. Like my extended network of family and friends, many are mainstream; they work, go to school, church or the market; they belong to various civic groups or social clubs; they parent, play and, while clearly Latino, are generally more native than "foreign." They are assimilated, like baseball more than *fútbol*, and their social and economic fate tends to rise and fall in sync with the rest of the nation. Right now, like most of our fellow citizens, my family is being impacted across the board by the economic downturn. But no one is jumping on the JetBlue flight back to San Juan, except for vacation.

The experience of my mostly working- and middle-class circle is fairly typical of the nation's long-term Latino population. The longer a particular person's family has been in the States, the tighter his or her bonds to

American popular culture and educational and economic systems. They range from those with advanced degrees to high school dropouts and, overall, are doing about as well as the rest of the country.

Some have opened small businesses: One owns a Coca-Cola distributorship in the Bronx, another heads a small neighborhood law firm, and still another owns a grocery store in El Barrio. We are also represented in the tony suburbs of Connecticut, where one of my cousins lives with her husband, the doctor. Others work for state or municipal agencies. One of them is a mailman like his dad; another works for the Port Authority of New York and was unlucky enough to be in the World Trade Center towers for both the truck bombing by the Blind Sheikh's gang in 1993, and the takedown by Khalid Sheikh Mohammed's bunch of kamikaze murderers on 9/11/01, miraculously emerging shaken but uninjured by either. Others have become teachers, steamfitters, airline mechanics and cops. Now, business is down. Future job prospects are limited. And there is a general unease about what lies ahead for the country. In other words, they are just like most other Americans.

Remember that my father was one of seventeen naturally born children of the same parents, Juan and Tomasa Rivera of Bayamón, Puerto Rico. That noble pair lived well into their nineties, having produced children into their fifties. Those children's upbringing on the island, though modest, was intensely loving and massively supportive. Some stayed in Puerto Rico; most came to the States; none stayed still, all traveling to and fro on a semiregular basis.

Happily, the mere scope of the Rivera clan presents a large universe from which to draw examples, with well over one hundred first cousins on my father's side alone. Every one of them speaks English. Their Spanish varies, but ranges from barely capable (i.e., mine) to fluent. Because the group is so big and, in a sense, so representative of three-quarters of the U.S. Hispanic experience, the settled three-quarters, I don't have to look far for classic examples of what has been called the Great American Assimilation Machine.

They are somewhat more religious and traditional than most Americans, but not obnoxiously so. And they are noticeably better educated on average than recent immigrants, particularly those from Mexico and Central America. They will survive our current economic plight more or less intact, if somewhat downsized.

The recession will impact the other 25 to 30 percent of Hispanic America far more drastically. "There is a push-pull phenomenon that is central to those people's lives," Dr. Juan Hernandez, president of the Organization for Hispanic Advancement and a former aide to the Mexican president, told me. "They leave Mexico because they can't put food on the table; that's the push. The pull is having the world's most prosperous nation steps away. The land of opportunity is hard to ignore, despite the obstacles."

Those relative newcomers, like Pedro Pablo of Guatemala, who came within the last few years, are a constantly changing cast made up mostly of younger men, more than half from Mexico, the rest from the Caribbean and Central and South America. These new immigrants have been among the primary beneficiaries of the rapid economic expansion that generated millions of new jobs in the United States in the past decade. And they are the group that is feeling the raw brunt of the Great Recession.

Timing is everything. The recent arrival who looked for opportunity in the United States in 2002–2006 saw it everywhere. From Texas to Georgia, North Carolina to New Jersey, Arkansas to Tennessee, from the foothills of the Rockies to Appalachia, Latino men became the heart of the booming construction business. As recently as 2006 and 2007, an estimated 300,000 Hispanic immigrants were joining the labor force each year, some headed to traditional immigrant jobs like meatpacking and agriculture, most others to the golden goose of construction. In all but the most strictly union or technically challenging jobs, like plumbing or trades requiring state licenses, like electricity, the arms pounding nails or sawing wood or wheelbarrowing concrete were brown and probably born abroad.

Almost all under thirty, they also came to dominate small manufacturing in Chicago, kitchen work in New York City, and dozens of other hard jobs in the four corners of the country. They made money and improved their standard of living and lifestyle here in the States. Three-quarters of them were even flush enough over the last several years to send surplus billions back to relatives in Latin America, much of the money earned in the physically demanding or unsavory work that most native-born have walked away from: on farms, in fast-food restaurants, carpet and upholstery factories, poultry-processing or meatpacking plants. And there, at least, most of the jobs remain.

But the real secret weapon in this recent march toward relative prosperity has been the tremendous number of comparatively high-paying jobs coming from the construction industry, especially in the exploding suburbs, and it was great while it lasted.

During the building trade's golden age, Latinos rose from one-fifth of the construction workforce in 2000 to almost one-third by 2006, according to the Economic Policy Institute. Millions chased the post-millennial boom. It became commonplace from New Jersey to Florida, Georgia to Nevada to Louisiana to see groups of young Latinos, unmistakably migrant, hanging at the local 7-Eleven or corner gas station waiting for the construction boss to swing by and pick up the usually robust number of day workers needed. In New Orleans they seemed to me to represent 90 percent of the crews reconstructing the hurricane-ravaged Big Easy.

Some of those crews are still around, familiar faces when you drive to the convenience stores or gas stations near my neighborhood here in the Hudson River town of Edgewater, New Jersey, across from Manhattan's West Side. I moved here to the river's edge in 1998 in search of the closest dock to my Midtown New York office. For the last ten years I have been happily making that fifteen-minute cruise from home, downriver to the 79th Street Boat Basin, the world's most pleasant commute. The scenery has changed, though. The Jersey side of the river was a melancholy mix of toxic dumps, fuel refineries, run-down amusement parks and warehouses when I first hit these waters almost fifty years ago. But for the last decade it has been the scene of an enormous boom in building. Lovely— or at least not ugly—low-rise, high-end condos have replaced the industrial morass.

Most of the spaces in between have been filled by new or refurbished homes. And most everything—certainly almost all of the smaller jobs, like the stand-alone private homes—has been built in part by these young

Latino nomads. The demand for labor attracted them here. The pay was good, immigration enforcement nonexistent, and the word went out to their brothers and cousins and later to their wives and children that this really was the promised land.

In those days no fence on earth could have stopped them from coming to America. Many settled and worked their way into the social establishment in nearby towns; roots were laid, and children schooled. But most of the jobs are either finished or stopped due to lack of buyers or mortgage financing. Some of those that aren't even finished aren't likely to be finished. And cleared sites bulldozed for new development aren't going to see building cranes anytime soon.

The Commerce Department reported in February 2009 that privately owned housing starts in January 2009 fell 16.8 percent from December to an annual rate of 446,000. That was the slowest pace since 1959, and less than half the rate of the year before. Now the Jersey real estate story is the omnipresent For Sale sign and foreclosures (and it is far worse in states like California, Nevada and Florida). So there are not as many young Latinos around my neighborhood as there were, a reflection of the rapid disappearance of their most reliable source of income.

For the random reason that a few years ago someone from back in Guatemala came and found a demand for labor here in Bergen County, along with a nonjudgmental populace and a de facto sanctuary policy in which local law enforcement does not inquire about the immigration status of even the obviously "foreign" day workers who hang out at the gas stations or convenience stores, this area near the river has been the perfect place for the young men from abroad to work.

Over time, many became assimilated, even legalized, but now that the jobs are going or gone, many are leaving. Two hardworking young cousins I know are typical. Alberto, the younger, twenty-two years old and single, is already back in Guatemala City, where I hear he is having a tough time finding a job, but where others similarly situated who would normally be heading toward the United States have been discouraged from doing so by Alberto's recent experience.

The other, Alfredo, three years older at twenty-five, is working only part-time but is desperate to stick it out because his wife and three young children are already here, living in a modest rental in West New York, the heavily Latino town downriver about across from Wall Sreet on the Jersey side of the Hudson, where the kids are enrolled in public school. When I asked him why he stays in the face of privation, Alfredo tells me that one perhaps ironic reason is the stronger border enforcement. He knows it will be more difficult for him to return once he leaves.

The official November 2008 unemployment rate among U.S. Hispanics was 8.6 percent, and that didn't count the undocumented workers, just the citizens and legal residents who field unemployment claims. Two months later, according to the Bureau of Labor Statistics, in January 2009, it was 9.7 percent. It is substantially higher today. By the end of 2008, the unemployment rate in the construction trade was already 15 percent. That was before the industry lost a hundred thousand more jobs in January, and that melancholy statistic was also heading straight up. Clearly, the effect of the sharp decline of the housing trades is dragging on the entire U.S. Latino community, legal and illegal.

Largely because of the collapse of the U.S. construction industry, in January 2009, for the first time in a decade, the amount of money sent back to Mexico by migrants living in the United States dropped. The so-called remittances by workers abroad are Mexico's second-largest source of foreign income, after oil. Those remittances dropped by more than 3.5 percent in 2008, to $25 billion. That $25 billion is still a whopping amount that should give a clearer picture of why emigration is the social safety valve for the Mexican Republic. Without the enormous prop of her sons and daughters sending money home to grandparents, parents, spouses and children, the entire Mexican economic system might collapse.

American citizens, even the recently unemployed or underemployed, are protected by the vast federal and state social safety net of unemployment insurance, food stamps and job assistance. Because they don't have to work to feed themselves, even in these distressed times, many won't take jobs at the bottom of the barrel. Not too many of the native-born are that into handpicking fruits and vegetables or cleaning public toilets wherever found, especially those really sticky ones in bus terminals and rest stops.

Immigrants don't have that choice. In fact, since the construction bust, undocumented workers are often working scared, doing longer hours for less pay. They have to work to eat or they have to go back where they came from, where they can earn even less money for even more work. A seven-dollar-per-hour job in El Paso and a decent meal easily morph into a one-dollar-per-hour job across the border in Juárez, and a plain tortilla and salt.

In addition to the gnawing bite of recession, hard times have amped resentment toward recent immigrants. I don't take it too personally. While there is and always has been a race-based component to anti-immigrant sentiment, it is primarily a matter of visibility. Since the middle of the previous century Hispanics have simply been the most widespread and obvious new arrivals. Now it is Target: Latinos, just as it was Target: Irish or Target: Italians, etc., before us. That we are the last ones over the bridge, however, has real-world consequences. A Zogby poll taken two days after the November 2008 election showed that 57 percent of Americans voting believed that offering amnesty to illegal workers would harm American workers. That is a polite way of saying that our nation's current economic travail has knifed deeply into not only the financial well-being of the Hispanic immigrant community, but has also spread disquiet through the larger Latino citizen population.

In the year and a half since the reform bill's defeat, I have fielded frequent complaints from citizen or otherwise legal Hispanic viewers and listeners who relate stories of harassment, usually in the form of racial profiling by immigration authorities and manifest discrimination at airports and border crossings. In the tough economic climate that prevails, scores have told me that their employers are "carding" them to ensure they are here legally. And these measures are being taken against a wide swath of the Latino community, including citizens born in the United States.

In the long, sour tradition beginning with that manifest resentment toward the legions of Irish pouring onto our shores 160 years ago, the sometimes violent reaction toward Chinese railroad workers who helped build the West in the latter part of the nineteenth century; and the raw discrimination against the white ethnics of the early twentieth century, especially the "foreign" Jews, who always got blamed as the consummate "outsiders" when their host country's economy collapsed, Latinos are now the prime target of the anti-immigration posse.

One particularly egregious example occurred near my old Long Island neighborhood in November 2008, when a thirty-eight-year-old Ecuadorian immigrant who had lived in the community for fifteen years was beaten to death by a group of sixteen- and seventeen-year-olds who were out "hunting Mexicans." The teenagers accused in the racially motivated stabbing death were later charged in a January 2009 indictment with taking part in a wave of violent attacks over fourteen months.

Most of the gang look just like the kids I played football with in high school: tall, skinny white ethnic teenagers with names like Hausch, Shea and Conroy. In all, seven of them from Patchogue, Long Island, are now charged with hunting down and attacking random Hispanic immigrants, injuring eight and killing one. They called their hobby "beaner bashing," and for a year it became an important part of their social lives.

According to prosecutors, the young men would prowl areas where migrant workers were known to congregate. Picking a target, they would then stalk him until he was alone; then with knives, pipes, fists and boots they would savage the victim, telling him they were going to kill him if he didn't go home where he belonged. The bashers overdid it with Marcelo Lucero, whose death capped the more than yearlong rampage that spread terror through the immigrant community in the still agricultural area of the same county that is home to the Hamptons. And even as word spread of the bashers' goal of ridding the region of Latino workers, the gang regaled their friends in high school with tales of their violent activities, which they viewed as righteous vigilantism.

Just a month later another Ecuadorian was beaten to death in New York City with an aluminum baseball bat, even as his attackers shouted anti-Hispanic and antigay slurs. Police and prosecutors said the man, José Sucuzhañay, was attacked as he was walking arm in arm with his own brother to keep warm on a frigid night. The attack left Sucuzhañay in a coma. He died several days later as his mother was en route from Ecuador to see him. His body was flown back to South America for burial.

"This horrible act appears to have been fueled by a deadly combination of ethnic and homophobic prejudice," said Mayor Michael Bloomberg, who after announcing the arrests of two suspects told family members attending a City Hall news conference in Spanish that victims of hate crimes should not fear reporting the attacks. The mayor added that he hoped the arrests provided some measure of comfort to the victim's family.

Hate crimes targeting Latinos have increased 40 percent since 2003, according to the most recent FBI statistics. "The wave of hate that is seeping through our communities threatens the fabric of our nation and is costing lives," argued La Raza's executive director, Janet Murguía. "Americans will not be cowed by those trying to advance intolerance—we must stand up to the presence of hate groups and extremists in our communities and speak with one voice to say we will not be dehumanized."

Blame the media. In this instance the old cliché about how antisocial activity is being encouraged by what kids see and hear on TV or the radio is true. I hear the anecdotal reports from Latinos across the country on a weekly basis: how even citizen Hispanic children are being teased by their classmates because they are "foreign," "different" or "trespassers." I will bet that the families of those "beaner bashers" attacking immigrants expressly and vocally agreed with the raging nightly anti-immigrant commentary from Lou Dobbs or Michael Savage.

The rise of hate crimes is serious and reflects the erosion of tolerance that always accompanies hard times. Even Saint Obama, in his 2006 book, *The Audacity of Hope*, admits to having "nativist sentiments," including feeling resentful when he saw Mexican flags waved at pro-immigration rallies, and frustration when forced to use a translator to speak with his car mechanic.

Before the crash, I remember fielding an angry call on live FOX radio from a construction worker in the Atlanta area complaining about how the "Mexicans have taken over." Jay Leno and I even had an on-air *Tonight*

Show conversation/debate in March 2008 in which Jay lamented how the old Italian roofing crews so familiar during the burgeoning heyday of the San Fernando Valley had disappeared under the wave of Hispanic workers who absorbed most of the mass construction jobs. It was the one area of real-world friction between the migrants and native-born, particularly when the industry began its brutal contraction in 2007 and the lavish job supply dried up.

Once the crash came, the boss with the pickup truck who had run a crew of two to four regulars, mostly those eager young migrants willing to work for ten bucks an hour and lunch, was reduced to driving himself around looking for handyman work. Statistics done by Pew suggest the severe hit Hispanics have recently taken. In a year, employment among Mexican immigrants dropped from 65.9 percent to 63.8 percent of their total population.

The recession/depression is now pervasive and spiraling into a danger zone in which social dislocation among the poorest threatens. And the last in are the first to suffer the adverse impact. From the third quarter of 2007 to the third quarter of 2008, about a half million Hispanics were newly unemployed. And of that number, most were migrants. The number of unemployed Mexican-born workers increased from 326,000 in the third quarter of 2007 to 498,000 in the fall of 2008. Over the last six months of 2008, a total of 2.2 million Latino workers became newly unemployed, according to Labor Department statistics.

As the flow of new Latino immigrants into the United States dries up, "A small but significant decline has occurred during the current recession in the share of Latino immigrants active in the U.S. labor force," says Pew's crack economist Rakesh Kochhar in his report "Latino Workers in the Ongoing Recession," explaining how the proportion of working-age Latino immigrants participating in the labor force has fallen.

That lack of employment opportunity is now provably affecting illegal migration to the United States. Census data released in May 2009 by Mexico's National Institute of Statistics and Geography confirm the dramatic decline in the number of Mexicans trying to make their way into the United States. Bearing in mind that the vast majority of those who leave Mexico are bound for the U.S., during the year that ended in August 2008, about 226,000 fewer people left Mexico than during the previous year, a decline of 25 percent. That decline will be even greater in 2009, when the effects of the swine flu epidemic are figured in. When the disease swept through Mexico, their government responded by locking down much of the nation's public life, making even internal travel more difficult, and crossing the international border even more daunting. The meaningful decline in Mexican immigration demonstrates clearly that immigration is driven by economic opportunity. Most of those who come here are coming to find a job; no work available means less immigration. Stripped of the rhetoric, thus it has always been.

The collapsed market for building trades workers has proven a much more effective weapon against the presence of illegal workers than all the overdone raids ever concocted by Immigration and Customs Enforcement. I can report from the Mexican border that the reality of a severe downturn in decent job opportunity in the States has been eloquently passed down the immigrant communications network and has resulted in a tightening of the spigot of new arrivals from Latin America. The real question is, What are those former immigrants doing back home? Is their presence destabilizing to their home countries? Will they come back when the U.S. economy recovers? And more immediately, as our own economic situation deteriorates, will resentment and discrimination against Latinos, citizens and immigrant alike, continue to fester and grow?

★ 7 ★

A *HOGAR* IS NOT A HOME

How Aspiration, Greed and Failed Assumptions Bankrupted the Latino American Dream

"By the end of the decade Latinos will share equally in the American Dream of homeownership."

—The Congressional Hispanic Caucus 2003 mission statement

"The American Nightmare: Strategies for Preventing, Surviving and Overcoming Foreclosure."

—A 2008 National Association of Hispanic Real Estate Professionals handbook

"At the height of the subprime lending boom, in 2005, banking and finance companies gave at least $2.3 million in campaign contributions to members of the Hispanic Caucus, according to data from the Center for Responsive Politics."

—*Wall Street Journal*, January 2009

When California congressman Joe Baca enthusiastically introduced me for a luncheon speech in connection to the Congressional Hispanic Caucus annual meeting in the nation's capital in September 2008, I was ready to roar. Addressing the crowd in the packed hotel ballroom, I ripped into the disappointing Homeland Security secretary, Michael Chertoff, for abandoning a balanced and reasonably conciliatory approach to immigration enforcement, and for beginning instead the series of brutal, senseless workplace raids aimed at arresting and deporting hardworking people. And I called passionately on President George W. Bush in his last days in office to remember his own originally moderate instincts on the topic and to pardon all undocumented aliens, whose only crime was their unauthorized presence here in this country, a low-level federal misdemeanor.

Many in the partisan crowd of mostly Latino Democrats that day were refreshing young strivers, the next generation of leadership who hold so much promise for our community's future. All enthusiastically responded to the speech; several promised to craft legislation or draft class-action lawsuits to help along the cause of a general presidential pardon for all 11 or 12 million living in the shadows of American society.

It was two months before the election, and the buzz in D.C. was about how the polls had all turned Obama's way, the Latinos' way, and most of the audience were congratulating one another about the coming dawn of a new political era in America. The scores of young men and women who had come to the nation's capital to intern or otherwise begin careers in or around government were especially psyched by my defiant, confident tone. They just couldn't get over the fact that I work at FOX News, which they perceive to be the bastion of conservative thought.

Events would soon prove—indeed, were already proving—the perils of political power and the dark side of dreams. Like almost every other American, we in that hall in the fall of 2008 were oblivious to the speed with which the U.S. economy was unraveling, and how the avalanche of one of the steepest downturns in history would take the dreams of millions of homeowners, including many Latinos, down with it.

As caucus chairman, the affable Congressman Baca has long been a power in Congress, a pillar of the Latino community who represents the district around San Bernardino, an hour east of Los Angeles. In that sweeping center of modern suburban living, he represents a district that is 58 percent Latino, many of them hardworking seekers of the dream of owning their own home. To further that goal, in 2003 the influential congressman and his colleagues in the caucus created a housing initiative called Hogar, which means "place" or "hearth" in English. They established as its mission to bring Hispanic homeownership up to the levels of other groups.

Lavishly funded by the mortgage industry itself, which was an inherent conflict of interest, the Hogar initiative came at the same time the barely regulated lenders, real estate agents, brokers and bankers hungry for new markets saw a dream of their own. There was a huge, largely untouched pool of unsophisticated consumers so eager to own their own homes for little or no money down that they would gladly accept mortgages that came with introductory interest rates, giving little or no thought to the fact that those rates would soon balloon and become unaffordable.

Coming in the midst of what was a quickly rising twenty-first-century tide of Latino employment, housing booms happened in traditionally Hispanic areas of Nevada, California, Florida and Arizona, and in North Carolina, Arkansas, Georgia and other places you don't usually associate with large concentrations of Latinos. Las Vegas, Orlando, Phoenix and Miami blossomed, and the new economy fueled an unprecedented boom in which even immigrant families, some still undocumented, were catapulted into the home-owning middle class.

Still at NBC News, I reported in 1999 from Vegas on the breathtaking explosion in the number of Latino immigrants who had landed union service jobs in the casino industry and who had parlayed those decent wages into a settled, promising life.

According to the U.S. Census Bureau, between 1994 and 2006 Hispanic homeownership grew from 41 percent of all Latino families to 50 percent. In 2005 alone, mortgages to Hispanics rose by 29 percent. More ominously, although not noticed by regulators, advocates or the news media, ultimately lethal subprime mortgages that year, 2005, to Latino families with questionable credit soared 169 percent, according to a Federal Financial Institutions Examination Council report cited by an important January 2009 *Wall Street Journal* investigation.

Latinos still lagged well behind the 74 percent rate of homeownership for non-Hispanic white families, according to the 2008 Hispanic Policy Agenda, but the period through 2006 represented real evidence that the American dream of homeownership was taking hold in the Latino community as well.

Everybody was happy. The mortgage industry was making a killing, and was only too glad to donate money, reportedly $2 million, to expand the Hogar initiative's homeownership goals; Hogar was a powerful, well-connected nonprofit whose avowed purpose was opening this brave new housing market, jump-starting equal opportunity for ownership. Who would complain when the activist, socially conscious Democratic legislators at the Hispanic Caucus and the entrepreneurial, presumably Republican investment bankers, hedge fund managers, and mortgage lenders like Countrywide, Washington Mutual, New Century Financial and AmeriQuest, not to mention Fannie Mae and Freddie Mac, were all on the same noble page? Not to mention the panting encouragement of real estate developers, builders, commission-seeking agents and brokers everywhere.

Angelo Mozilo, the now widely reviled ex-chief of busted Countrywide Financial, spoke at the 2006 Place Your Bets on Home Ownership convention Hogar sponsored in Las Vegas; so did Henry Cisneros, former HUD secretary turned real estate baron and the bought-and-paid-for $5 million face of Countrywide. This brings to mind the old cliché, "with friends like these, who needs enemies?"

Cisneros served on the board of Countrywide from 2001 to 2007, when, powered by promiscuous credit, Latinos were being seduced to inflate the housing bubble. Interestingly, in a move that should attract attention from any future employer or agency, he resigned just days before Countrywide reported a $1.2 billion quarterly loss in 2007, and that a third of its borrowers were late on their mortgage payments. It was the beginning of the end of the housing bubble, a grim harbinger of hard times to come in the United States and around the world, and almost nobody knew just how catastrophic the ultimate collapse would be.

Cisneros, the scandal-plagued former housing secretary, reluctantly admitted in February 2009 during a "Back to Basics: Restoring Latino Financial Security" telephonic symposium sponsored by La Raza and the Center for American Progress, a left-leaning D.C. think tank, "Did Countrywide go too far? In retrospect, maybe so."

No shit, Sherlock.

Cisneros added, "Step one . . . we have to curb unscrupulous business practices." He did not say, "Beginning with my own company," but perhaps he should have. I saw Cisneros in Washington during one of the Latino inaugural events. A tall, charismatic, good-looking man who as mayor of

San Antonio and later HUD secretary had everything going for him, he quickly turned and walked the other way when he saw me. Not wanting to taint the festive atmosphere, I did not pursue him.

During the boom times, the real estate agents and mortgage brokers were making a fortune selling homes or loans to just about anyone with a pulse. Openly counseling mortgage seekers on how they could misrepresent income and commit other fraud, it was no secret that only the constantly rising value of real estate was keeping the system intact. Yet few complained: The banks, brokers and investors were making a fortune, and the quasi-governmental companies like Fannie Mae and Freddie Mac could find comfort in the fact that they were doing God's work in eradicating homeownership inequality. When the bubble burst, we must admit that it was a function not only of greed, but also of good intentions.

To afford those new homes, like too many other Americans, Latino families went deeply into hock, cheered on by those quasi-governmental policies that encouraged minority homeownership, and by lending institutions that abandoned prudence for profit, secure in the assumption that housing prices were destined always to keep rising. Companies like soon-to-be insolvents Fannie Mae and Freddie Mac, and now-bankrupt Washington Mutual, Countrywide Financial and AmeriQuest, all jumped on the bandwagon of throwing money at naive buyers who barely had a pot to piss in.

In the parlance of the trade, they were often so-called NINA loans, for buyer/borrowers having "no income, no assets." (There were also some NINJA loans—no income, no assets and no job either.) Campaigns pushing these come-one, come-all loans appeared "to target borrowers who would have trouble qualifying for a mortgage if their financial position were adequately disclosed," said a Freddie Mac memo obtained by Congress and reported in the *Wall Street Journal*. Of those toxic NINA loans, according to the memo, "It appears they are disproportionately targeted toward Hispanics."

For fear of diluting public sympathy and eagerness for change, when I reported on the grim conditions inside the nation's institutions for the mentally retarded back in the early 1970s, I made a point of deemphasizing the fact that the institutional populations were disproportionately minority. I didn't want the systematic abuse and neglect to be perceived as a black or brown problem. When the subprime catastrophe is analyzed it will become graphically clear that minority homeowners are the majority of the willing victims who bought houses they could not afford, with loans they could never repay. According to several sources, as many as 40 percent of all subprime mortgages nationwide are held by Hispanics. Hopefully that won't dilute America's resolve to help those home owners out.

The bipartisan Fair Housing Commission, using data from the Federal Reserve, told Congress that 47 percent of Hispanics who got mortgages had received subprime loans, as opposed to 17 percent of whites. A common real estate advertisement in Spanish-language media read, "*¡Sin verificación de ingresos! ¡Sin verificación de documento!*" ("No income verification! No documentation!")

"We would say, 'Is he breathing? Okay, we'll give him a mortgage,'" Tim Sandos, the president of the National Association of Hispanic Real Estate Professionals, told the *WSJ*.

As a community heavy with renters and young adults, Latinos, citizens, legal and illegal immigrants alike represented one of the last great untapped pools of buyers for U.S. banks, mortgage finance companies, brokers and other real estate professionals who all made a ton of money during the boom. Everybody could be a real estate broker in those heady days, and everybody else could own a home.

Many first-time Latino home buyers paid swollen prices for their homes at the worst possible time, that period from 2004 to 2007 when the market was bubbling. Worse, they bought or refinanced their homes with exotic mortgages written in English and containing a time bomb designed to blow up interest rates after a short grace period. One common scheme among predatory lenders is called an "option-adjustable rate" mortgage, or ARM, which Latinos were twice as likely to receive as white borrowers.

Buyers begin with a low monthly payment and are unknowingly adding a balance to their mortgage each month. Eventually, the payments "reset"; that is, they increase significantly. From 2008 to 2009, 1.8 million ARM mortgages reset. Because of an upcoming explosion of resets, the peak of foreclosures for Latino households will be in late 2009–2010, according to Janet Murguía, president of the National Council of La Raza, who added, "NCLR is deeply concerned that a generation of Latino wealth is under attack."

The *Journal* profiles Gerardo Cadima, a Bolivian immigrant who works as an electrician in suburban Virginia and bought a home for $300,000, with no money down. When work slowed and the higher adjustable interest kicked in, "I started to think, is this really worth it?" he told the *Journal*. He stopped making payments and the house was sold at auction for $180,000. Emotional cost aside, because he had made no down payment Mr. Cadima and tens of thousands like him walked away from their home once its value dipped below what they owed on it; they literally had no vested interest. No-down-payment real estate buying is bad business and bad public policy.

Worse was a disastrous idea pushed by a nonprofit housing corporation called AmeriDream: a seller-financed down-payment program. The cost of the loan to make the down payment was simply added to the monthly mortgage payment, which was a time bomb designed to explode in much higher monthly payments at some designated period down the road. Seller-financed down payments have since been outlawed.

In chronicling the boom/bust in another of those surprising concentrations of Hispanics, the carpet factory town of Dalton, Georgia, *New York Times* reporter Peter S. Goodman profiled the Perez-Torres family, which had ridden the wave of easy credit to success in a taxi service that ferries Latino workers from home to jobs in the factories. Their first car was purchased in 2001 with no money down. The bold gambit worked for the family, which had emigrated from Mexico and arrived in small-town Georgia after fleeing the mean streets of Los Angeles.

By 2005, the family business was earning a profit of $40,000. Goodman writes that they bought a four-bedroom home with a swimming pool for $240,000, also with no money down. Then the factories their business served started laying people off or cutting their hours. The cab company was forced to idle three of its six cars. The so-called promotional mortgage payment of $1,700 per month jumped in early 2007 as scheduled in the fine print to $2,500.

With their car service losing money, they stopped making payments on their home. Ultimately they lost it to foreclosure. According to Goodman, they were one of 111 Dalton families in that period between January and March 2008 to lose their homes, four times the number of the previous year. Now, the reporter says, the family is camping in the taxi company office, doing their laundry at a Laundromat and cooking with a hot plate.

The increase in Hispanic homeownership in places like Congressman Baca's San Bernardino, California, district is proving to be like the improvement in athletic performance with steroids. The average Latino family has increased its debt load, even as unemployment is spiking and the value of their homes has plummeted in some cases by more than half. And no group was so seduced, or as effectively targeted by predatory lenders. Even those Hispanics whose credit scores could have qualified them for more consumer-friendly fixed-rate standard or prime loans were steered toward subprime mortgages. using extremely low "teaser rates" to draw borrowers into their malignant embrace.

"This was not only a problem of regulation on the mortgage front, but also a targeted scourge on minority communities," said Shaun Donovan, secretary of Housing and Urban Development, in a May 2009 speech at New York University. The secretary was quoted in an excellent analysis by Michael Powell and Janet Roberts in *The New York Times*, who add, "Roughly 33 percent of the subprime mortgages given out in New York City in 2007, Mr. Donovan said, went to borrowers with credit scores that should have qualified them for conventional prevailing-rate loans. For anyone taking out a $350,000 mortgage, a difference of three percentage points—a typical spread between conventional and subprime loans—tacks on $272,000 in additional interest over the life of a 30-year loan."

Advocates put the number of doomed subprime mortgages in the nation as high as one in four of all policies written. A Pew Hispanic Center fall 2008 study shows that almost one in ten Latino families has skipped a mortgage payment or was not able to make a payment last year. It also says that more than a third of Latinos have fears that their homes may face foreclosure. If accurate, that is the most chilling statistic of all—that one out of every three Latino families fears they could lose their home to future foreclosure. In the spring 2009, the U.S. Latino homeowner foreclosure rate is already around one in every nine homes.

Even now, in Hispanic neighborhoods from Florida to Arizona, Nevada and California, including in Congressman Baca's San Bernardino district, For Sale signs are everywhere and foreclosed homes sit vacant and poorly maintained, accelerating the decline in the value of occupied houses nearby. There are reportedly more than nine thousand home foreclosures in Mr. Baca's district. Home ownership fueled by subprime mortgages is proving the wreck of dreams to many Hispanics.

The challenge now facing Hispanics and the larger American community is, first, to survive the recession. Native-born Hispanics had a 9.5 percent rate of unemployment in the fourth quarter of 2008, and, "The current recession is having an especially severe impact on employment prospects for immigrant Hispanics," according to Pew. Interestingly, the fact that Latinos were not as heavily into homeownership to begin with might ultimately prove a saving grace. A renter has less leverage, less debt than a homeowner. And the renter is spared the direct impact of declining home values. Like those Hispanics who didn't qualify for credit cards because the applicants were deemed too risky even for predatory lenders, the renters may have the last laugh, particularly if declining prices make homes more legitimately affordable.

Whenever the U.S. economy contracts, the people who suffer most are those who can afford it least. And right now the squeeze is tightest on Latinos. Hopefully, the job market will improve as the impact of various stimulus programs kicks in. In terms of homeownership, those who got a too-good-to-be-true deal on a house they could never hope to afford, and which may now be worth much less than the owner owes on it, have to do some hard reckoning.

Many, like Gerardo Cadima and the Perez-Torres family, will walk away from those deals and seek to pick up the pieces of their lives else where. Our Hispanic American dream of homeownership is no different from that of any other segment of the population. But we all have to be careful what we wish for, remembering that if a deal sounds too good to be true, it is probably not true. Our leaders like Joe Baca and Henry Cisneros also have to be scrutinized with the same vigor as any other public servant or businessperson. Good intentions don't forgive responsibility for the consequences of actions taken that hurt innocent people. And some of the pain the community is now enduring is clearly self-inflicted.

While the jury is out on Cisneros, I don't believe Congressman Baca or Hogar acted dishonestly in trying to spread the housing wealth. If the *Wall Street Journal* is correct and members of the Hispanic Caucus received over $2 million in campaign contributions from mortgage lenders, then it suggests our Latino representatives are as susceptible as the next to morally corrupt but pervasive and probably legal Washington lobbying.

Enthusiastic about what they saw as the ultimate win-win of a happy, generous industry serving happy, voting consumers, those officials were no more to blame for impoverishing home buyers than the stock broker who in 2008 still advised us to buy "safe" S&P 500 stocks, only to see the Dow Jones average plummet from above fourteen thousand to below seven thousand points.

With all the real pain and suffering within the Latino and broader American community, perhaps predictably some of the same ideologues who blamed immigrants for everything that ailed the nation before the housing bubble burst, like disease, job stealing and crime, are now blaming government efforts to expand affordable housing to minorities as the cause of the collapse of the banking system.

As recounted in the left-leaning, but usually accurate Web site Media Matters for America, on February 20, 2009, right-wing political analyst Pat Buchanan alleged on MSNBC that "the feds leaned on banks and threatened some of these banks, 'You've got to make more loans,' and pushed them out—you gotta help, frankly, in minority communities. And they pushed them out and the guys put nothing down and stuff, and then the banks sell the loans off to Fannie and Freddie." To which host Joe Scarborough responded, "And that's what happened. Banks made bad loans. They sold it to Fannie and Freddie, Fannie and Freddie sold it to Wall Street," and so on to the end of the world as we know it.

The problem with this harsh analysis is that it conveniently overlooks the central fact that in the fifteen most populous metropolitan areas, 84.3 percent of subprime loans were not made by traditional banks that then passed them on to Fannie and Freddie, destroying the financial integrity of those two quasi-governmental entities. That is not what happened. More specifically, that is not most of what happened. In minority neighborhoods the companies throwing money at lenders who could never hope to pay it back were financial institutions not regulated as depository institutions. Rather the predators were the creepy, greedy, loan-sharky concerns like Henry Cisneros's Countrywide Financial, AmeriDream and Ameri-Quest. The motive of the nondepository institutions was to make as much money as fast as they could before the bubble burst. They were a cut above Bernard Madoff, but just a cut.

The big busts that took down the world economy—like Bank of America and Citicorp, Goldman Sachs, JPMorgan Chase, Morgan Stanley, Merrill Lynch and Bear Stearns, HSBC and Wachovia, and all those other international, national and regional banks and financial institutions that went for the short money and then got caught short—all got in trouble or failed without any help from poor brown and black people. Blame Greenwich, not south Los Angeles, Las Vegas or Orlando.

With the various government proposals coming down the pike in the Obama administration designed to stem the pain and suffering of those who were honest victims of the housing debacle, there is reason to hope that the deals worth salvaging will be saved. The president unveiled the Homeowner Affordability and Stability Plan, a $75 billion proposal that includes helping home owners who are behind in their monthly payments but could keep up if their mortgage terms were eased, a situation that includes many Latinos. By the time you read this, some expensive bailout or other will have been enacted. Undoubtedly some jerky, greedy, yuppie house flippers will benefit from the taxpayers' largesse, but in that cascade of free public money hopefully the minority community will receive a share commensurate with its size and relative innocence.

Going forward, lenders must be open-minded about refinancing and homeowners prudent about what they can afford. As important, controversial but powerful and effective advocacy groups like ACORN must be careful to craft realistic goals rather than trying to force a radical housing agenda. Every family does not deserve to have the government—meaning taxpayers—buy them a home. Where I was raised, we believed homeownership was a reward for hard work and prudence, not a roll of the dice on a day trip to Atlantic City.

Homes have never been as legitimately affordable as they are today to anyone who has saved a few dollars and has a job and a plan. Unless the federal or state governments decide they want to foster a policy under which homeownership is mandatory for every American, just like they have bailed out fake and unsupportable businesses like AIG, then we've got to cool our jets about forcefully advocating a free lunch. While all of us have the right to life, liberty and the pursuit of happiness, that doesn't mean we can't rent.

★ 8 ★

ENDING THE EDUCATION SIESTA
Because If We Don't, Nothing Else Matters

"The most urgent problem for the American education system has a Latino face."

—Patricia Gándara, Civil Rights Project, 2008

"Respect, responsibility, and results."

—Village Academy (California) motto,
cited by President Barack Obama, 2009

The biggest anchor holding back America's Latino community is not racism, anti-immigration sentiment or even the economy. It is lack of education. As a national community the Latino school dropout rate and the related frequency of unmarried teenage pregnancy continue to rival those of the Third World. That is beyond doubt or contradiction. What is more difficult to determine is why so many of us remain at the bottom of the education barrel, with the fewest over-fourteen-year-olds eventually getting a high school diploma, the most over-twenty-five-year-olds having not completed a single year of high school, and by far the most who are functionally illiterate, having completed just the fourth grade or less.

Again, the truth cannot be spun. In 2007, 18.7 percent of all U.S. Hispanics age twenty-five or older possessed less than five years of elementary-level education, according to the U.S. Census Bureau. That means that about one out of every five Latino adults walking around and looking for a job in America today is armed with less than a sixth-grade education. Is there any wonder their opportunities are severely curtailed, their odds of breaking poverty's bonds so long?

Boston Globe reporter James Vaznis wrote in February 2009 that in his

state, "Little more than half of the Hispanic male students last year graduated from high school within four years, a slight decline from the previous
year" in Massachusetts, "the lowest rate of any student group broken down
by race, ethnicity, and gender since the state began tracking graduation
rates three years ago." Vaznis quotes Gary Orfield, codirector of the Civil
Rights Project, based at the University of California at Los Angeles:
"Latinos need to get mobilized. This is a life-or-death issue for their
future. . . . Not getting a high school diploma is a life sentence to margin-
alization and poverty and living on the streets. It's a horrible threat to the
future of a community."

Nationally, only 60.3 percent of Latinos had completed high school or
higher in 2007, which compares to 82.8 percent of blacks and 90.6 percent of whites. Part of the reason is surely the vicious cycle of mandatory
employment. A kid may be just sixteen years old, but if his family needs
his or her labor to survive, he or she will drop out of school to work. The
story is even bleaker among recent immigrants, who comprise most of the
least well educated. Among those hard-pressed newcomers, that urgent
need for even the youngsters to work is part of their heritage, officially
encouraged by very low or even nonexistent minimum mandatory-
education age requirements in the country of their origin.

Although Mexico requires that its thirty-one states and Federal District
provide "compulsory" education up to ninth grade, i.e., lower-secondary
education, that really means that the states must provide the education, not
that the students must actually attend classes. As a practical matter kids can
drop out of school in Mexico after sixth grade, when they are twelve or
thirteen years old. Our neighbor's educational deficit is a severe handicap
to Mexico's hopes for the future. As former Mexican president Vicente
Fox said in his book *Revolution of Hope*, a lack of educated workers "leads
to underemployment and low wages in a global economy that demands
more and more intellectual ability."

In this regard, the slowing of immigration into the United States will
also necessarily mean that fewer uneducated or undereducated migrant
children will be enrolling in stateside schools. That is not a bad thing, at
least not for us. Gradually, and depending on individual circumstance as

well as the overall economy, those already here will become better educated. Studies show they are learning English at a faster rate than their forebears.

Changing this situation won't be easy and probably needs massive federal government attention, a necessary priority along with immigration reform, because "Unfortunately, Latino students share demographic characteristics that are strongly correlated with low levels of school readiness and poor academic achievement. Latino children tend to have higher levels of poverty, lower levels of parental education, and higher levels of linguistic isolation than their white peers," according to a 2008 report by the Hispanic Education Coalition, a group of twenty-six organizations dedicated to improving educational opportunities for the nearly 50 million Latinos living in the United States and Puerto Rico.

"Only 6 percent of Latino students are proficient in reading by the 4th grade compared to 41 percent of white students . . . approximately 600,000–700,000 Latino students drop out of school each year . . . four times the rate of white students," says the Coalition's 2008 report.

But why should the rest of American society care? "It is apparent that the success of our public schools largely depends on our ability to address the educational crisis facing the Latino community," adds the report.

American Latino youngsters hold the short end of the educational stick. "The characteristics of high schools matter for student performance. Careful statistical studies have found that schools with larger enrollments are associated with lower student achievement and higher dropout rates," says Pew. Look at the three largest Los Angeles high schools, all predominantly Hispanic: L.A. High with forty-seven hundred students, Roosevelt with five thousand, and Belmont with fifty-two hundred, the nation's largest. That is an intense concentration of mostly poor kids, stuffed into very large classrooms, with enormous baggage from the surrounding communities, including gang affiliations.

On March 12, 2009, the Chicago Public Schools recorded their twenty-sixth student killed since the start of the school year, tying last year's total with three months remaining in the school year. He was Franco Avila, age seventeen. "He just was trying to get on the right track," Avila's stepfather, Dennis Kuhn, told the *Chicago Tribune*, with "his voice breaking and his body trembling" as he explained to the *Tribune* reporters that his boy didn't want to belong to a gang anymore, but the gangbangers killed him anyway.

So the social and economic condition of our children's lives plays the major role in handicapping their educational attainment. They have the toughest row to hoe. But you knew that. More challenging is the question of why so few manage to break poverty's bonds. One much maligned theory is the notion that a "culture of poverty" exists, a voluntary pattern of life that forms a kind of social prison. Anthropologist Oscar Lewis was first to write about it in *Five Families, The Children of Sanchez* and *La Vida*. While the Mexican-American immigrant "Sanchez" family that Lewis wrote about was eager to break free from poverty's grip, the Puerto Rican "Rios" family, U.S. citizens living *la vida loca*, were exerting only enough energy to get by. It seemed not so much a culture of poverty as a culture of cynicism. "I'll never amount to much, so why try too hard? There's always welfare or some scam or other available. I'll get by."

A couple of points: No one is more proudly Puerto Rican than I am, Boricua to the core. (Boricua means a person from Boriken, which is the name our aboriginal relatives, the Taino Indian, had for Puerto Rico). And there is no doubt that Puerto Rico's colonial status is a drag on our self-confidence. Another part of the problem is historic, the destruction of the island's agrarian-based society, replaced by the short-lived and ultimately disastrous rush to urbanization spurred by no-longer-existing tax breaks and long-gone companies who took their jobs with them when they fled Puerto Rico, often leaving nothing but their pollution behind.

The dislocation and division of Puerto Rican society led to fragmenting, which can be summed up by describing two of its faces. First and foremost is the *jíbaro*, the dignified, hardworking, God-fearing, child-raising, wife-and-mother-loving country farmer who is our cultural ideal man, our national hero. Even though my father, Cruz Rivera, came to live in New York City in 1937 as a young man, he kept the heart of a sugar-cane-cutting *jíbaro*, always trying his best and lamenting his inability to do more to make his parents proud. There is a statue in a roadside park between the capital of San Juan and the small southern city of Playa Salinas where I have a home, of a *jíbaro* bearing his ever-present sugarcane-cutting machete, his wife and child by his side, that always makes me think of my dad and his dad, my noble *abuelo*. The other side of the national personality is the *jaiba*, a.k.a. *mujeriego* or *sanguijuela*. It is street-slang for the hustler, the good-for-nothing city con who exploits anyone and everything he can, as long as it doesn't take too much energy. Like the 'goodnuff', *chavala, chilango, malinche,* or *lacra* in Caribbean, Latin American or Chicano culture, he's the guy who keeps impregnating girlfriends whom he doesn't support, so they can get government assistance in the form of Aid to Dependent Children, which he in turn can live off.

I've known scores of them over the years. These days they tend to have baggy pants, hoodies hiding neck tattoos, jailhouse workouts and criminal records as long as their arms. This is the crew that makes obscene noises when girls walk by, and sadly every culture has a version of them in varying degrees.

Remember that there are a thousand structural reasons why too many Latinos are impoverished, often attending those bad schools with stuffed classrooms and disinterested teachers in bad neighborhoods, suffering bad health, discrimination and so on. To suggest, however, as too many progressive young thinkers do these days, that the poor *jaiba* bears no responsibility for his social and economic plight is to demean the true grit and determination of the uncounted *jíbaro* men and women who through hard work and sacrifice have led themselves and their families out of the social and economic abyss.

After my upwardly mobile working-class childhood spent on Long Island, and having grown to manhood on Avenue C in Manhattan's Lower East Side, I can distinguish between a scammer and a striver from a block away. One maintains his dignity even in the face of a demeaning job and hardscrabble circumstances. The other is a parasitical leech who throws his garbage out the window because to take it outside is to play "the Man's game."

Even during the recently departed boom times, and understandably more so now, a resigned "why try" vibe firmly grips the souls of too many

Hispanics, entrenching us in a semipermanent caste, like India's social "untouchables," existing on the edges of American society, English or Spanish. Too many of us are too cool for school. For reasons that vary regionally, household instability is endemic, and the effect on prospects for our young people is deeply troubling. It is bad in East L.A., and it is particularly aggravating in the community I know best, New York Puerto Ricans, the original Caribbean Hispanic immigrants and still among the worst off.

Until the recent worldwide economic cataclysm, relative prosperity continued trickling down into Latino barrios from Oxnard to Miami to San Antonio as sweat-built equity. Even today, shaken as they have been by rising unemployment and collapsing home values, most middle- and working-class Hispanic neighborhoods in the West, Midwest, South and Southwest remain intact. The men and women are stressed, but they have not surrendered. There are, however, noteworthy pockets of institutionalized poverty in the North and Northeast that predate the current crisis.

Together, the New York City neighborhoods in East Harlem and the South Bronx represent the capital. Many better-off Puerto Ricans have fled to New York City's outlying neighborhoods in Queens, Staten Island, the high Bronx or the suburbs of New Jersey or Long Island, leaving behind a more or less permanent underclass. In this original barrio the shopkeepers and entrepreneurs tend to be non–Puerto Rican Hispanics, increasingly from the Dominican Republic or Mexico. Camden, New Jersey, and North Philadelphia across the Delaware River have similar permanent, self-perpetuating, underclass ghettos filled with American citizens of Puerto Rican descent.

Guess what year the study for the U.S. Department of Education called "The Losers: A Report on Puerto Ricans and the Public Schools" was written? Quoting: "Puerto Rican youth lag behind white and Negro students in mathematical and verbal ability and reading comprehension." Answer? May 1968. When it comes to Puerto Ricans shaking off the legacy of underachievement, the saying "the more things change the more they stay the same" has never been truer.

Puerto Ricans have spread far and wide from our original stateside barrio, that enclave on the Upper East Side of Manhattan, roughly between

106th and 135th streets, between Fifth Avenue and the East River. But though many of us are proudly established in suburban neighborhoods from central Florida to Long Island now, it is pathetically easy to find third- or fourth-generation inner-city families still mired in poverty in East Harlem, Brooklyn or the South Bronx.

Bearing in mind that unlike every other Hispanic subgroup we Puerto Ricans are citizens by birth, the failure of our community to attain broader educational achievement is galling, especially in the New York City cradle that both nurtured and retarded our assimilation into larger American life.

Discrimination and persistent language difficulties obviously play a big part in keeping our community outside the economic and social mainstream. But to place all blame on the shortcomings of American society is pathetically obsolete, so 1960s. The "blame the Man" ethos of my early days also ignores the enormous, if ill-conceived taxpayer charity dumped on our community since the Great Society, by now in the many hundreds of millions.

These days an ad hoc patchwork of government programs provides just enough of a social safety net to foster dependency and rob Puerto Rican youngsters of ambition, while keeping their families stuck in decaying rentals or in public housing that has the appalling, unintended consequence of concentrating poverty and its attendant problems in neighborhoods where fathers are absent, 40 percent of mothers have less than a high school education, school generally is considered a dispensable luxury and where television is stuck on melodramatic *telenovelas* or gaudy "reality" shows like *MTV Cribs* day and night.

"We need to free up our spirit, our willingness to be creative and work hard," Puerto Rico governor Luis Fortuño told me. "I believe to a great degree some of the social programs from the federal government have killed that work ethic and desire to succeed and the belief that if you work hard in our society, you can get ahead no matter where you were born. Of course, there are exceptions. If you're ill or elderly or you don't have someone to take care of your kids and you're the only one at home. But in most cases, I believe federal programs have failed our families and actually helped in the breakup of our families."

Disadvantaged Latino boys from hard-core urban areas also face another grim distraction from getting a good education. They "are often able to gain some form of peer status through violence, which clearly undermines educational attainment," according to the National Longitudinal Study of Adolescent Health. "They are Chicanos and they don't know what that means. And there is no one guiding them in terms of what that means. So they are trying to figure it out and it comes out in this weird, aggressive, violent way," explained one Minneapolis-based community organizer quoted in "The Other Family: How Gangs Impact Latino Families and Communities," a 2005 report by HACER (Hispanic Advocacy and Community Empowerment Through Research). Gravitating toward the mean street life is obviously putting them, "at much greater risk of high school dropout than other students," says the NLSAH report.

President Obama addressed our youngsters directly when he spoke to the Hispanic Chamber of Commerce in March 2009. "Dropping out is quitting on yourself, it's quitting on your country, and it is not an option—not anymore. Not when our high school dropout rate has tripled in the past thirty years. Not when high school dropouts earn about half as much as college graduates. And not when Latino students are dropping out faster than just about anyone else. It is time for all of us, no matter what our backgrounds, to come together and solve this epidemic."

The dropout epidemic is just one devastating effect of multigenerational poverty. Our urban young have more persistent and severe health problems, too many infants have low birth weight, our children miss school because of illness or inconvenience, and frustration leads to child, spouse and elder abuse. When the economy jerks downward, our marginally employed are the first to get dumped.

"The people in the culture of poverty have a strong feeling of marginality, of helplessness, of dependency, of not belonging. They are like aliens in their own country, convinced that the existing institutions do not serve their interests and needs. Along with this feeling of powerlessness is a widespread feeling of inferiority, of personal unworthiness," wrote Oscar Lewis in 1998.

Lewis's original vision of a permanent Hispanic underclass has been attacked by later, more idealistic sociologists, but in my experience too many Puerto Ricans are stuck in a status quo best described as quiet desperation, isolation, resentment and resignation. There is a social shyness and an unspoken defeatism; a smoldering anger and at times rejection of the stateside, i.e., American value system, including the English language that is passed down from generation to generation. An attitude of "why bother?" Imagine how tough it is for a Puerto Rican teenager from an impoverished, stubbornly or lazily still Spanish or Spanglish-dominant one-parent family to leave the familiar if melancholy 'hood to seek employment in the outside world. What is he or she going to wear? Who's the connection to give them the inside scoop on employment opportunities and steer them to something other than a grueling minimum-wage job schlepping boxes in the Garment District, if that job still exists in these tough times? How are they going to outhustle the immigrant arriviste who will toil at whatever job, however long and dirty, if it pays enough to survive and maybe send a couple of dollars back home to Tegucigalpa, Oaxaca or San Salvador?

It is a crippling environment, which predates the current economic crisis by decades, and exists even in the best of times. When seeking access to entitlement programs like welfare or food stamps becomes a career, and youngsters are sexualized and victimized, where no stigma attaches to dropping out of school and where drug abuse saps aspiration, it is hard to be idealistic.

I used to be. In 1988 I "adopted" a class of twenty-four eighth graders at the Rafael Cordero Middle School in East Harlem and promised to pay for their college education, only to lose seventeen of them along the rocky road to high school graduation, dropouts to the bruises and bangs of inner-city life.

I understand that it is politically incorrect to say so, but it is nevertheless part of our reality that a higher percentage of Puerto Ricans live in poverty than any other Hispanic group; we have a higher percent of households headed by females, and yet we have been here longest. We have the same DNA as our fellow Caribbean islanders, roughly the same colonial historic antecedents, our religious affiliations are more or less the same, so why the dramatic differences in important measures like high school graduation rates and per capita income?

If we remember that this fluid population comes and goes from the island to the States on a regular basis, one concrete problem is the disastrous public education system in Puerto Rico itself. We are importing students ill-equipped to handle stateside public education. According to *Education Week*, students on the island perform disastrously worse on standardized tests when compared to students in any of the fifty states. "Virtually no students in Puerto Rican [public] schools scored at the Proficient or Advanced levels on the National Assessment of Educational Progress test [in] 2005," according to the Web site devoted to New York's vast public education system, GothamSchools.org.

Language was not the issue, since the tests given in Puerto Rico had been translated into Spanish. The new governor, Luis Fortuño, agreed. "I took the tests myself. I didn't send an aide. I realized the tests were translated correctly. Our kids are simply not getting the level of education that they should. And I want our kids to compete with the other kids in our nation, not have special treatment. I want to make sure that we stick to the same requirements, academically speaking."

According to UCLA professor Patricia Gándara and Frances Contreras of the University of Washington, coauthors of 2009's *The Latino Education Crisis: The Consequences of Failed Social Policies*, "Growing up in a primarily Spanish-speaking environment does NOT in itself affect college-going. Many Spanish-speaking students from solid middle-class homes go to college and succeed. Their families are able to prepare them well for school and as a result they do well. However, if the family does not have sufficient resources and the schools that their children attend are impoverished, as is the case with the great majority of Latino students in the United States . . . then the data speaks for itself—the consequences are negative."

According to the authors, poverty crushes educational opportunity in another, more practical way. "It is important to remember that there is an extremely strong correlation between [standardized test scores], and family income and parent education levels. So, poverty and poor schooling are the real culprits that simply get expressed in these scores."

Long-established advocacy groups like ASPIRA ("aspire") work to keep kids engaged, but have had uneven success. According to the group's Web site, its 16th Annual Citywide Youth Conference at Hunter College in Manhattan "attracted 500 high school students from across the city to participate in workshops about college admissions, urban policy, personal finance, environmental issues, career choices and immigrant rights." AS-PIRA's literature also points to success stories like Jose Estrada, who moved to Chicago with his family at the age of thirteen. "I didn't speak a word of English but I refused to give up," he recalls, becoming valedictorian of his graduating class. I wish we could bottle Jose and spread him around.

Aside from all the social problems Latino youngsters must overcome to succeed, Puerto Rico, unique in the U.S. Hispanic world, has another exacerbating factor: the wretched partisan political stink that infects every aspect of official Puerto Rican life.

Remember that since 1952, Puerto Rico has been a commonwealth— that is, a semi-self-governing territory of the United States—it has a schizoid identity. It is neither a state nor an independent country, but something in between. Its primary language is Spanish, but English is spoken widely, particularly by those in the tourist business or with a high school or better education, the latter of whom fare far better than their less educated countrymen on either the island or the U.S. mainland.

For all its rich history and manifest charm, its gorgeous climate and the gregarious, live-and-let-live spirit of its residents, *La Isla del Encanto*, the "Enchanted Island" is a mess in some ways. Today's mainland recession hit there four years ago. The government is the largest employer on the island, which is racked by deep double-digit unemployment officially approaching 25 percent, but almost double that if you factor in the "informal", i.e., cash economy where no records are kept. After finding that his predecessor had neglected to pay the bills and that the government was virtually bankrupt, the new governor announced thirty thousand public-employee job cuts, mostly through attrition.

Aside from its manifest economic difficulties, the island also remains bitterly divided roughly between those who want Puerto Rico to be part of the United States and those who want it to remain a subsidized stepchild in the family of nations, taking what America has to offer, sometimes serving in her military, but avoiding a full commitment to the nation that has been the island's overlord for 111 years. After that century-plus of second-class status, the island possesses a colonial mentality that is deeply engrained. There is a legacy of dependence that saps individual vitality more subtly, but just as surely as slavery did African-Americans'. There is a pervasive feeling among many that Puerto Ricans don't own the island; Uncle Sam does, just like Señor Spain did before America's conquest in 1898.

Until it fell in the November 2008 election landslide, the largely dysfunctional procommonwealth party *Partido Popular Democrático* (PPD) ran the island, whose last leader, Harvard-educated ex-governor Aníbal Acevedo-Vilá, got bounced only after a massive federal indictment accused him and his cronies of corruption. The first governor to be charged with a crime, Acevedo-Vilá was ultimately acquitted by a hometown jury on nine counts of conspiracy, money laundering and lying to the FBI. Although several of his alleged cronies pled guilty, he beat the raps, which would have meant twenty years behind bars, but the damage his administration had wrought to the island's institutions was done.

As the politicians had fought to stay out of prison, the students suffered profoundly. In 2006, the island's recurring budget crisis caused the public schools to be shut down for two weeks. In February 2008, they were closed again for ten days by a teachers' strike. There are constant complaints about the woeful physical condition of the schools, and teachers are demoralized, overpoliticized and generally underpaid.

But Puerto Rico's version of the educational siesta may be ending. Unlike the pro–status quo, procommonwealth officials he replaced, the impressive new governor wants Puerto Rico to be our fifty-first state. Me too—either a state or an independent country. In a sharp break from his legally challenged predecessor's secretary of education, a man named Rafael Aragunde-Torres, who blamed the students' abysmal standardized-test scores on the structure of the tests themselves, even asking the U.S. Department of Education for permission to withdraw from participating, Governor Fortuño insists that commonwealth students continue to participate in the National Assessment of Educational Progress (NAEP) exams.

The governor told me he blames the poor performance of the students on the prior administration's policies advocating an unrealistic, outdated, naive nationalism that makes little sense in the twenty-first-century world. "For reasons that actually escape my understanding, in the last few years, the state government has tried to deemphasize the teaching of English, when that is the trend all over the world. We are U.S. citizens. We must speak English. It is great that we can speak Spanish. My kids speak three languages. We all gain by speaking as many languages as possible."

He wants to improve their education, not avoid responsibility for the system's failure to educate them. If the island's educational system can be improved, fewer unprepared students will be imported into New York or Philadelphia. The same goes for public schools in Mexico, the largest provider of uneducated youngsters to the United States. Cities with large Mexican immigrant populations, like Dallas and Chicago, struggle to educate children handicapped by limited English skills and no real tradition of extolling the virtues of education. Obviously, the older those children are when they arrive, the less chance the public education system has to teach them English and other skills they need to move up the ladder of opportunity.

President Obama's choice of Arne Duncan, the former superintendent of Chicago's public schools, to head the Department of Education is inspired, because Duncan totally gets the special needs of the recent arrivals. One powerful remedy to alleviate the handicap these youngsters face when they get to the United States would be broader, deeper mandatory English-language education in Mexico's public schools. That reform by Mexico could be part of a wider agreement reforming cross-border life.

Of my several laments toward the end of a long public career, one is the lack of widespread crossover success among Puerto Ricans in the broader context of American society. We have our stars and go-getters, but not nearly enough of them. At different times in our specific lives we various Riveras lived in the ethnic and economic ghetto; some of us still do, but all refuse to be either confined or defined by those old geographic constraints. In some cases, the way out was the military; in most others it was education. In my particular case, blessed with a two-parent home, which is still the single most important indicator of future success, my siblings and I were drilled on the importance of staying in school. Even in tough times, my parents offered what financial support they could, their support more often taking the form of cheerleading and encouragement. "Oh, son, we're so proud of you," became so familiar a refrain I thought they were passive-aggressively ensuring that I would never drop out.

My upbringing was positively upscale and privileged compared to our community's brightest new star, Sonia Sotomayor, the Bronx-born federal judge, who, as I write this, has just been nominated by President Obama in a stirring White House ceremony to replace retiring U.S. Supreme Court justice David Souter. Raised in a housing project, one of those dreadful high-rise ghettos where crime and other social problems are raw, unavoidable and everywhere, she, like the president, has a rags-to-riches story that should inspire our youngsters, indeed our nation, with the certain knowledge that despite all obstacles, with education anything is possible. After Judge Sotomayor's dad, a Puerto Rican-born immigrant factory worker, died when she was in third grade, she and her younger brother (now a doctor) were raised by their diligent and devoted immigrant mother, who was a nurse (and a veteran of World War II) and also worked another job to put her kids through school. "Her mom insisted on education, fair play and hard work," said my delighted friend, Bronx-based congressman Jose Serrano, who added that Judge Sotomayor "never forgot where she began."

Earlier, President Obama had raised some eyebrows when he stated that "empathy" was one of his prerequisites for his Supreme Court pick. He brought it up again during his announcement of Sotomayor's nomination to the high court: "As Supreme Court Justice Oliver Wendell Holmes once said, the life of the law has not been logic—it has been experience. Experience being tested by obstacles and barriers, by hardship and misfortune. Experience insisting, persisting and ultimately overcoming those barriers. It is experience that can give a person a common touch and a sense of compassion. An understanding of how the world works and how ordinary people live. That is why it is a necessary ingredient in the kind of justice we need on the Supreme Court," indicating that Sonia Sotomayor was exactly the kind of person Justice Holmes had in mind.

After telling the crowd in the White House and the rest of the world over live television that "my heart today is bursting with gratitude," and praising her mother for all she had done, "I stand on the shoulders of countless people, but there is one who is special," Judge Sotomayor told those gathered in the East Wing for the president's historic announcement that "I try never to forget the real-world consequences of my decisions."

How could she not remember the "real world" after her own difficult path? Fatherless and suffering from childhood diabetes from the age of eight, the judge attended parochial schools, graduating from Cardinal Spellman, the principal Catholic high school in the north Bronx. Dazzled by her many and varied achievements in high school, she was accepted by Princeton University, graduating summa cum laude in 1976. From there, this incredible young woman went on to edit the Law Journal at Yale.

After a noteworthy stint as an assistant district attorney in New York County, where I once worked, she became the youngest federal judge in Manhattan's important Southern District, appointed by Republican President George H. W. Bush, becoming the first ever Hispanic federal judge in New York State. "She is not intimidated or overwhelmed by the eminence of power or prestige of any party, or indeed of the media," said another judicial pioneer, Jose Alberto Cabranes, the Mayaquez, Puerto Rico–born, also Bronx-bred appellate court judge who became her colleague on the bench after Democrat Bill Clinton nominated Sotomayor to the U.S. Second Circuit Court of Appeals, the most prestigious intermediate appellate court in the land.

In naming Judge Sotomayor as one of the most influential people of the twenty-first century, Esquire magazine said of the deeply impressive fifty-five-year-old, who is generally regarded as a judicial centrist, "In her rulings, Sotomayor has often shown suspicion of bloated government and corporate power. She's offered a reinterpretation of copyright law, ruled in favor of public access to private information, and in her most famous decision, sided with labor in the Major League Baseball strike of 1995. More than anything else, she is seen as a realist. With a likely twenty years ahead on the bench, she'll have plenty of time to impart her realist philosophy."

Handicapping the prospects of Senate confirmation of potential judges to the Supreme Court is difficult, but Sotomayor's nomination has already been attacked by ideologues from both sides. Most infuriatingly, she has been criticized from the left in a hatchet job in *The New Republic*, which claimed the former *Yale Law Journal* editor was "not that smart" and quoted an anonymous law clerk as saying, "She has an inflated opinion of herself, and is domineering during oral arguments, but her questions aren't penetrating and don't get to the heart of the issue." Because she is an observant Catholic, some pro-choice advocates are worried about the eventual firmness of her commitment to abortion rights, and she has also been criticized by several other liberal commentators for being the "next token justice" (like the disastrous, nearly mute and corrosively bitter, ultraconservative, African-American justice Clarence Thomas, who was certainly nothing like the pioneering black judge he followed to the high court, Thurgood Marshall).

Sotomayor has also been attacked by the hard right for saying during a frank and honest 2001 speech at the University of California, Berkeley that family background, gender and ethnicity invariably play a role in a judge's opinions on social and other issues. "I would hope that a wise Latina woman with the richness of her experiences would more often than not reach a better conclusion than a white male who hasn't lived that life." I have always maintained that we are products of the bundle of our personal experiences, and that someone, say from a derelict housing project, would be more sensitive to tenants' rights than someone from an affluent suburb. But her frankness already has numerous critics crying that Sotomayor will not be impartial, as if most judges really are.

Furthermore, she has been criticized for 2005 judicial conference remarks at Duke University asserting that a "court of appeals is where policy is made." Suddenly realizing that she had just fueled a controversy over judges who "make law instead of just interpreting it," she hurriedly added, "And I know—I know this is on tape, and I should never say that because we don't make law. I know. OK, I know. I'm not promoting it. I'm not advocating it. I'm—you know. . ." her voice trailing off to nervous audience laughter and scattered applause.

By the time you read this, Judge Sotomayor will have been raked over the coals by conservative media and by Republican senators like Orrin Hatch and John Kyl fearful of her "judicial activism," and therefore opposed to her confirmation as the nation's first Latina Supreme Court justice. (Actually, she is the first Hispanic on the high court of either gender, unless legendary justice Benjamin N. Cardozo, whose family came to the U.S. in the eighteenth century and who was of Portuguese-Jewish descent, is counted.)

More to the point of this essay, the personal/professional trajectory of Judge Sotomayor demonstrates conclusively the central role education can play in shaping a life story. As the president said, "When Sonia was nine her father passed away. And her mother worked six days a week as a nurse to provide for Sonia and her brother, who is also here today as a doctor and terrific success in his own right. But Sonia's mom bought the only set of encyclopedias in the neighborhood, sent her children to a Catholic school called Cardinal Spellman, out of the belief that with a good education, here in America, all things are possible." Judge Sotomayor is an extraordinary person, but as she and the president consistently maintain, with education and ambition, there are many others from the Bronx to Hawaii who could also attain heartening success.

In his March 2009 speech on education to the Hispanic Chamber of Commerce the president vividly described how his own mother worked to overcome material disadvantages to make sure her son was educated.

"When I was a child, living in Indonesia with my mother, she didn't have the money to send me where all the American kids went to school so she supplemented my schooling with lessons from a correspondence course. I can still picture her, waking me up at 4:30 in the morning five days a week to go over some lessons before I left for school. And whenever I'd complain or find some excuse for getting more sleep, she'd patiently repeat her most powerful defense—'This is no picnic for me either, buster.'"

But while the virtue of education is preached in many Hispanic families far less advantaged than the president's or mine, it falls on deaf or disinterested ears when the children are expected to go to work as soon as possible to help support their folks, or the girls get pregnant early enough to be considered babies having babies.

Between 1968 and 1970 I was part of the problem. As a fire-breathing storefront lawyer at Harlem Assertion of Rights, and later at Community Action for Legal Services, during that period of social turmoil I represented minority high school and college students and their parents in various demonstrations, lawsuits and acts of civil disobedience, which, viewed dispassionately from the perspective of four decades, aggravated educational underachievement. One of my targets—who later became my dearest mentor, the late Professor Julius C. C. Edelstein, vice chancellor of City University—once told me he estimated the cost to the city of my activism at several million dollars.

At the time, the nation's youth were consumed with opposing the Vietnam War, their opposition based on fear of being drafted as much as compassion for the Vietnamese. Urban America was being burned and disrupted by widespread rioting in cities like nearby Newark and Asbury Park, New Jersey. Columbia University had barely recovered from a long series of war-related demonstrations against every organization having anything to do with Vietnam, from ROTC to recruiters from the CIA and Dow Chemical, the manufacturers of napalm.

That tense buildup reached the breaking point in 1968, when Students for a Democratic Society leader Mark Rudd condemned the university's "morally corrupt, unjust . . . racist policies" concerning admissions, and Columbia's campus expansion at the expense of nearby slums. "What would you do if somebody came and took your property!" shouted one student in the buildup to one of the most prolonged and disruptive student takeovers in American history.

By 1968 large-scale student insurrections at the university level were more than matched by a rapidly deteriorating public school system that was being ripped by racial tensions and a bitter fight to politicize school boards and give communities control of public education. The city teetered on the edge of anarchy.

The incumbent New York mayor, a patrician, limousine-liberal Republican named John V. Lindsay, maintained a tenuous peace by frantically engaging radical activists in negotiations, thereby elevating far-left groups like my main clients, the Young Lords, to the status of legitimate community organizations. As one of the principal lawyers of the group, which was a kind of Latino Black Panthers, I remember the intoxicating power our elevated status under Mayor Lindsay bestowed. Here we were, negotiating on an equal basis with the city's elite.

Following a two-week occupation of seventeen buildings at the south campus of City College in 1969, activists forced the formerly highly regarded jewel of CUNY to accept more minority students. Open admissions was born, and tens of thousands of students, many of whom had made it through high school on social promotions based on their age or other nonacademic qualification, were then admitted into City College, rather than one of the many available two-year schools. The faculty was also shaped by activists who rallied and protested whenever a popular teacher was reprimanded or denied tenure.

"An institution for higher learning may waive standards, but I know that the outside world will not," warned my original role model, former congressman Herman Badillo, at the time, 1969, the Bronx borough president and a candidate for mayor. He added, "The disillusion will be deeper, since it will be founded upon greater expectations."

Although harshly criticized by many of today's Bronx- and barrio-based ethnic elected officials, Badillo, who became chairman of the City University board of trustees, was right. New York's well-intentioned, forty-year experiment with community control of the city's public schools—open admission at its public colleges and universities, plus other politically inspired programs like bilingual education, which was really just a segregated, separate but unequal system of Spanish-language education— all contributed to the massive failure by the Puerto Rican community to climb the academic ladder.

We had the power to politicize public education. We wielded that power and should have been more careful. The result was a system that until recently has failed to educate tens of thousands of Puerto Rican young people and left many utterly unequipped to make it in the outside world. As Badillo predicted, the widespread failure led to frustration and disillusionment. Parents who were either bashful, apprehensive or too stressed by the harsh social and economic circumstances of their own lives then played little or no effective role in keeping their kids in school.

New York's current mayor, another liberal Republican but a far more practical man than Lindsay, Michael Bloomberg, reversed open public-college admissions and community control of public schools. Now schools are better, safer; tests and admissions are standardized, and our community's achievements or lack of them are revealed. It is lamentable that there is a move to restore community control and increase the power of the public school unions. Both moves will further handicap our children, who already have their hands full coping with life on the mean streets.

The truth is that, considered as a whole, U.S. Hispanics trail our fellow Americans in all important indicators of social success, especially education. Latino youth are now the largest minority enrolled in our public schools. In 2005 there were 10.9 million Hispanic students comprising approximately 20 percent of all U.S. public school enrollments, but "Latinos are the least well educated segment of the American population," says the Pew Hispanic Center, recalling that "In the United States today people with more education tend to live longer and healthier lives, remain married longer and earn more money."

"Hispanics must set aside talk of their great culture, their music, and their traditions and instead focus on educational accomplishment," Badillo wrote in his 2006 book *One Nation, One Standard: An Ex-Liberal on How*

Hispanics Can Succeed Just Like Other Immigrant Groups. Because he chose to couch his argument as an ideological struggle between liberals and conservatives, between Republicans and Democrats, Badillo was widely ridiculed, labeled a turncoat and effectively exiled from the Puerto Rican establishment. Still, his "I told you so" gives him the last laugh—if you can laugh through your tears.

I'm not for putting aside culture, music and tradition, because they inspire our pride and sense of belonging, but the virtue of education must become the central theme of the urban dialogue. Real Latino men and women help with or at least encourage their kids to do their homework. The good news is that it is happening in other places. According to the 2000 Census, the education, income and English-language proficiency levels of Puerto Ricans in central Florida, as one example, were much higher than in New York.

The Census found that 73.6 percent of Puerto Ricans in the Orlando area had completed high school, as compared to just 55.2 percent in New York. Granted, some of that imbalance is a function of the fact that most of Florida's Boricuas were better off to begin with. "Puerto Ricans who have settled in and around the Orlando area are relatively well-off economically and have a higher educational level and a more thriving business community than earlier generations of Boricuas who settled mostly in the U.S. Northeast," wrote journalist Robert Friedman in a 2000 paper titled "Florida Now 2nd Most Populous P.R. State."

As we bear in mind America's inescapable economic crisis, "Today's young Hispanics are the first generation that is expected not to do better than their parents," said Maite Arce, Vice President of the Hispanic Council for Reform and Educational Options (Hispanic CREO), adding, "This is not only a tragedy for our Hispanic community, but it is a disaster for our nation. Without improving our educational system, we will see a lack of skilled, productive workers and our economy will suffer."

But the consequences of lack of resources and the language barrier are being overcome by millions of Latinos, who, like their fellow Americans, go out to work or school every day. And therein lies the reason for optimism despite these grim times, because if they can hold on and graduate high school, native-born Hispanics fare almost as well as similarly educated whites. The challenge, as I found with my adopted class and see daily on the streets of New York or Los Angeles, is getting Latino youngsters out of high school.

Once that level of achievement is attained, they are almost as likely as their non-Hispanic peers to get a job, join the military or be accepted into college. The biggest failing of affirmative action programs as they are currently structured is that most target those least in need, the already college-bound. While it is pleasant to see Latinos accepted into prestigious colleges and universities, the communities those youngsters left behind are about the same as they would be if those same high school grads were attending a less renowned institution.

I'm happy for the lucky kid who's on the fast track. Harvard, Yale, Princeton and Columbia benefit tremendously from their presence, because those campuses are culturally richer and more diverse, but I would be just as proud of them and confident of their ultimate prosperity if they had attended Fresno State, Hostos Community College in the Bronx or the University of Arizona. That's one of the reasons why I don't particularly like affirmative action. The programs breed tremendous resentment from those not eligible, without delivering much social bang for the buck.

Like Princeton's Sonia Sotomayor, any student accepted to a top school on either an academic, athletic or social basis was probably heading out of the underclass on a scholarship anyway. The dire need is keeping them in junior and senior high schools, a public education the Supreme Court's *Plyler v. Doe* decision (1982) mandates that even children here illegally are entitled to. "Already disadvantaged as a result of poverty, lack of English-speaking ability, and undeniable racial prejudices," wrote federal judge the honorable William Wayne Justice at the time, "these children, without an education, will become permanently locked into the lowest socioeconomic class. That lockout would be tragic for America, because they are our children. It is not their fault that they grew up to find themselves in a country without documentation." Fortunately, the high court in one of those seminal 5–4 rulings recognized the wisdom of the brave federal judge appropriately named Justice, affirmed and affixed his decision.

It also makes sense to offer all resident children, if qualified, and regardless of immigration status, the same discounted tuition for community colleges, vocational schools and four-year colleges as those lucky enough to have been born here. It is where the rubber meets the road in education, and it is where the nation's prime focus should be. Hopefully the Obama administration, however burdened by the weight of the world, will undo the crushing defeat in the U.S. Senate in 2008 of the DREAM Act.

The Development, Relief and Education for Alien Minors (DREAM) Act would have provided tens of thousands of undocumented children who arrived in the United States before the age of sixteen years old a clear path through high school and toward higher education, complete with in-state tuition at public universities or access to a career in the military, with its explicit promise of permanent legal residence and, with service, citizenship.

Isn't that the way to go? Fifty-two senators agreed, but they fell eight votes short of the amount necessary to break a promised filibuster, and so the Senate rejected even the attempt to begin debate on the legislation. The DREAM Act is necessary and proper, and advocates for children hope it is high on Barack Obama's to-do list.

If we care about fairness and the nation's fiscal health, our Hispanic youngsters, like other Americans, must be prepared to make a decent living. But many of the current programs miss the mark of effectiveness. The Federal Pell Grant Program for college, for example, is a terrific program, and I am happy it was augmented in Obama's first budget. I would have loved a grant when I was borrowing money to stay in the University of Arizona. But the number of kids saved from poverty's resilient grip would be much higher if that same amount of money were invested in keeping them in junior and senior high school, and then, through the DREAM Act and other programs directed at the urban poor, giving them unfettered access to public colleges and universities.

Pilot programs offering cash rewards to parents keyed to their children's school attendance records, with bonuses for parents and students for grades attained, in my view represent one possible way forward. Break the bonds of poverty by offering the streets a direct competitor: financial incentives to stay in school and do well. Keep kids in middle and high school through a system of performance-based payments to their families. Couple the payments with huge public investment in public school facilities and incentive pay for teachers based on their students' performance.

Nothing could be more of an economic stimulus than an educated, able, prepared, more socially mobile and confident former underclass.

Dramatic action is necessary, because the devalued priority of education in Latino society must be overcome. While it is risky to generalize, there has not been the same broad respect or ambition for education among Latinos as that existing in mainstream society in the United States today. The consequences of continuing what Badillo calls our five-hundred-year education siesta are troubling for the nation.

"If Hispanics' education and skills continue to lag, the nation will be less competitive in the global economy," Dr. Steve Murdock, the Texas state demographer, told *Parents' Alliance* magazine. "Given the projected growth of the Hispanic population over the next quarter century, compromising the future economic prospects of Hispanics by underinvesting in their education will likely compromise the nation's future as well."

The president spoke of one Hispanic student during his address to the Hispanic Chamber, but he was really speaking to all of our youngsters.

"I want children like Yvonne Bojorquez to have that chance. Yvonne is a student at Village Academy High School in California. Now, Village Academy is a 21st century school where cutting edge technologies are used in the classroom, where college prep and career training are offered to all who seek it, and where the motto is—"respect, responsibility, and results.

"Now, a couple of months ago, Yvonne and her class made a video talking about the impact that our struggling economy was having on their lives. And some of them spoke about their parents being laid off, or their homes facing foreclosure, or their inability to focus on school with everything that was happening at home. And when it was her turn to speak, Yvonne said: 'We've all been affected by this economic crisis. [We] are all college-bound students; we're all businessmen, and doctors and lawyers and all this great stuff. And we have all this potential, but the way things are going, we're not going to be able to [fulfill it].'

"It was heartbreaking that a girl so full of promise was so full of worry that she and her class titled their video, 'Is Anybody Listening?' So, today, there's something I want to say to Yvonne and her class at Village Academy: I am listening. We are listening. America is listening. And we will not rest until your parents can keep their jobs and your families can keep their homes, and you can focus on what you should be focusing on—your own education; until you can become the businessmen, doctors, and lawyers of tomorrow, until you can reach out and grasp your dreams for the future."

Obama's speech was honest, realistic and inspiring, but to understand the true extent of the obstacles facing young Yvonne, listen to what CNN's hateful, proudly anti-Latino commentator Lou Dobbs said following the president's remarks, and, specifically, about where Mr. Obama chose to deliver them.

"Making a decision to talk about a national initiative on education from the U.S. Hispanic Chamber of Commerce, which is effectively an organization that is interested in the export of American capital and production to Mexico, and Mexico's export of drugs and illegal aliens to the United States. This is crazy stuff."

Could a phrase more accurately reflect the odious depth of anti-immigrant racism in America than Dobbs's suggestion that the U.S. Hispanic Chamber of Commerce is interested only in importing drugs and illegal aliens from Mexico? Following Dobbs's March 2009 remarks, *El Diario*, the major New York–based Spanish-language newspaper, editorialized, "To impute that Hispanic-American businessmen are working against American interests is demagoguery of the vilest sort. To associate them with the drug trade is slander."

Dopes like Dobbs aside, and without flogging the woe-is-us, when it comes to education, all children are not created equal in America. A significant proportion of the nation, fortunately not anywhere near a majority, believes Yvonne and others like her should be grateful for what they've got. "It's better than they would get in Mexico." But reasoned observers agree that these now American children need a hand, most importantly help from their own parents. It is in the nation's interests to provide quality public education. Remember, educated young Latinos will earn and spend vastly more than their less accomplished colleagues. Remember also the role young Latinos could play in saving Social Security. The awesome potential of this huge, dynamic new population is that it could and hopefully will become an essential part of the financial and social backbone of the nation, as America flies inexorably toward her twenty-second-century Hispanic majority.

There is no magic bullet. Government must fund the supplemental help these children often need to compete: extra hours of class study, and smaller classes, tutors too, charter schools where appropriate, and yes, on a limited, transitory basis, bilingual educational opportunity must be made available to the newer arrivals.

But the key lies in something less tangible, a rejection of the cynicism of the *jaiba* and an embrace of education as a cherished goal as a proud *jíbaro*. Check out this statistic: Asian-American kids are just 14 percent of New York's 1.1 million public school student population. As one example of their disproportionate achievement, they now make up more than two-thirds of elite Stuyvesant High School's 3,247 students, up from 48 percent in 1999. Hispanics are barely represented, and the percentages in the city's other elite high schools are not much different.

Why the disparity between them and us? It is not genetic, geographic, racial, dietary, environmental or, ultimately, even economic. Some of those Asian parents proudly watching their children graduate with honors from prestige high schools work in Laundromats or Chinese restaurants. I was going to say that the difference is character, but that is too harsh. But the difference is values and the sooner we understand our responsibilities as parents to extol the virtue of education to our children, the better for them and for our country.

★ 9 ★

THE (NOT SO) FOREIGN LEGION
The Latinization of America's Military

"I believe that there is no greater calling for a man or woman than to serve in the military of a free nation. I believe that it is a calling that transcends all others because imbedded deep within the soul of every free man or woman is the knowledge that every freedom we have was earned for us by our ancestors, who paid some price for freedom. Each and every generation must relearn those lessons, and they are best learned by doing. The strength of every free nation depends on this transfer of knowledge. Only through the transfer of knowledge* from generation to generation will free men survive."

—M.Sgt. Roy P. Benavidez, winner, Congressional Medal of Honor, quoted in *Medal of Honor: One Man's Journey from Poverty and Prejudice*, March 2005

It was like a scene out of a Rambo movie. In the sweltering Cambodian jungle and hills west of Loc Ninh, South Vietnam, a twelve-man Special Forces reconnaissance team on a secret mission was overrun by a superior Viet Cong force. The first helicopter-borne rescue team sent in to get them out was shot up in an intense firefight. With the craft incapacitated and the unit pinned down, Sergeant Benavidez came in aboard a second chopper. Still under intense fire from the hidden enemy, the sergeant was hit several times and was bleeding heavily. Still, he managed to save the lives of eight Green Berets despite his wounds and heavy loss of blood. At first awarded only a Distinguished Service Cross by then–General William Westmoreland, when survivor accounts were later tallied, Latino advocacy and veterans' groups suggested that the true magnitude of the soldier's exploits deserved greater recognition.

On February 24, 1981, President Ronald Reagan agreed, presenting Master Sergeant Benavidez the Medal of Honor, making him the forty-third Latino to receive the nation's highest military award. As he presented it, the president turned to the gathered press and said as only the Great Communicator could, "You are going to hear something you would not believe if it were a script," whereupon President Reagan read Master Sergeant Benavidez's remarkable story for the assembled crowd.

"Realizing that all the team members were either dead or wounded and unable to move to the pickup zone, he directed the aircraft to a nearby clearing where he jumped from the hovering helicopter, and ran approximately 75 meters under withering small arms fire to the crippled team. Prior to reaching the team's position he was wounded in his right leg, face and head. Despite these painful injuries he took charge, repositioning the team members and directing their fire to facilitate the landing of an extraction aircraft, and the loading of wounded and dead team members. He then threw smoke canisters to direct the aircraft to the team's position. Despite his severe wounds and under intense enemy fire, he carried and dragged half of the wounded team members to the awaiting aircraft. He then provided protective fire by running alongside the aircraft as it moved to pick up the remaining team members. As the enemy's fire intensified, he hurried to recover the body and classified documents on the dead team leader. When he reached the leader's body, Sergeant Benavidez was severely wounded by small arms fire in the abdomen and grenade fragments in his back. At nearly the same moment, the aircraft pilot was mortally wounded, and his helicopter crashed.

"Although in extremely critical condition due to his multiple wounds, Sergeant Benavidez secured the classified documents and made his way back to the wreckage, where he aided the wounded out of the overturned aircraft, and gathered the stunned survivors into a defensive perimeter. Under increasing enemy automatic weapons and grenade fire, he moved around the perimeter distributing water and ammunition to his weary men, re-instilling in them a will to live and fight.

"Facing a buildup of enemy opposition with a beleaguered team, Sergeant Benavidez mustered his strength, began calling in tactical air strikes and directed the fire from supporting gunships to suppress the enemy's fire and so permit another extraction attempt. He was wounded again in his thigh by small arms fire while administering first aid to a wounded team member just before another extraction helicopter was able to land.

"His indomitable spirit kept him going as he began to ferry his comrades to the craft. On his second trip with the wounded, he was clubbed with additional wounds to his head and arms before killing his adversary. He then continued under devastating fire to carry the wounded to the helicopter. Upon reaching the aircraft, he spotted and killed two enemy soldiers who were rushing the craft from an angle that prevented the aircraft door gunner from firing upon them. With little strength remaining, he made one last trip to the perimeter to ensure that all classified material had been collected or destroyed, and to bring in the remaining wounded. Only then, in extremely serious condition from numerous wounds and loss of blood, did he allow himself to be pulled into the extraction aircraft."

Perhaps the reason why it took the military so long to recognize the obvious merit of Benavidez's conspicuous gallantry was because it happened inconspicuously, during a secret CIA-run operation that took place in Cambodia, a nation we did not officially invade until two years after the firefight that claimed so many of his fellow soldiers' lives. Still, the backstory of the GI known throughout the army by his call sign, "Tango Mike Mike," is a telling example of the social potential of the Latino military experience.

Born in south Texas, Raul Perez Benavidez was a sharecropper's son who barely knew his parents, Salvador and Teresa Benavidez. They died a year apart, leaving him and a younger brother, Roger, to live with an uncle, Nicholas Benavidez. The family worked as migrant laborers, toiling in sugar beet and cotton fields from west Texas to Colorado. Like so many other young Latinos, Benavidez was forced to work to help support his family, managing only to finish eighth grade, "and though he faced discrimination in the 1940s he vowed to master English and his life. Benavidez found his high school diploma, and upward mobility, in the Army. A stint in airborne school persuaded him to make a career of the service and, he said later, 'to become a soldier and be the best,'" according to his official biography.

Benavidez died at the age of sixty-three on November 29, 1998, at

Brooke Army Medical Center in San Antonio, Texas. Five days later, more than fifteen hundred family and friends gave Tango Mike Mike one final salute as he was buried in the shade of a live oak tree at Fort Sam Houston National Cemetery. Three years later, the navy named its seventh and last *Bob Hope*–class strategic sealift ship after him. More than three football fields long, it is one of the few naval vessels named for a soldier.

And while Benavidez's story is extraordinary, many of the best people I know have served or are currently serving in the military. Further, I believe that the services I know best by personal experience, the frontline army and Marine Corps units, to be the best agencies of the federal government, the highest functioning, the most committed, professional and diverse. Especially after the last eight years of intense warfare, through thick and thin I have watched them experience life and death on a scale that has been both grand and intimate. On the walls of my office at FOX News there are pictures of since-dead GIs and me arm in arm in scenic and obviously deadly places. They gave their lives in service to their nation, and we grieve their passing even as we respect and honor their service.

The Iraq War opened with a terrifying wave of Latino casualties, including two undocumented immigrants, José Antonio Gutierrez, an orphan who had hopped a train up from Guatemala at the age of eleven, and Jose Angel Garibay, who came up from Mexico as an infant with his mother. Both had somehow managed to enlist in the U.S. Marines, despite the specific prohibition against recruiting illegal immigrants. Their deaths in the war's opening salvo led critics in the Hispanic community to allege that Latino youngsters, particularly immigrants, were being lured by the promise of citizenship or legal residency to be used as cannon fodder, or that the machismo of our young people was being exploited to assign them the riskiest missions. A Pew study in 2003 revealed that while only 10 percent of all enlisted personnel were Latinos at the time, almost 18 percent found themselves in frontline combat units, no doubt a function of their lower educational attainment prior to enlisting. That disparity in suffering caused some critics of military recruitment, including Rodolfo Arcuña, professor of Chicano Studies at California State University,

Northridge, to suggest an insidious pattern going back to the disproportionate Latino casualties in the Vietnam War era, a propensity to "let others do the dying for you," a charge the Pentagon denied.

The Pentagon is right on this one. Now that the war has dragged on, Latino combat losses are commensurate with and proportional to their total numbers in the armed services. By January 10, 2009, according to the Department of Defense, 450 Latino soldiers, marines, sailors and airmen had lost their lives in Iraq, 10.7 percent of the total U.S. casualties. Ironically, neither brave Garibay nor Gutierrez would be allowed to enlist today, given their undocumented-immigrant status. Because of that counterproductive and unfortunate immigration hang-up, which excludes perhaps 20 percent of the nation's Latino youngsters from enlisting, until hard times hit, the military had been struggling to recruit enough young men and women to reflect our percentage of the general population. According to the Pentagon's most recent statistics, in 2007, Hispanics made up 17 percent of the nation's population ages eighteen to forty, but only 11.4 percent of army recruits and 15 percent of navy recruits.

A February 2009 study by the RAND Corporation blames several factors. On the plus side, the best-qualified Hispanics have excellent civilian job or college prospects, making the military a harder sell for the best and brightest. On the other hand, our youngsters' woeful high school graduation rates, poor test scores and, more prosaically, our failure to meet military weight standards also severely limit access to a military career. More bluntly stated, too many of our children are too fat to serve.

Beth J. Asch, the lead author of the RAND report, proposes several options to build Hispanic enlistment, including expanding existing programs to build English proficiency, relaxing weight standards while maintaining strength standards, and, for those hard-to-find top-tier candidates, a greater emphasis on the monetary and other benefits available. The army's lead recruiter, Maj. Gen. Thomas Bostick, told reporters when the RAND report was published that the armed services were even considering the establishment of a "fat camp" to help overweight recruits meet physical standards, pointing out that 40,000 of 250,000 youngsters failed their physicals in 2008 due to weight issues. I can just picture the new Telemundo reality-TV show, *Latino Boot Camp*! The problem is the rice and beans, and our mamas telling us that we look skinny or that we have to eat to stay strong.

But the effort to qualify for the armed services is worthwhile for many youngsters, because despite the understandable fears of service members' families and friends, and remembering that there are a total of nearly forty-four hundred honored American dead so far in this fight, most of our 1.1 million–strong military, including the more than one hundred thousand Hispanics serving on active duty in all branches of the U.S. Armed Forces, do not become casualties of war. They serve, experience, learn, travel and accumulate memories and education, and earn themselves a brighter future. Even putting aside intangibles like patriotism, camaraderie and tradition, those are some of the practical reasons a stint or even a career in the military is a wonderful choice for many of America's young people, including Hispanics. Let Uncle Sam pay for your college education, housing and many other benefits for your family. My dad was able to buy our first home because of the GI Bill.

It is not for everybody, and I respect those who oppose wars in general or oppose the conflicts in Iraq and/or Afghanistan specifically. There is an admired and substantial grassroots movement here in the States and in Puerto Rico to counteract the aggressive efforts by the military to recruit Hispanics, especially the Delayed Entry Program (DEP), that targets big-city Latino teenagers in junior and senior public high schools. Some of the opposition is based on conscience, some on ideology, and some on sheer anxiety. Whatever the motivation, I can relate, having opposed the war in Vietnam, and having used every angle I could to beat the 1960s draft, including college, marriage and law school. If those didn't work I might have claimed homosexuality, polygamy or chronic athlete's foot or all three; so I was never drafted, but my not serving when eighty thousand other Hispanics like Master Sergeant Benavidez did in Vietnam haunted me for decades. It is the principal reason I later became a risk-everything war correspondent who volunteered to report on scores of occasions from front lines spanning the globe, garnering a sort of personal "Red Badge of Courage."

Feeling redeemed, my personal failure cauterized by the subsequent fire of frequent combat, I have come to deeply respect our armed forces and appreciate the promise service holds for our youngsters. If you do not oppose our military's various missions and objectives, and if college is not for you, at least not yet, and if your job prospects aren't what you would like them to be, then the military might be a fit for you—or your children, as the case may be.

In the early days of what was then called the War on Terror, or more precisely, "the war against terrorists of global reach," to be associated with service people was to be hanging out with rock stars. They—and, through them, to a much lesser degree, war correspondents like me—were wrapped in a grateful nation's warm embrace whenever we went into harm's way. Now the fighting has dragged on for so long, as of this writing eight years and counting, that I have forged friendships with middle-ranking young officers who are now commanders. We have watched one another's children grow up and our hair go grayer. We have mourned fallen comrades, followed the ebb and flow of careers, and tracked changes in leadership, military and civilian. How could I not believe that this noble calling was anything but a one-way ticket to social acceptance and respectability?

Even after the war fell out of favor and then out of the headlines, and even though the audience has stopped watching war stories because they're preoccupied by news of the Great Recession, Americans still care deeply and sincerely for our service members. You see that affection at airports, train stations, bus depots or wherever the public and soldiers, sailors, marines, Coast Guardsmen or airmen meet: a feeling of intimacy and gratitude, a sense of "thank you" that no other calling elicits. Our divided country is united in appreciation for our GIs. By association, if I were to label the best of what I am, it would be "warrior journalist."

Why can't immigrants, including undocumented youngsters who have been here for most of their lives, enlist in the armed services? That is one of the bigger reasons I want the DREAM Act to become the law of the land. It is the perfect combination of causes. One provision of the bill would allow accomplished, though undocumented high school graduates to get in-state tuition at public colleges and universities if they arrived in the United States before the age of sixteen. That access to a relatively low-cost education would allow them to maximize their potential contributions to their families and to society. "Many American students graduate from college and high school each year, and face a roadblock to their dreams: they can't drive, can't work legally, can't further their education, and can't pay taxes to contribute to the economy just because they were brought to this country illegally by their parents or lost legal status along the way," explained Change.org.

Specifically regarding military service, another of the bill's provisions would allow children who are undocumented, but who have lived here for years, to serve their adopted country in the military and, by serving, become citizens, officially and legally part of the country.

Likewise, the comprehensive immigration reform bill (S 1639) authored by senators Ted Kennedy and John McCain, which sadly also failed to pass the Senate in June 2007, would have bestowed legal permanent residency on any "alien [who] has served in the uniformed services for at least two years, and, if discharged, has received an honorable discharge." Isn't that a great idea? Implicit in the language of the bill is the ability of youngsters here illegally to enlist and, by enlisting, make themselves part of the process of becoming officially an American.

Absent any new legislation, since shortly after the September eleventh attacks, the Pentagon has had specific wartime authority to sign up permanent noncitizen, legal immigrants, with the emphasis on *legal*. In the last several years only about eight thousand green card holders annually have signed up, often becoming naturalized citizens as a result. While that sounds like a practical expansion of military eligibility during times of crisis, it really is not. In the days before Lou Dobbs and the current wave of anti-immigrant hysteria—that is, before 2006—the all-volunteer armed services could enlist almost any person they deemed fit for service.

That fact is not being adequately or accurately reported: The Pentagon has always had the general authority to recruit foreigners in wartime, even undocumented immigrants. In several recent published interviews, Lt.

Col. Margaret Stock, the legendary immigration attorney and professor of military law at West Point, explained the recent shrinking of traditional immigrant eligibility.

"During World War I, World War II, Korean hostilities, Vietnam hostilities [and] other periods of military hostilities, citizenship was granted solely on the basis of three years of honorable service or honorable separation from service, whether or not the person ever lived in the United States . . . In January 2006 Congress made it harder for the Pentagon to recruit foreigners who are not Lawful Permanent Residents. It used to be that anyone could join the military in wartime—even undocumented immigrants—but now the Service Secretaries have to find that an undocumented person's enlistment is 'in the vital interests' of the United States."

Anti-immigration sentiment distorted and polluted every aspect of every decision in virtually every nook and cranny of the second Bush administration, including who could serve in the military. Even in the period when the bloody situation in Iraq and Afghanistan made military recruitment extremely difficult, and recruiters were hard-pressed to meet quotas and were perennially coming up short, especially for infantrymen, the Defense Department was still so freaked out by the harsh rhetoric of the immigration debate, it bent over backward to keep illegal immigrants from enlisting. It was another example of the counterproductive, ultimately anti-American nature of the nativist movement.

The Pentagon is still afraid of comparisons to the French Foreign Legion of *Beau Geste*, so much so that its aversion to immigrant enlistees borders on paranoia. Yet, that enlistment of undocumented immigrants happens; some say it happens a lot, others only rarely, but why the hesitation at all? If a kid has been in the United States since his parents brought him here from Mexico at the age of seven, what is wrong with offering that youngster a pathway to citizenship by service? We grant waivers allowing citizens who are convicted criminals, guilty of committing violent felonies, to enlist in our armed forces.

What logic prevents undocumented immigrant teenagers who have never done anything illegal, except being in this country, the same right to enlist? Are citizen felons more fit to serve than innocent, noncriminal immigrants? Let's do the tough background checks, find out exactly who these potential recruits are, but then let's do the right thing for them and our nation by giving the children of undocumented immigrants the chance to earn legitimacy in the only country they have really ever known.

Under existing laws, those who manage to serve and serve honorably can apply to become citizens on the first day of active duty and take the oath in as little as six months. Few ceremonies are as emotionally satisfying as watching noncitizen GIs taking the oath of citizenship in faraway places like Camp Liberty near Baghdad or Bagram Air Base outside Kabul, Afghanistan.

I was excited in early 2009 when the military announced a pilot program that would also allow skilled legal immigrants with only temporary visas the chance to become U.S. citizens in as little as six months if they enlisted. Beginning in New York, the pilot program was looking to recruit about 550 temporary immigrants who speak one of thirty-five languages, including Arabic, Chinese, Hindi and Russian, which is all well and good. But then to my deep disappointment, I learned that the Pentagon, again in deference to the Minutemen and Michelle Malkin, specifically excluded Spanish-language proficiency as one of the skills they were looking for in potential immigrant recruits. In other words, temporary but legal Latino immigrants—tourists, say, or students or visiting children—need not apply. If the troubles along the Mexican border continue to worsen they'll be sorry they devalued the useful skill of Spanish speaking.

The awkward intersection of the military and immigration law is clearly demonstrated in the case of twenty-year-old army Pfc. Armando Soriano, who was assigned to the howitzer battery, 3rd Squadron, 3rd Armored Cavalry Regiment out of Fort Carson, Colorado. Born in the U.S.A., he was an ambitious kid who had worked ever since the age of twelve trying to help his impoverished, undocumented parents get by, earning money in construction or restaurant jobs until he joined the military soon after graduating from South Houston High School. "The main reason he took off to the Army was that he wanted to help out his parents and to try and be somebody and learn," his lifelong friend Alex Castellano told the Associated Press. "He would think about everybody else before he thought about himself."

Joining over the strong objections of his parents, Armando gradually convinced them that he had made the right choice, sending letters and photos of himself sailing through basic training. "I was real proud of him," his mother, Clotilde Soriano, told the AP reporter. "He was being somebody."

In February 2004, Armando Soriano was killed in Haditha, Iraq, when his armored Humvee rolled over while traveling in a two-vehicle convoy in harsh weather through an enemy-held area. Back in Texas, he was buried with full military honors and was awarded the Bronze Star posthumously. After his death, his parents, both illegal immigrants, benefited from the unwritten policy that often grants immediate relatives of service members killed in action legal residence, a green card. His mom was quickly approved for lawful permanent resident status. But Armando's dad, Enrique, had a problem.

As the *Houston Chronicle* newspaper first reported, Enrique Soriano had once been deported from the United States in 1999 after falsely claiming to be a U.S. citizen. He had sneaked back across the Rio Grande to be with his family, including his four children who are U.S. citizens. Immigration officials learned of Enrique's unlawful return to this country only when his green card application was filed following his son Armando's death. Facing deportation, the forty-seven-year-old Soriano received a helping hand from Houston-area Congressman Raymond Green, who intervened on his behalf, convincing immigration officials to defer deportation for a year. Congress is considering a private bill, which is the only way he can now obtain a green card. Sacrificing a son is apparently not deemed sufficient legal cause to circumvent immigration laws in the current political climate.

"I think it would be a travesty for these parents to be deported after their son died in Iraq fighting for our country," said Congressman Green, who as of this writing remains confident a private bill will be passed.

The issue of immigrants aside, Hispanic citizen teenagers make up the fastest-growing pool of potential military recruits, and, taken as a whole, few ethnic groups are more patriotic. On the occasion of the eightieth anniversary of the civil rights group the League of United Latin American Citizens (LULAC), I gave the keynote speech at their founding local lodge in Corpus Christi, Texas. The evening started with everyone in the hotel ballroom standing and reciting the Pledge of Allegiance.

When was the last time you were at a function where, with neither resentment nor embarrassment, the entire crowd stood and recited the pledge? Grade school? That was followed by the singing of the national anthem. Then my dear friend and former LULAC president Tony Bonilla proudly introduced his grandson, Tony III, who is in the marines and was just back from Iraq. The entire crowd stood again to applaud the young man, who looked sharp in his dress blue uniform.

LULAC is extraordinarily promilitary, even sponsoring recruitment seminars, which bring Latino students from across the U.S. and Puerto Rico to hear how an army career could enrich their lives. Their February 2009 evening was just another example of a more central fact: As the grateful sons and daughters of immigrants, or as immigrants themselves, Hispanics are often extremely patriotic. All surveys show that once in the service they are more likely to complete boot camp, serve honorably and reenlist than any other group in the military. There is a sense that service is the honorable way to repay the nation's welcome. Military recruiters are no fools; they understand the gratitude Hispanics hold for the opportunities America provides, and they stress those noble aspects of service in their pitch.

To other potential recruits, especially during these hard times, the savvy recruiters stress the suddenly competitive service salaries, the education and on-the-job training. Even in the best of times, Hispanics tend to be so relatively disadvantaged that a military salary is often their ticket out of small-town or inner-city poverty. I wish I could recruit half of East Harlem. I mean that. Four years in the military would be beneficial for many of these youngsters. One of my "adopted" kids from El Barrio, Rey Lopez, is now a staff sergeant serving in the elite 101st Airborne Division. Rey is married, has a new baby who, like my older son, is named Gabriel, and has just been accepted as a combat photographer, which is a great fit for his career aspirations once he returns to civilian life to become a network cameraman.

Despite widespread racial and ethnic segregation and mistreatment, Hispanics have been an integral part of America's military history since before the beginning of the Republic. During the Civil War over thirteen hundred Mexican- and Cuban-Americans fought for the Confederacy, mostly in units from Texas, Louisiana and Florida. During the Spanish-American War the original Troop F was a unit of about a hundred Spanish speakers led by Captain Maximiliano Luna of Santa Fe, New Mexico. They were part of Teddy Roosevelt's Rough Riders, who charged up San Juan Hill and into history. Among the five hundred thousand Latinos who served during World War II, about a quarter of the Bushmasters, the 158th Infantry Regiment, was Mexican-Americans. Gen. Douglas MacArthur praised the unit as "one of the greatest fighting combat teams ever deployed for battle."

Warrior Latinos have held and continue to hold high commands in the U.S. military. Because of space constraints, I can't do justice to all who have honorably served the nation, but we have had secretaries of the army (like the Honorable Louis Caldera; the Harvard-educated eldest son of Mexican immigrants, who served under Bill Clinton and was later appointed Director of the White House Military Office by President Barack Obama. (Unfortunately, in May 2009 Caldera was forced to resign the White House post after authorizing a truly bone-headed photo-op flyover of Ground Zero by *Air Force One* that caused panic in downtown Manhattan). We have had secretaries of the Navy like the Honorable Edward Hidalgo, who served with distinction under Presidents Jimmy Carter and Ronald Reagan. Born in Mexico City Hidalgo was the first Hispanic to serve as Navy Secretary. We have had chiefs of the National Guard like Lt. Gen. Edward D. Baca of Santa Fe, New Mexico; and we claim David Glasgow Farragut, the first Hispanic-American admiral in the United States Navy, who during the Civil War in 1864 from the bridge of his flagship the U.S.S. *Brooklyn* issued the immortal battle cry, "Damn the torpedoes," and led the Union fleet ordering, "Full speed ahead," thus overwhelming the Confederate stronghold in Mobile Bay, Alabama. His father, Jorge Farragut Mesquida, was born on the Spanish island of Minorca. Jorge immigrated to America in 1776 and served during the American Revolution.

The first Hispanic-American to graduate from the United States Naval Academy and reach the rank of admiral was Robert F. Lopez, class of 1879. There have been many flag officers since; in more recent years, in 1964 Adm. Horacio Rivero Jr. became the first four-star admiral from Puerto Rico and the second Hispanic full admiral after Farragut. Two years earlier, in 1962, Rivero commanded our amphibious forces off Cuba as the United States went to the brink of Armageddon in the missile crisis following the ill-fated Bay of Pigs invasion. Since I was a second-year lowly cadet ordered to remain on board the New York State Maritime College training ship *Empire State*, which was put on hold by the U.S. Navy for possible reserve duty if war broke out, you could say that Puerto Rican sailors bookended our naval forces in the October 1962 crisis from the very bottom to the top.

Gen. Richard E. Cavazos, the first Hispanic four-star general in the U.S. Army, was born in Kingsville, Texas, and served for thirty-three years with distinction, retiring as head of the U.S. Army Forces Command. In February 1953, during the Korean War, then-lieutenant Cavazos served with the famed 65th Infantry Regiment, the mostly all-Spanish-speaking Puerto Rican Borinqueneers, receiving the Silver Star for extraordinary heroism after leading his men in a raid on the entrenched enemy. Mockingly called the "Seeexty Feeeth" at the time by critics who still longed for the day when black and brown units were segregated and used only in kitchen duty, this National Guard regiment served gallantly in Korea, garnering four Distinguished Service Crosses, more than 125 Silver Stars and numerous other commendations. Even in such distinguished company, Cavazos's bravery was extraordinary.

Braving heavy hostile fire, he stayed behind to extricate his fallen comrades as his unit retreated following a massive attack by the Communist Chinese army. He located five of his wounded and then dragged them out, one at a time, to a point where they could be rescued. Fourteen years later, in Vietnam, then–lieutenant colonel Cavazos was awarded his third Distinguished Service Cross for valor in repulsing a Viet Cong attack on his unit. On December 17, 1967, per General Orders No. 6479, Lieutenant Colonel Cavazos was awarded his third Distinguished Service Cross for his actions on October 30, 1967. His citation reads, "Constantly exposed to savage hostile fire and shrapnel from exploding grenades, he moved among his troops directing the counterattack. His brilliant leadership in the face of grave danger resulted in maximum enemy casualties and the capture of many hostile weapons."

Courage of the sort demonstrated by General Cavazos brings to mind an infuriating side story about Puerto Rican service and patriotism. With nearly seventy dead in fighting in Afghanistan and Iraq since September 2001, it is clear that units from the island have suffered disproportionately in this latest fight. Mothers Against War, a group supported by Puerto Rico's tiny independence movement, is particularly active, especially as casualties mount.

One deeply traumatic death for islanders came on January 2, 2005, when Sgt. 1st Class Pedro Muñoz of Aguada, Puerto Rico, was killed in action in Afghanistan. A forty-seven-year-old Green Beret, he had earned great deference from soldiers half his age, and was known respectfully as the "old man" by his troops. New York Congressman José Serrano said that "with his death, our community has lost a great *compatriota* who knew what it was to love both Puerto Rico and America."

But here is the rub. With their incredible record of service over the years it is maddening that, unique to all the troops serving in harm's way, these Puerto Rican-based soldiers have no right to vote for their commander in chief. It is another reason the island residents have to resolve their national status sooner rather than later. Like Sergeant Muñoz, they are both true Puerto Ricans and real Americans. They should have the right to vote.

I remember with pride joining a courageous Puerto Rican National Guard unit at Camp Victory outside Baghdad just before Christmas 2007 in singing a robust, if slightly off-key version of my old friend José Feliciano's "Feliz Navidad." We were live on FOX News, and, without overstating it, I felt my heart swell; I knew that everyone was watching these brave soldiers demonstrate their own pride of self, community and service. And speaking of pride, no Puerto Rican service member is getting more buzz than a former sergeant in the United States Marine Corps Reserves, Joseph Michael "Joe" Acaba.

The forty-one-year-old schoolteacher is the first person of Puerto Rican heritage to become a NASA astronaut, rocketing to the International Space Station on March 15, 2009. The first Boricua to fly into space, Joe was the mission specialist educator on the flight to deliver the final set of solar arrays that will keep the ISS humming after the space shuttles are retired next year. By all accounts he performed well, including on a space walk to install batteries and antennae at the far end of the space station's newly extended solar wings. He did put one bolt in backward, but nobody is perfect.

Watching it live, I experienced one breathtaking moment. Acaba and his partner, Steven Swanson, were loosening bolts holding down the batteries, when a space station alarm went off. It turned out that the gyroscopes that were maintaining the position of the station–shuttle complex became overloaded from the astronauts' work at the end of the truss. In the end, mission control sorted it all out and Joe and his partner were able to return to the shuttle, as Puerto Ricans everywhere breathed easier.

Acaba is a former educator, Peace Corps teacher and hydrogeologist, a renaissance man who carried a Puerto Rican flag into space with him, waking his crew one "morning" with a rousing sing-along to the beloved folkloric tune, *"Qué Bonita Bandera, La Bandera Puertorriqueña"* ("What a Pretty Flag, the Flag of Puerto Rico").

Another favorite and uniquely appropriate old folk song, "*Boricua en la Luna*" ("Puerto Rican on the Moon"), was also frequently mentioned in reference to this hero. Acaba made Puerto Rican *abuelas* everywhere happy when they heard that among the relatives attending his shuttle launch was his beloved ninety-year-old grandmother, Jovita, who told the *New York Daily News*, "We all feel very close, very happy, and support him in everything." Then Grandma explained how something in his youth hinted at his future in space: "He always liked those action movies." While Joe was the first Puerto Rican in space, he wasn't the first Latino. He was preceded by a Cuban, a Costa Rican and a Mexican. Also, as he was a teacher in space, Joe's status carried special resonance after the death of the first teacher-astronaut, Christa McAuliffe, in the 1986 *Challenger* disaster. *Challenger* was no doubt on the minds of NASA engineers this time around when they found and finally repaired a leaky gas venting system that postponed Joe's historic flight for a week.

Continuing my Hispanic service honor role, on August 2, 2006, Brig. Gen. Angela "Angie" Salinas became the first Latina to become a United States Marine Corps general officer, as commanding general of the Marine Corps Recruit Depot San Diego. Brig. Gen. Carmelita Vigil-Schimmenti hails from a ranch near Albuquerque. She was born to a family that traces its New Mexico roots back to 1695; in the 1950s her family moved to Atrisco, New Mexico, to work on the railroad, where she recalled signs reading, SPANISH-SPEAKING PEOPLE, NEGROES AND INDIANS NEED NOT APPLY.

Disgusted by society's persistent discrimination, and discovering as a civilian nurse working on an air force base the increasingly color-blind military, she enlisted in the air force. Working her way up through the ranks in various billets around the world, she became the first female Hispanic to attain the rank of general in 1985. General Vigil-Schimmenti served in the Pacific theater during the Vietnam War, receiving the Distinguished Service Medal and the Legion of Merit, among many other honors.

They haven't all ended their careers so magnificently. At the time of his selection to command all coalition ground forces in Iraq in June 2003, Lt. Gen. Ricardo Sanchez was the highest-ranking Hispanic in the armed forces, another wonderful rags-to-riches story, another dirt-poor kid from the Rio Grande Valley in Texas who worked his way to the top.

I remember telling him how proud of him I was, and what a terrific role model he was for Latino young people when we met in his office in one of Saddam Hussein's palaces in Camp Victory in June 2003. He was at the time of his ascension to command among the most junior three-star generals in the service, which to some in the service had the taint that perhaps he was selected over Lt. Gen. Thomas Metz, his second in command and someone more senior, because Sanchez was in essence a Bush administration affirmative action hire. It is a charge that may be true.

Worse, from the point of view of his detractors within the armed forces, he was a product of ROTC who never had the backing of the West Pointers who run the Army, despite the fact that he had won the Bronze Star as a battalion commander during Operation Desert Storm in 1991.

Sanchez was elevated from commander of the 1st Armored Division to commander of all ground forces in Iraq three months after the March 2003 "shock and awe" invasion that drove Hussein into hiding. When I first interviewed Sanchez in the summer of 2003, some cracks were already becoming visible in our strategy over there. A disturbing Sunni insurgency was spreading; Shiites in Sadr City were restive, and sectarian violence and attacks on U.S. and other coalition forces were on their way to becoming effective and deadly.

To complicate matters, Sanchez had an awful relationship with his civilian counterpart, Ambassador L. Paul Bremer, who had been instrumental in dismantling the Iraqi army, which was the only agency at the time that had any chance of maintaining civic order, and Bremer was in the process of throwing money at any Iraqi who seemed sympathetic to United States efforts.

Ivy-educated and aristocratic, Ambassador Bremer seemed also to have nothing but disdain for blue-collar General Sanchez. The two men complained about each other constantly. They hated each other, and the bitter feelings aggravated the divide between Bremer's State Department and Sanchez's military and was already complicating efforts to find an effective, comprehensive Iraq strategy.

Even the good news on their watch seemed tainted. When on July 22, 2003, our forces received a tip giving up the hideout of Saddam's crazy sons, Uday and Qusay, it took an extraordinary force from the 101st Airborne Division and heavy weapons like TOW missiles six hours to finally kill them. Then, the day after the fierce minibattle, a vocal group of demonstrators picketed our northern base to protest their "wrongful" deaths. And in the weeks and months to come, the brothers were immortalized as heroic martyrs.

Still, the brothers who had squandered their nation's riches on piggish lifestyles, indulged every obscene excess and terrorized their nation during their father's brutal reign were dead, and I congratulated General Sanchez when we first met in his office inside Saddam's ornate Al Faw Palace, which we called the Water Palace, located in sprawling Camp Victory on the outskirts of Baghdad.

To see this humble and soft-spoken Latino success story at the pinnacle of his career was enormously appealing. He had none of the swagger and bravado of many officers I've known over the years. In fact, he looked more like a small-college president than a three-star general. He seemed almost stunned that his military career had brought him to command here in war-torn Iraq, and he reacted with modest pride, a small smile and lowered eyes when I asked about the likelihood that his next assignment would yield a further promotion and a coveted fourth star.

Despite a deteriorating situation in the country later that year, General Sanchez had at least one good day during his service in Iraq. On Sunday, December 14, 2003, he got to make the following statement:

"Today is a great day for the Iraqi people and for the Coalition. Last night at approximately 8:00 p.m. local [time], forces from the 4th Infantry Division commanded by Major General Ray Odierno [now a lieutenant general and Sanchez's well-regarded successor] together with Coalition Special Operations Forces conducted Operation Red Dawn to capture the former Iraqi dictator Saddam Hussein. This was done during a cordon and search operation at a remote farmhouse near the city of Tikrit. There were no injuries, and in fact not a single shot was fired. Saddam Hussein, the captive, has been talkative and is being cooperative."

But by the time we spoke next, in June 2004, General Sanchez's career was in shambles.

Beginning with a scathing Dan Rather *60 Minutes* exposé three months earlier, followed by an even more eviscerating article by Seymour Hersh in *The New Yorker*, the world came to know about a former Hussein horror house called Abu Ghraib prison. Only this time the allegations of torture, abuse and sodomy of prisoners, all backed by shocking and sickening photographs, were being made against our own forces. And Congress had already dragged the general back to Washington to answer hard questions about the ensuing scandal that had spread like wildfire, especially through the Muslim world. It was a fixture on Al Jazeera.

At that critical juncture of the war, with our military on the verge of turning over nominal control of the country to appointed Iraqi civilian authorities, which was considered a necessary first step in restoring civic order, making elections the following January 2004 possible, the enemy was using the Abu Ghraib scandal to undermine support for that move and to encourage violent resistance. Improvised explosive devices (IEDs) were coming into common use, suicide bombings were increasing and everybody was looking for someone high-ranking to blame for the prison scandal. And whether General Sanchez knew it when we spoke next, the crosshairs were fixed squarely on him.

In the immediate wake of that first round of hostile congressional hearings, the general and I did our second Iraq interview. Awkwardly, we were situated in front of assembled GIs standing by their armored vehicles on a parade ground not far from the Water Palace, where our initial interview had taken place what seemed like a long time earlier. He was on the way out, clinging to dignity and barely suppressing his resentment. The word was out that he was being replaced by the four-star general George W. Casey Jr., the army's vice chief of staff himself. The officers around Sanchez treated him respectfully, but as if he were already gone.

"When I saw you testifying before Congress in the Abu Ghraib prison scandal hearing my heart broke," I started, revealing my bias immediately. "You know that I'm a big fan of yours. But are you being made the scapegoat for what happened in Abu Ghraib?"

"I don't believe so," he answered equivocally, then, getting more politically correct, "Absolutely not. What is going on is legitimate; investigations are ongoing to establish what the true facts were. Abu Ghraib was . . . I would call it a defeat for us. It is something that America must delve into, establish very objectively what those facts are, and the investigations will clearly establish what occurred at Abu Ghraib and we will take action against those accountable."

"When you hear the terrorists using the prison scandal as fuel for their propaganda machine, does it break your heart?"

"That's something our forces in the country did not need and something we definitely need to recover from," he answered, his voice trailing off.

By this time, deeply depressed myself and seeing the writing on the wall, first and most important about the prospects for increased violence in Iraq, but also the certain end of this humble man's career, a fact this good soldier was perhaps overlooking, I asked, "Can we recover from it?"

"I think here in the country, when you talk to the Iraqi people or politicians here, they understand these things happen and remind us very, very clearly about what they went through under the Saddam regime. That's important that we shouldn't forget that." He sounded like a defense lawyer making an argument he knows is a loser.

"It seems as if people are forgetting those years of repression and in-discriminate injustice," I added realistically.

"What happened is inexcusable. We all recognized that based on American views and other own individual value systems; we can't allow what happened here to occur again," he insisted, and I include it for the historic record.

"Did you permit, condone or order that kind of treatment against those people?" I asked the first question last.

"As I stated in the hearings, absolutely not," he said.

"I believe you," I replied, not really sure what the truth of Abu Ghraib would finally reveal, but wanting to give my brother Latino the benefit of the doubt. We shook hands and he marched off to his waiting flight of Blackhawk war choppers and was soon gone into the dusty air toward the Green Zone in Baghdad.

I want to love him, but in retrospect General Sanchez had apparently acquiesced to the iron-fist policies promulgated by Vice President Dick Cheney and Defense Secretary Donald Rumsfeld, and Sanchez's fate was sealed when documents signed by him were later uncovered, seeming to authorize military and CIA interrogators to go to "the outer limits of our authority." The memo implied that use of torture on recalcitrant prisoners was approved by him personally, a charge he angrily denied during later congressional hearings on the matter.

But the die was cast, and General Sanchez was out. Congress wanted a ranking officer to join trailer-park-trashy Private Lynndie England and the other West Virginia–based military police reservists photographed abusing, taunting, torturing and humiliating their Iraqi prisoners. The disgraced and criminally charged soldiers' defense was that they were just following orders. So, as senior commander in Iraq at the time, Sanchez was doomed, even though he said he knew nothing about the foul abuses being perpetrated by these miscreant, perverted rogues wearing the uniform of the United States.

Passed over for promotion to a fourth star, Sanchez retired after thirty-three years in the military in November 2006. On his way out he became the most senior retired general to criticize the war effort, saying, "There has been a glaring, unfortunate display of incompetent strategic leadership within our national leaders. As a Japanese proverb says, 'Action without vision is a nightmare.' There is no question that America is living a nightmare with no end in sight." Further, "There has been a glaring and unfortunate display of incompetent strategic leadership within our national leaders," who were "derelict in their duties," and guilty of a "lust for power."

He later said that the "surge" of forces proposed in 2007 by brilliant Gen. David H. Petraeus was "a flawed approach to stave off defeat." Happily, events in Iraq are proving him wrong on that count. General Sanchez retired to Texas, and historians have not been kind. When he made a highly critical Democratic rebuttal to a President Bush radio address, and advocated a congressionally imposed certain date for withdrawal from Iraq as a condition of further funding for the war, a *Real Clear Politics* piece by Jack Kelly said, "Though Ricardo Sanchez had lots of help in becoming a failure, and lots of company, the fact is that he was a failure, and that most of the responsibility for being a failure rests on the shoulders of . . . Ricardo Sanchez."

Sanchez implies "that somehow he was a blameless bystander and not the one entrusted with day-to-day operations during the critical year following regime change in Iraq," Kelly quotes the *Small Wars Journal.* "It appears that Sanchez did not have a problem with U.S. strategy at that time. Moreover, as the senior commander he had the authority to take measures that could have lessened the impact of a failed or nonexistent strategy had he so desired."

I disagree, because Sanchez was never really in charge. Every book written about the time frame around and following Abu Ghraib, including my own observations and reporting, shows that General Sanchez was far enough down the command food chain, and just far enough removed from his officers in the field, to have been neither the architect of the prisoner policies nor the implementer. If the care and treatment of the Abu Ghraib prisoners can be placed at the feet of anyone other than their dysfunctional reserve unit prison guards, then look to the powerful men who also created Guantánamo Bay.

Sanchez was treated like a junior military leader who was fielding an undersize force of about 125,000, more than half of which was noncombat support staff, while facing a malignant insurgency. All that while attempting to deal with Iraq's civilian czar Bremer, whom many in the military regarded as a condescending snob with a Napoleon complex. It is also telling that Sanchez had a reputation for doing whatever the White House and the Defense Secretary wanted.

What I find fascinating is how this supposed military giant was eaten alive by his Pentagon and White House bosses—a breathtaking reminder of how little power he apparently ever really had.

Sanchez was the victim of the military politicians' irritating practice of playing musical chairs of responsibility, which, to mix metaphors, often leaves the last commander standing holding the bag. Sanchez was a scapegoat too of what's left of the military's old-boy network. When push came to shove, not being a West Pointer, he had no powerful clique to watch his back. His experience is a bitter reminder too of the days when the armed forces were segregated and minorities undervalued.

I ran into Ricardo Sanchez at the 13th Annual U.S.-Mexico Border

Issues Conference in Washington in March 2009. He introduced himself, perhaps thinking I would not recognize him out of uniform. Maybe I wouldn't have. Again I was struck by his professorial appearance, more small businessman than former commander of all our Iraq ground forces. I asked how he was doing, and he told me he was a San Antonio–based "consultant" on international trade issues, and that he was looking for business at the big conference. I introduced him to the audience, calling him a hero, with a big flourish that got only polite applause from the savvy crowd who knew the record. It was sad, and I wish him well. There is a lesson here for ambitious Latinos that I'll get into deeper later. In quick strokes it's this: If, for whatever reason, you get a shot at the big time, don't let gratitude trump judgment and responsibility. You can't say you were just following orders. History extols honor over loyalty.

Despite General Sanchez's melancholy fate, our military achievers far outnumber the losers. As an exercise in understanding the enormous contribution Hispanics in uniform have made in defending freedom and giving everything, including their lives, for the United States, consider just those killed in action with the traditional Latino surname Perez. I want to restrict it just to the fighting since 9/11, but I would be remiss if I didn't mention Pfc. Manuel Perez Jr., the Mexican-American Oklahoma boy who won the Medal of Honor posthumously after singlehandedly attacking Japanese positions in the Battle of Luzon during the campaign in the Philippines in World War II. Realizing that enemy pillboxes were holding up the advance of his division, as lead scout he charged the fortifications, killing eighteen enemy soldiers before being mortally wounded. He was buried with full military honors in Oklahoma City, and the reserve center of the 221st Unit Army Hospital there is named in his honor.

Flash forward to the War on Terror, and the first Perez to fall in 2004 was a Spaniard, Cmdr. Gonzalo Perez Garcia of that country's Civil Guard. After weeks in a coma, he died after suffering serious wounds sustained in a shoot-out in southern Iraq, about twenty-five miles from Diwaniyah, where the Spanish troops were based. His death helped fuel the antiwar movement in Spain, which then helped elect a socialist prime minister, José Luis Rodriquez Zapatero, who promptly pulled that nation's fourteen hundred troops out of Iraq.

The fourteen other coalition soldiers named Perez who had lost their lives in Iraq and Afghanistan as of January 2009 were all Hispanic-Americans.

They are, in alphabetical order:

Cpl. Andres H. Perez of Santa Cruz, California, a marine who died as a result of enemy action in Anbar province, Iraq, on November 14, 2004. Anbar totally sucked in 2005; I remember a memorial service for a slain soldier in which his comrades honored their fallen comrade in a memorial service that had as a centerpiece the dead man's boots. I had to leave the room, because to see these brave, sincere young men say good-bye to their brother in arms was so poignant it broke my heart.

Sgt. Christopher S. Perez of Hutchinson, Kansas, died of wounds received in an indirect fire attack on May 23, 2005, during combat operations against enemy forces in Ramadi, another Sunni insurgent stronghold.

Second Lt. Emily J. T. Perez, who died of injuries sustained when a roadside bomb exploded near her Humvee during combat operations in Kifl, Iraq, on September 12, 2006, is the only Perez woman in this hall of heroes.

Marine Pfc. Geoffrey Perez of Los Angeles also went down in Anbar, succumbing to hostile action on August 15, 2004.

S.Sgt. Hector R. Perez of Corpus Christi, Texas, was killed on July 24, 2003, when the military convoy he was in came under fire north of Hawd, Iraq, another scary shithole of a place.

Sgt. Joel Perez III of Newark, New Jersey, was killed in a convoy ambush on November 2, 2003, in Taji, Iraq.

The 1st Armored Division's Spec. Jose R. Perez of Ontario, California, died from injuries suffered from enemy small-arms fire in Ramadi, Iraq, on October 18, 2006.

Pfc. Luis A. Perez of small-town Theresa, New York, was killed when his convoy vehicle hit a roadside bomb in Fallujah, Iraq, on August 27, 2004. Fallujah was a killing field for our servicepeople in that terrible year when things started unraveling and deaths that had been coming in ones and twos began coming in wicked piles of four, five and six a day. This was when Fallujah metastasized into the stronghold of the insurgency, and when it became clear that all the optimistic projections about "Mission Accomplished" came unraveled. This was the year we stopped thinking about winning and started thinking about getting the hell out of Iraq.

Marine Lance Cpl. Nicholas Perez of Austin, Texas, died due to hostile action in Anbar province, Iraq, on September 3, 2004. Anbar was another awful killing field: a vast desert that stretches to the borders of Syria, Jordan and Saudi Arabia. To be assigned to this dusty, arid, hostile moon-scape was to count the days until you got out carrying your shield or being carried out lying on it.

The 2nd Cavalry Regiment's Spec. Orlando A. Perez of Houston, Texas, died of wounds suffered from small-arms fire during dismounted operations in Baghdad, Iraq, on February 24, 2008.

Las Vegas native Lance Cpl. Richard A. Perez Jr. died as a result of a nonhostile vehicle incident, again in the sinkhole Anbar province, Iraq, on February 10, 2005.

And finally, Spec. Wilfredo Perez Jr. of Norwalk, Connecticut, was killed when a grenade was thrown from a window of the Iraqi civilian hospital he was guarding in Baghdad, Iraq, on July 26, 2003. I've been to this high-rise hospital, which was reopened in 2007 and now serves a huge and needy swath of the capital city. Although it has been refurbished and reequipped, the scars of grenade blasts and shot impacts are still clearly visible under the new coats of paint. Driving home along the Connecticut Turnpike (I-95) last week, I thought of Perez and that Baghdad hospital when I drove over the bridge named in his honor outside Bridgeport.

My melancholy Perez KIA memorial complete, I still believe with all my heart that military service by Hispanic youth will continue to be one of their best avenues for self-advancement. Moreover, our heroes will help our fellow Americans understand that we are all in this together. Pass the DREAM Act.

★ 10 ★

THE BOY SCOUTS GET IT

The Importance of Latinos to U.S. Institutions

"Scouting is an enormously important and useful discipline for young people, particularly young boys. It can build character and can awaken an appetite for learning."

—Raul Yzaguirre, president, National Council of *La Raza*

"Scouting reinforces values you brought from home. It gave us an opportunity to share them with others whose values were not as strong."

—José Niño, president and chief executive officer, El Niño Group, and former president, U.S. Hispanic Chamber of Commerce

"Scouting! *Vale la Pena.*" ("Scouting! It's Worth the Effort.")

—One of many Spanish-language posters "designed to assist in promoting scouting's awareness in Hispanic communities," according to the Boy Scout Web site.

The first dramatically different father-son activity my dad and I took up upon leaving our teeming, ethnic, urban Williamsburg, Brooklyn, neighborhood for the new, emerging blue-collar suburb of West Babylon, Long Island, around 1950 was the Boy Scouts of America.

Although less than forty miles from Brooklyn, our new hometown could not have been more different from the one we left behind. In that era, before its twenty-first-century yuppie gentrification, Williamsburg had been an exotic Puerto Rican/Jewish stew: bustling, noisy and crowded. As a rare combination of these lively yet disparate groups, we young Rivera children had not encountered much of the big-city tension that often flared between those ethnic rivals (and sometimes still does). We moved easily among relatives from either group. But the American dream beckoned to my parents from the affordable, emerging suburbs opening up along the recently expanded Sunrise Highway.

Reversing Horace Greeley's admonition to go west, we followed that promising highway east into Suffolk County. More precisely, we followed my mother's brother Louie Friedman, who, with his wife, beloved Aunt Amy, had left Brooklyn a year before us, after landing a job in the Babylon branch of the U.S. Post Office. Amy would spend a long and admired career in the circulation department of the *Long Island Newsday*. Her daughter, my cousin Estelle, still works there.

In these formative years, West Babylon was almost exclusively Irish and Italian, a rapidly expanding, newly incorporated area of just-constructed or about-to-be-constructed modest frame homes, most purchased by World War II veterans like my dad with the help of the GI Bill. (Fortunately, sub-prime loans weren't around in those days.) Our brand-new, four-bedroom, two-story wooden home standing on what felt like a huge one-hundred-by-one-hundred-foot lot at 614 Ninth Street cost my parents less than ten thousand dollars. It was right across the street from the Friedmans', whose grandchildren still live there. My brother Wilfredo and his extended family still live in our old place, now greatly expanded, with a two-car garage attached.

Unlike in neighboring Babylon, a centuries-older, more prosperous and established community bordering the Great South Bay and, most important, on the other side of the Long Island Railroad tracks, the families in our town were largely headed by men like my dad, Cruz, who worked at one of the two large defense plants located nearby, Republic Aviation, which made jets for the U.S. Air Force, and Grumman, which made them for the navy, both now defunct. Pop ran the almost exclusively Puerto Rican kitchen staff of Republic's main cafeteria concession. Uncle Louie later joined my still Brooklyn-based, Puerto Rican-born uncles Ramon, Augustín and Carlos, all working hard for dad.

With its largely ethnic, working-class, Catholic population, West Babylon was what would now be described as a basically conservative, family-values neighborhood, inhabited by folks later called Reagan Democrats. In these formative years it was an undramatic neighborhood of modest new homes set on sparse lawns, adorned by skinny young trees and behind scrawny hedges that well masked whatever secrets there might be behind. Even in this era of *Peyton Place*, I don't remember a single scandal other than a mild, mostly voluntary outing of the theatrical gay guy who staged the high school plays, the death of one classmate in Vietnam and, much later, legendary *New York Post* reporter Steve Dunleavy's successful midnight pursuit of the disgraced but colorful televangelist Reverend Jim Bakker's young paramour Jessica Hahn, who lived in a two-story rental near Sunrise Highway.

Because the GOP represented the town of Babylon's long-established local power structure, our village tended to vote Republican, which was easy because widely admired former general Dwight D. Eisenhower, the victorious World War II Supreme Allied Commander, would soon defeat a strange Democrat named Adlai Stevenson for the presidency. Anyway, you had to register Republican if you wanted your kid to get a government summer job, as I later did with the Babylon Town Highway Department. That followed several earlier all-season stints as a *Long Island Press* newspaper bicycle delivery boy.

The neighborhood families respected and aspired to the American ideal of opportunity and, ultimately, they earned their way into the upper working- or middle-class's relative prosperity. They were mostly religious or at least churchgoing, though secular and conservative in lifestyle. And while it was certainly no *Peyton Place*, it wasn't really much of anything but a bedroom community for these defense plants nearby. What the neighborhood really lacked was a geographic heart. Only recently bulldozed out of the scrub pine and sandy soil of the South Shore, its one saving grace was that, unlike the ultimate postwar suburb Levittown over in Nassau County, at least our homes weren't all cookie-cutter matches. But unplanned West Babylon had no center, no village square and no downtown. There were no malls or movie theaters, fast food had yet to be invented, government buildings were scattered along Sunrise Highway, and the community lacked fundamental institutions like libraries, parks, churches or synagogues (though the fact that there were no other Jews in West Babylon at the time made that latter problem mostly moot). Several years later, when the time came for my bar mitzvah, a small, mostly newly arrived reform congregation had been established in a volunteer fire department hall near the LIRR stop across Route 109 in adjacent North Lindenhurst. The crowd that day was mostly from the much larger Puerto Rican side of the family, a fact I remember as charming, though weird.

Most of my friends attended Our Lady of Perpetual Help, the big Catholic Church on North Wellwood Avenue, the main street in the long-established village of Lindenhurst, where, being religiously ambidextrous, I often joined them for services and even confession. Community events and not-for-profit organizations based in West Babylon tended to use public school buildings, like my grade-school alma mater Santapogue School, about a mile from the new house on Ninth Street.

The Boy Scouts met there at least once a week. Attracted to their family-values agenda and keen to be and appear to be totally assimilated in this otherwise non-Hispanic environment, my dad dutifully enrolled me in Cub Scouts. He went even farther, volunteering to be one of the assistant scoutmasters who supervised the weekly drills in the elementary school gym, and accompanied us on the Scout jamborees held farther out east, near Lake Ronkonkoma.

Excepting one sleepless camping trip following a vampire movie and fireside ghost stories about the resident witch called the Lady of the Lake, who was going to drown some random camper, the Cub Scouts was a positive experience for me. I didn't amount to much later as a Boy Scout, though, not getting past Tenderfoot after my priorities shifted abruptly in adolescence to sports and girls. By the time I dropped out, several other Hispanic families had trickled into town, similarly attracted to the Scouts, which brings me to the point.

Even in this age of Obama-inspired volunteerism, the Boy Scouts of America are still the nation's largest youth organization, claiming 2.8 million members. But as the venerable organization approaches its one hundredth birthday in 2010, various crises are upon it. The organization has been racked by scandals involving allegations of sexually predatory adult mentors and, more mundanely, by a controversy over inflated membership tallies. It has been further ripped by bitter public battles involving bans on gay or atheist members, and for those and other reasons has consequently been barred from using most public facilities (like old Santapogue School).

Bizarrely, the group's ban on homosexual Scouts and troop leaders became an issue in the 2008 presidential election campaign. McCain supporter and Texas governor Rick Perry, a proud former Eagle Scout and the author of a book on his scouting experiences called *On My Honor*, attacked McCain's rival Republican candidate Mitt Romney. Perry alleged that when Romney was drafted to save the troubled 2002 Winter Olympics in Salt Lake City, he bowed to the homosexual rights lobby and barred the Boy Scouts from the Games.

"In 2000 [Romney] put out a published call for volunteers. . . . The Great Salt Lake Council of the BSA, the largest in the nation, with some 80,000 Scouts and 35,000 adult leaders, answered Romney's call for volunteers. Sometime that fall, however, the Scouts were advised that they were no longer welcome to participate," wrote Governor Perry, who further pointed out that the 2002 Games were the first to openly welcome gay participants.

To his credit, Romney responded during a 2007 debate that, "I support the right of the Boy Scouts of America to decide what it wants to do on that issue [of gay membership]. I feel that all people should be allowed to participate in the Boy Scouts regardless of their sexual orientation." Me too—gay kids should have the same rights of access to this otherwise wonderful organization as straight kids. Homosexuality is a natural condition, not a contagious disease. Diversity is a virtue and an American value. But to the point of this essay, the debate is largely irrelevant. Because of the Hispanic community's inherent social conservatism, the ban on homosexual Scouts and Scout leaders is unlikely to have much impact on Latino membership.

More fundamentally problematic, the BSA is still a mostly white organization that has largely failed to attract many minority members, especially Hispanic. "Many newly arrived immigrants from Mexico and parts of Central and South America, and a large number of second-generation families perceive Scouting as a youth program reserved for wealthy families," admits Scouting.org, the BSA's official Web site. "When a child brings a Cub Scout flier home from school, the conclusion many of these parents draw is that Scouting can't possibly be for them." As a result of its various travails, the BSA is only half the size it was during scouting's peak during the supposed counterculture, the year of the Nixon landslide and Watergate burglaries, 1972.

"We're either going to figure out how to make Scouting the most exciting dynamic organization for Hispanic kids, or we're going to be out of business," Rick Cronk, former national president and chairman of the World Scout Committee, told the Associated Press bluntly.

Cronk's bleak assessment is another small but meaningful indicator of America's demographic eruption. Despite the fact that nearly one in four kids of scouting age is Hispanic and the fact that the Scouts'"brave, thrifty, clean and reverent" ethos fits right into the prevailing values of the Latino community, Hispanics make up just 3 percent of all Scouts.

"More than a third of the Hispanic population is younger than 18," Robert J. Mazzuca, the organization's chief Scout executive, told the *Latino Business Review* in March 2009. "There's a lot at stake. We're not fulfilling our mission as an organization if we don't see this incredibly rapidly growing and dynamic part of our population and do everything we can to reach out to them."

To their credit, and unlike other large quasi-public national organizations, like the ultimately self-defeating 2008 edition of the Republican Party, the Boy Scouts are moving aggressively to attract Hispanics to their flock by emphasizing the shared values of respect, discipline and community involvement. The BSA has a plethora of brochures including, "Cub Scouting: *Tiempo Bien Utilizado*" ("Time Well Spent"), "Cub Scouting: *Un Buen Programa para Nuestras Familias*" ("A Good Program for Our

Families") and "Scouting—*Sí Funciona Para Sus Niños*" ("It Works for Your Youth").

Mazzuca told the *Review* about a campaign involving bilingual radio and TV spots, bilingual and bicultural staff representatives and, more uniquely, *fútbol*. "One of our pilot programs over recent years has been Scouting in soccer, using the attraction of the soccer game to gather Hispanic families around." In what should be the model for not-for-profit organizations and educational institutions throughout the nation, in 2009, Boy Scout outreach programs were planned in heavily Hispanic markets like Houston, Fresno and Orlando and partnerships formed with various churches that emphasize traditional values, especially Catholic and evangelical.

Bearing in mind that most Hispanics don't have a long tradition of scouting in their families, "Council executives who are serious about serving their growing Hispanic American/Latino communities should keep in mind that it will take some time . . . to establish the trust and confidence of . . . parents about a program that is fairly new to them," says the Scout Web site. Dads like my pioneering pop back in West Babylon are being actively recruited by a group that understands that the only way to succeed in Nuevo America is to become part of the fabric of a cautious community resistant to strangers.

"I was not too convinced," one mom who only reluctantly decided to get involved in scouting told the *Review*. "I was actually scared, like most Hispanics. We tend to hold onto our kids even when they're older." As she was convinced by the local Latino Cubmaster, mom relented, reassured. "They teach them respect, responsibility and, you know, they're more self-confident in their decisions. I noticed that in my son, and I'm very happy."

The Scouts also understand that they have a way to go, totally appreciating their need to absorb and be absorbed by Hispanics to survive; but the frank sentiment expressed by one official could as easily describe a broader future for institutions ranging from the Masons to the community college to the local chamber of commerce.

As Marcos Nava, the director of the Scouts' newly established national

Hispanic Initiatives Division, told the AP, "One hundred years—that's a great benchmark for us. But we have to remember that to Hispanics, we [the Scouts] [a]re just at the introduction, the basics. Because if we don't get past that stage, we won't live to see another hundred years." How is that for urgency?

★ 11 ★

HISPANICS AND THE NEW UNION MOVEMENT

"There's a new sheriff in town."
—U.S. Labor Secretary Hilda Solis in her first public appearance
after being confirmed, AFL-CIO Executive
Council in Miami, March 2009

On the day the planes hit the World Trade Center buildings and changed all of our lives, my brother Wilfredo, a union steamfitter, and his colleagues were working on the new police headquarters building in Lower Manhattan. After one fully loaded 757 plowed into the first building, Willy and his mates pondered what they thought was a terrible accident. Since some of these same steamfitters, including Willy, had installed the extensive sprinkler system in the Trade Center, they wondered when it would kick in, extinguishing the flames. Then, as they watched the second aircraft hit, they knew no sprinkler system on earth was going to put out those fires.

Willy was the first of our family to become a member of a union, and he had to fight for the privilege. A union card thirty years ago was a ticket to upward mobility and respectability, and they weren't easy to come by, especially for a Puerto Rican. Union membership and entrance to the "halls" where jobs were assigned were part of a restricted world, jealously guarded by those lucky enough to be the relative or connected friend of a previous or current member, virtually all of whom were white guys, either Irish, Italian or German, depending on the trade. As far as I know, Willy was the first Puerto Rican to be admitted to his steamfitter local, and only grudgingly, after his tough Irish friends from the neighborhood campaigned tirelessly on his behalf, refusing to take no for an answer, and finally convincing fellow members of the local that it was time.

Excluded for various social, ethnic and racial reasons from the glory days of American organized labor, Latinos are now in the forefront of a new union movement. The largest is the Service Employees International Union, representing over 2 million workers in the United States, Canada and Puerto Rico, many of them Latino and a large percentage of them employed in hospitals and health care, one of the few expanding sectors in our withered economy.

The union's "Justice for Janitors" campaign, which organized thousands of Texas-based building services workers effectively, doubled their salaries from $5.15 per hour to almost $10 in 2006. The SEIU also played a pivotal role in the 2008 presidential election, putting tens of thousands of janitors, nurses, child-care providers and other campaign workers in the field to register new voters, knock on doors, work in phone banks and squeeze every possible vote out for Barack Obama.

The result, according to SEIU executive vice president Eliseo Medina, is that "from the palm trees of Southern Florida to the snowy mountains of Colorado, millions of first-time, long-time and infrequent Latino voters have raised their voices and changed the course of history."

In appointing former California congresswoman Hilda Solis his Labor Secretary, President Obama was remembering the debt to Hispanics in organized labor, which has thought fondly of Solis since her early sponsorship of a California bill to raise the minimum wage from $4.25 to $5.75 back in 1995, a raise which had been strongly opposed by manufacturers and the restaurant industry. And, after a shaky start, she has proven a delight to labor activists, although for a time it appeared she wasn't going to make it.

The problems for the California congresswoman picked to become the nation's twenty-fifth Labor Secretary began with revelations of sixty-four hundred dollars in outstanding tax liens owed by her husband Sam H. Sayyad's Los Angeles auto repair business. I thought it was a rinky-dink issue, especially after Sayyad paid up and the liens were released, but the tempest in a teapot came at the same time various other Obama cabinet nominees were being forced to withdraw or were being embarrassed by missteps ranging from not paying taxes on nannies to failure to pay any taxes at all, in the case of the Treasury Secretary.

More important, Republicans were threatening to invoke a rule that would have forced a filibuster-proof sixty supporting votes for confirmation in the Senate. "Unfortunately, based on my review of her background, I am concerned that Representative Solis lacks the management experience needed to meet the demands of the job," said Wyoming Republican senator Michael B. Enzi, the ranking member of the Senate Committee on Health, Education, Labor and Pensions to the *Los Angeles Times*. The congressman pointed out to the paper that the relatively inexperienced Solis would be in charge of the Labor Department's $53 billion budget and nearly seventeen thousand employees.

The antiunion, probusiness conservatives were also freaked about Solis's role in a nonprofit that lobbied for a bill that would have made it much easier for workers to form unions. She gave them an opening to use that advocacy against her, because the secretary apparently failed to mention the association on her mandatory House disclosure forms. Because the GOP saw her as a union activist, her husband's lien could have been for sixty-four thousand dollars or even sixty-four cents and she still would have had problems.

In late February 2009, despite her vague and shaky testimony during which she seemed a deer caught in the headlights, Solis was confirmed by a vote of 80–17, including twenty-four Republicans, among them Enzi of Wyoming. Opposition to her nomination had been swept away following payment of the silly little tax lien and, far more important, by a cascade of support in the form of demonstrations, petitions, e-mails, faxes and angry telephone calls from groups ranging from the United Farm Workers to the Congressional Hispanic Caucus, LULAC and the Service Employees International Union. Latinos weren't going to let the negative vibe surrounding Obama's other failed nominations bring Solis down; the GOP blinked and history was made.

She was sworn in by Vice President Joe Biden and thus became the first Hispanic woman to serve as a cabinet secretary in American history. It was a stirring moment for this daughter of immigrants, her dad from Mexico, her mom from Nicaragua. And since both parents had been blue-collar union members, dad a teamster, mom an assembly worker for Mattel toys, who met as both were studying for their citizenship tests, her ascension electrified supporters of the movement that is changing the face of American labor. The path traveled by the Solis family is the essence of what I wish for all Latino immigrants.

SEIU's fire-breathing president, Andy Stern, captured the significance of the moment when he put it this way: "As the daughter of two immigrant workers and union members who met in a citizenship class, today's vote to confirm Hilda Solis as Secretary of Labor proves the American Dream is still alive. Working men and women now have a Department of Labor they can count on to stand up and fight for them because Secretary Solis personally understands the challenges workers face in the global economy. For Secretary Solis this is not just another job, but the culmination of a lifetime of action serving as a voice for people who work."

"The failing economy has put millions of Americans out of work and millions more are wondering if their job will be next," said California congressman George Miller upon her confirmation. "The Department of Labor will have an important role in our nation's economic recovery, and I am very confident that Hilda Solis is the right leader for the job."

The new chair of the Congressional Hispanic Caucus, the stylish and influential Representative Nydia Velázquez, of whom you will be hearing great things, said, "The influence of the Latino community continues to grow, and today, Hilda Solis helps pave the way for generations of Latinos to come."

In introducing her in Miami for that first formal appearance as our new Labor Secretary, AFL-CIO president John Sweeney praised Solis as "the only labor secretary in recent memory from a working family, and a union background. We know she does not plan to be a secretary of the bosses or the CEOs. I say the same thing about the secretary as I have said about Barack Obama: I trust Barack Obama. I believe what he told us during the campaign are promises that he's going to stick to, whether it's healthcare, financial security, employee free choice, education. The list is long."

Solis didn't disappoint the long-suffering *unionistas* who had been bruised, battered and otherwise ignored during the two Bush administrations. She enthusiastically reassured the crowd that one of the Obama administration's top priorities is protecting workers. "If you take care of an employee, that employee will produce. Productivity by our workforce, especially union members, has increased. But we don't see the same value in terms of their wages going up. So there has to be some morality placed there."

In light of union president Sweeney's remark about the length of Obama's to-do list, it will be interesting to see whether the White House will push aggressively on the issue most important to the resurgent labor movement, the Employee Free Choice Act.

If passed, the act would make it easier for workers to organize by eliminating the seventy-three-year-old law requiring secret elections. Instead, workers would simply fill out a card that states their preference to have a union. If a majority of workers signed the cards stating their preference for a union, then that union would be permitted to organize that shop. It's called the "card check," and if it is passed the union movement could flourish big-time, awash in new members, and armed with mandatory arbitration of all substantial disputes. You want more or less overtime, brighter lights, a new watercooler? The boss says no; let's arbitrate.

But as with comprehensive immigration reform, the question is whether the president is willing to fight another death match with Republicans (and some conservative, Blue Dog Democrats) over a bill that is bitterly opposed by business groups, including "progressive" companies like Costco, Starbucks and Whole Foods. Worried that union organizers could pressure workers into signing the card expressing preference for a union, in the same way management has historically pressured workers into not holding secret elections, business groups are pulling out all stops to oppose it. Deciding to pick this fight with the economy still in the toilet might be something the president postpones until a more propitious time.

Whether they get the drive-by card check for new members whom they seek, or are forced instead to abide by the existing secret-ballot requirements, unions are entering a new phase. Long before either the government or business saw the promise of Hispanic potential, the unions did, understanding that the postindustrial era would have a Spanish face.

It wasn't always that way. Following the Civil War, and before civil rights, unions reflected America's segregated workforce. From the mid-1940s through the mid-1960s things were flush for everybody, at least relative to the Great Depression. Still, unions were for "real" working Americans, like those dust-blackened coal miners and bold steelworkers seen on progressive posters and murals. Then the flattening planet's global economy began outsourcing to India and China, even as get-tough bosses stepped up the fight, battling American unions tooth and nail. Pensions declined, health care began evaporating and wages stagnated. Organized labor was on its heels. With globalization snatching up high-end industrial jobs to be done cheaper and, in some cases, better somewhere else, it seemed like the end was near.

Labor's decline from its heyday didn't happen overnight. For decades, the original momentum gained from Depression-era legislation worked well in expanding protection of the rights of workers to organize and fight for better working conditions, job security, health care, retirement and better salaries. But even before free trade, organized labor's appeal faded as traditional blue-collar workers graduated to the suburban middle class, the general standard of living improved, and traditionally unionized industries like manufacture declined. At organized labor's peak in 1970, the number of union jobs in the private sector was nearly 17 million. By 1984, it was down to 11.6 million and shrank further to 8.2 million union jobs in 2004.

The percentage of union members declined from 15.5 percent of the private-sector labor force in 1984 to just 7.9 percent in 2004. That year saw labor in disarray. The movement was divided and having failed to get Democrat John Kerry elected over George W. Bush, its leaders feuded internally over how to stem the alarming erosion in membership and political clout. But even as they scrapped, there was already something else going on that would come to represent the future of the movement. There was still a vast untapped reservoir of potential members who could get jobs, and who might be interested in joining a union. Some of the labor bosses and the antiunion CEOs weren't noticing the little jobs like the barmaids, bellhops, cooks, dishwashers and maids working the Vegas strip, the nurses in hospitals and all those invisible service workers looking for job security and a decent wage.

Many of them had a brown face. The fastest-growing ethnic group in the U.S. workforce, by 2007, Latinos made up 14 percent of all American workers, union and non-union, up from less than 5 percent in the 1970s, according to the Center for Economic and Policy Research (CEPR). In those ensuing decades, Latinos working in low-wage and physically demanding jobs came to understand the power of collective bargaining just as their mostly ethnic white brethren did in the days before and during the Great Depression. There is a direct line from those coal miners and steelworkers and the newly unionized hotel, hospital and service workers of today.

Latinos have become the labor movement's heart and soul in recent decades, vital to its future. As with Social Security, these immigrants or children of immigrants are the force reenergizing the labor movement, which had stalled and was shrinking. Just considering unionized workers alone, Latinos are almost 12 percent, according to the Center for Economic and Policy Research. They now represent the fastest-growing group in the nation's battered union movement. Those unions have become the ticket to their upward mobility. From fields to processing plants to kitchens, according to CEPR, "Unionization substantially improves the pay and benefits received by Latino workers." On average, in 2007 a unionized Latino worker made 17.6 percent—that is about $2.60 more per hour, more than similar Latino workers who were not in a union. When you are making $15 to $18 an hour, that $2.60-per-hour pay difference is the difference between blue-collar dignity and bare subsistence.

Cesar Chavez, his partner, the wonderful Dolores Huerta, and their United Farm Workers were the inspirations for other Hispanic labor leaders to follow. More organizer than saint, Cesar understood the essential economics of labor: The more workers there are available, the less they're going to get paid; where supply and demand meet, you find price. That was the reason the UFW opposed illegal immigration and urged tighter border controls and severe restrictions on temporary workers, a platform that would be considered hard-core today.

Eventually, unions including the UFW discovered the crucial role even undocumented workers could play in their movement, as Hispanics moved out from the fields to factories and beyond in jobs ranging from meatpackers to municipal workers to maids. Although I have mixed feelings about organized labor, given its checkered history, the activism of units like the United Food and Commercial Workers International Union on behalf of undocumented workers swept up in those hideous workplace raids has made me a firm believer in the essential nobility of the movement.

I marched with one of labor's most powerful leaders last year at New York's Puerto Rican Day parade, the crazy, colorful, chaotic but grand event that bills itself as the world's largest parade, bigger than Mardi Gras in Rio. Dennis Rivera, the longtime head of New York's Local 1199 SEIU, was grand marshal. A native of Puerto Rico who attended college in the small, mountain island town of Cayey (which has some of the best traditional food in Puerto Rico and is by chance just a short drive from where I am writing this in the village of Playa Salinas), Dennis began his career as a union organizer in PR. He came to New York in 1977 to help organize its vast network of hospital and other health care facilities, ultimately becoming one of the nation's premier labor leaders, and a potent political force who can conjure a horde of legitimate new voters, as he and his colleagues did for Barack Obama in the crucial swing states of Nevada, New Mexico, Florida and Colorado; or fill a neighborhood with outraged protesters, as he did when the nomination of Labor Secretary Solis was in doubt.

The emerging union job trend Dennis's ascension represents was most visible in Las Vegas during the hotel and building boom of the 1990s. As the first megaresorts like the Bellagio, Mandalay Bay, Mirage and Luxor went online, an entirely new workforce was needed to clean those thousands of hotel rooms, wash millions of dishes, plant, mow and groom all those acres and carry all those bags.

The Hotel Employees and Restaurant Employees International Union's Culinary Local 226 began furiously organizing the thousands of Latinos pouring into town looking for jobs, many of them female. The ladies proved a powerhouse, flocking to the union, and, putting aside their traditional gender deference, many assumed leadership roles. Some tough, clear-eyed Latinas came out of the kitchen or mop closet to reinvigorate organized labor.

Geoconda Arguello-Kline, a Nicaraguan immigrant, became the first female president of Local 226, while another Latina, Maria Elena Durazo, the daughter of Mexican immigrants, became president of the union's Local 11 in Los Angeles. Together they helped negotiate reduced workloads for the maids and others, and won salaries approaching twenty dollars per hour for the almost sixty thousand kitchen workers, bellmen, maids and waitresses. With that decent wage, long the portal to the American middle class, their members could put down roots and anchor lives in respectability. Arguello-Kline also campaigned aggressively for Barack Obama in Nevada during both the primary and general elections.

Together, the United Food and Commercial Workers, the giant Service Employees International Union (SEIU), the Teamsters, UFW, UNITE HERE, which is a textile, restaurant and hotel employees' union, Change to Win, and other components both inside and outside the old AFL-CIO banner seem to have stemmed the erosion in union membership, which hit its nadir in 2006, when it represented just 12 percent of all American workers. Since then, total union membership has ticked up to 12.6 percent, largely driven by those new Hispanic health care and service workers.

But since Hispanics continue to have the lowest percentage of all unionized workers, their potential for reinvigorating the labor movement is clear. As with the Boy Scouts and innumerable other U.S. institutions, Latinos are the vast and still largely untapped reservoir from which the labor movement can draw its future. The big question is whether those various labor unions vying for Hispanic affection can put aside their sometimes ferocious internal differences to continue appealing to workers worried about losing their tenuous jobs in an economy that is scorching them disproportionately.

The fading economy was definitely on the minds of the many thousands who rallied in seven locations around New York State, including New York's City Hall, in March 2009. They were protesting proposed state and city budget cuts to public services, public education, health care and other programs, which they feared would have a devastating impact on the poor. To help prevent those cuts, Dennis Rivera and his robust former local 1199 SEIU, joined by such enemies of conservatives everywhere as ACORN, AFSCME District Council 37, AFT Local 2 United Federation of Teachers, and including activist groups like the Hispanic Federation, the NAACP, and the New York Immigration Coalition, hit the streets.

The group, with its sea of black and brown (and some Asian and white) faces, represents the new union movement I'm talking about. This powerful if fractious coalition wielded more power at the polls in November 2008 than they had since Franklin Roosevelt's day. Now it is pushing hard with street protests and a scary radio campaign to increase income taxes on New Yorkers earning $250,000 and more, which the group says would generate an estimated $6 billion annually. According to their literature, they were also advocating for "the governor and the legislature to take steps that will ensure the federal stimulus funding is spent efficiently and effectively."

What was impressive about the New York actions and similar moves across the country in the spring of 2009, including the outpouring of support for Hilda Solis when her nomination as Labor Secretary faltered, is that for the first time in several years, organized labor seems . . . organized. The vicious civil war between UNITE HERE, the textile, restaurant and hotel employees' union, and the Service Employees International Union, which it accused of raiding members, and the similarly bitter battle between rival factions of the AFL-CIO and breakaway federation Change to Win, had made the withered unions seem pathetic and dysfunctional. "If there's ever been a moment where having one unified voice is important, it's this moment," complained Steve Elmendorf, a Democratic operative, to the Associated Press in an article about how labor infighting undermined its political clout.

That rapprochement was followed that same month, March 2009, by an announcement that two of the nation's fastest-growing unions, the SEIU and the California Nurses Association, had ended the yearlong public brawl they were having as they competed to unionize registered nurses. "We have buried the hatchet," Rose Ann DeMoro, president of the California Nurses Association, told *New York Times* reporter Steven Greenhouse.

In what is still the best analysis of the man and his mission, another *New York Times* reporter, veteran Sam Roberts, interviewed Dennis Rivera seventeen years ago, shortly after Dennis became head of the huge 1199 health care workers' local. Roberts wrote how then-congressman Bill Richardson in his role as head of Hispanic PAC USA introduced Rivera at a Washington cocktail party. "Dennis may not be an elected official, but he controls about nine million votes," Richardson said to rousing applause.

Whether he was really that powerful back in 1992 or even whether he is now, Dennis Rivera of Aibonito—who is no relation that I can find to my father, Cruz Rivera, of Bayamón, although we would gladly claim him—understands the essential truths about the labor movement. It must unify and it must embrace Latinos and the new world economic order, or it closes down. As Roberts quotes him, "If 84 percent of all American workers do not belong to a labor union, labor is not the problem," Rivera concludes. "Labor is irrelevant."

★ 12 ★

DISFRUTE

Hispanic Impact on the Multibillion-dollar Style, Fashion, Arts and Entertainment Industries

"Siento Hermosa." ("I Feel Pretty")

—Lyric translated into Spanish for a 2009
bilingual revival of *West Side Story*.

I n 1961, John Kennedy was president, Mickey Mantle and the New York Yankees ruled the world and I graduated high school. After the prom, my friend Frankie DeCecco, our dates and I drove his father's car in from Long Island and parked under the then elevated West Side Highway to make out. The fact that it felt dangerous was exactly the appeal. I was sick of feeling safe in West Babylon. Besides, Frankie, who had moved to Long Island from Greenpoint, Brooklyn, just two years earlier, had dared me. It was also a cheap date. At that time, the darkness around the docks was a spooky extension of adjacent Hell's Kitchen, where rival ethnic gangs were fighting for territory.

The musical *West Side Story* had finished its run on Broadway in 1960 and I never got to see it. In fact, the first play aside from high school productions that I ever saw was *Flora the Red Menace* with Liza Minnelli five years later. But the bare outlines of the plot were well-known and enticing enough to lure us to the West Side, because as we knew in real life, the Puerto Ricans were moving in on the Irish guys' territory, and the city's street power structure was in flux. Newspapers were filled with stories of lurid gang violence. As a wannabe tough guy, I found it alluring. Having been associated with both the Corner Boys and the Valve Grinders in high school, which were blue-collar, relatively harmless, suburban versions of the Sharks and the Jets, I felt an affinity with their swagger.

When the movie came out that fall, I saw it in the Bronx in the drive-in near Fort Schuyler and was both transfixed and a little put off. There was so much dancing and singing, and who knew Natalie Wood was Puerto Rican? (She wasn't; her birth name is Natalie Zakharenko.) Anyway, Anita (Rita Moreno of Humacao, Puerto Rico, who won the Best Supporting Actress Oscar) was the one I really fell for: more fire, less angst.

The musical retelling the whole Tony and Maria/Romeo and Juliet saga marked one of those cultural turnings of the tide in New York City history. By the time I got back in town to live here permanently in January 1966 after the University of Arizona and after working in clothing stores on the West Coast, the West Side of Manhattan had become an extension of El Barrio, another mostly poor Puerto Rican enclave where recently arrived families lived on the edge, balancing hope and despair, cultures clashed on the fringes, and only the lucky ones made it out unscathed. Tony and Maria wouldn't recognize the neighborhood today. The Puerto Ricans who replaced the Irish and Italians have themselves been replaced by yuppies and other upwardly mobile strivers. I don't think many even know the neighborhood as Hell's Kitchen anymore, not since Lincoln Center and the Metropolitan Opera moved in a few blocks uptown.

In March 2009 *West Side Story* was revived on Broadway and it is far grittier and more realistic than when actors Richard Beymer, Russ Tamblyn, George Chakiris and a chorus line of sleek dancers in brown-face makeup went jumping around in the original. Centrally, the violence between the ethnic white Jets and the Puerto Rican Sharks now feels visceral and real, especially the rape of Anita. "We don't treat them as lovable little thugs," Arthur Laurent, the ninety-one-year-old who wrote the musical's original book and the remake, told *The New York Times.* "We treat them as what they were then and what they are now."

More to the point of this essay, the Puerto Rican Sharks are all played by actual Latinos who speak many of their lines and sing their lyrics in Spanish. New York–born Lin-Manuel Miranda, who created the smash-hit musical *In the Heights*, tweaked and translated Stephen Sondheim's original lyrics, so when Maria sings "I Feel Pretty" it's now "*Siento Hermosa*" and it sounds like she really means it, as does the new Anita, fiery Karen Olivo, who is of mixed Dominican, Puerto Rican and Chinese descent, when she spits out "*Un Hombre Así*" (a.k.a. "A Boy Like That"). Leonard Bernstein would have loved the edginess of it.

The fact that the Sharks and the Jets are now separated by a barrier of language, as well as ethnicity, helps us understand the raw animosity between the groups. The Jets not only saw these newcomers as a threat to their neighborhood sovereignty; they were also different, other, and foreign. Their reaction was not much different from this letter sent to the *Chicago Tribune* commenting on a review of the revival.

"I don't understand the need to have many of the characters speaking Spanish, when 90 percent of any audience will not be able to comprehend what is being said. How does this improve or advance the experience of attending such a performance? It sounds like this was meant to attract the notice of critics, not the theater-going public. What is next? *The King and I* with characters speaking Thai? I have never seen *West Side Story* live, but look forward to the chance—but I'll pass on this version."

That complaint echoes that of those who dislike the availability of Spanish-language instructions at banks or from 411 operators. But it is trying to sweep back an inevitable trend toward acceptance of a multicultural ideal that is positive and uniquely American. To me, the new version of *West Side Story* is a tidy way to sum up how Latinos have evolved in the half century since I graduated high school in terms of the best of how we are portrayed in various media. When a production is conscientious without being tiresome or politically correct, the payoff is immeasurable. If only the trend were more widespread, because there is little doubt that overwhelmingly, Hispanics are still most often stereotyped as negative fringe characters: lazy, venal, dumb, dark and violent, or fit mostly for gardening, child care and housekeeping—not that there is anything wrong with those jobs; they are just not typically roles for the leading man or woman.

But with successful, sometimes spectacular actors like longtime heartthrob Antonio Banderas; *Battlestar Galactica*'s Edward James Olmos; Puerto Rico's brooding favorite son Benicio Del Toro, who most recently nailed a portrayal of Che Guevara; intense Javier Bardem, who scared the pants off moviegoers with his chilling role as the soulless assassin in *No Country for Old Men*; and gorgeous Penelope Cruz, to name just a few of those near the top of the game, things do appear to be opening up.

As Colombian-born (with a Puerto Rican father) John Leguizamo once said, "The human experience is the human experience, no matter what color, race, religion, whatever you are. It's the same damn thing, with different packaging. All the leading roles are opening up. You don't have to be a drug dealer or gang member, or the villain of a movie, or die in the first thirty seconds. You can last the whole movie."

I've known John for a long time and I am a big fan, especially of his live one-man shows. He did a Spanish-language film called *Crónicas* in which he played a tabloid reporter from Miami named Manolo Bonilla who tracks down a child serial killer in Ecuador. He told reporters that the character was modeled after me: "Geraldo Rivera is the only one that I can remember having that sort of power and that celebrity, and also that investigative reporter need to really find the truth and really sort of solve it. I mean, he was, to me he was a big idol earlier in his career when he was such a purist."

Although not sure of my purity then or now, I was flattered. But the bigger point is the burgeoning influence of Latinos on the entertainment world. The number of U.S. Hispanic TV households is approaching 12 million, and they are the only ethnic group to experience growth in the key eighteen-to-thirty-four demographic that advertisers covet. If your TV show is a hit among those Spanish kids, then your show is a hit period.

In December 2008 the highest-rated network television shows on Wednesday and Friday nights among those young adults were Spanish-language Mexican-made *telenovelas* on Univision: *Fuego en la Sangre* (*Fire in the Blood*), about two brothers tracking down the man who kidnapped their sister, and *Cuidado con el Ángel* (*Don't Mess with the Angel*), which, set in Caracas, Venezuela, follows the love life of a young woman who grew up an orphan. Again, those shows outrate competing shows on CBS, NBC, ABC and FOX in that key eighteen-to-thirty-five-year-old demographic.

Both shows are terrific examples of a genre that is one of Latin America's biggest exports to the United States and the rest of the world. They are wildly popular melodramatic soap operas rich with romance, intrigue, betrayal and deceit. My dad, who worked the rough early-hours shift in the kitchen of a defense plant, used to put the *telenovelas* on when he got home so he could hear Spanish being spoken and perhaps feel closer to his life back home in Puerto Rico.

There is another thing these popular shows do for Spanish-speaking and bilingual audiences in the United States and elsewhere (they are translated into various languages for countries around the world and are huge in Russia). Even more florid and flamboyant than our own daytime soaps, they are morality plays that act out the great and not so great social issues of the day, from upheaval to upward mobility, from lust to liposuction.

Those two mentioned above are tame compared to a Colombian show whose title ranks among the medium's most daring: *Sin Tetas, No Hay Paraíso* (*Without Breasts, There Is No Paradise*). That title is meant to be taken literally. The show is about a young prostitute who joins forces with drug bandits and other bad guys because she needs money to pay for the breast enhancement that she feels she needs to succeed in her chosen career, the world's oldest profession. "Johnny, help me; I'm desperate for those double-Ds."

A fascinating mystery is how they will translate "*Sin Tetas*" in the English-language version now that NBC has purchased this highly rated scorcher. NBC hopes *Tetas* follows *Yo Soy Betty la Fea*, which the fabulous actress and role model for millions of young Latinas Salma Hayek bought and turned into *Ugly Betty*, leading its star, America Ferrera, to crossover prominence, and the show to a fourth season on ABC.

According to Christopher Goodwin of the UK's *Guardian* newspaper, "It's not just *telenovelas* that are popular in America." After an in-depth review Goodwin was shocked to learn of the intense popularity of reality shows like *Bailando por un Sueño* (*Dancing for a Dream*), a Mexican-produced version of *Dancing with the Stars*; *Sábado Gigante* (*Big Saturday*) and *Don Francisco Presenta*, both variety shows that feature the kinds of acts Ed Sullivan used to present, everything from Elvis to the little doggy on the flying trapeze; *Cristina*, a Miami-based talk show featuring the Cuban-born hostess Cristina Saralegui, who can command every subject from AIDS to sex aids; and *Aquí y Ahora* (*Here and Now*), a kind of populist *60 Minutes*.

In February 2009 *CNN en Español*, which has become an important and objective source of news to and from the Spanish-speaking world, scored an exclusive interview with Venezuela's elected president, the erratically anti-American Hugo Chávez. Meanwhile, White House chief of staff Rahm Emanuel scheduled his boss, President Obama, for an early interview with the Telemundo network, saying, "We should have a conscious strategy of communicating through Hispanic media. It's one of the fastest-growing groups in the country. Telemundo is one of the most significant media outlets."

Our three-and-a-half-year-old, Sol Liliana, is enamored with *Dora la Exploradora* (*Dora the Explorer*), a public television show so effortlessly bilingual you don't notice until your little girl starts saying "*sube*" when she wants to jump, or "*abajo*" when she sits down. Regatón or Reggaeton is a variation of Jamaican reggae that has become a whole genre of Spanish music that started in Panama and found widespread prominence in Puerto Rico.

Seven-time Grammy winner and Cuban-born Gloria Estefan, who claims her 2009 Latin America tour was her last, has sold 90 million albums worldwide; perhaps more impressively, more than 25 million of them were sold in the United States. Why is she giving up the road? "We [with husband Emilio, cocreator of the Miami Sound Machine] have eight restaurants, three hotels: I am working on a third book and on films." Remembering the smash hit her friendly rival Jennifer Lopez had when J.Lo portrayed the late, great Tex-Mex singer Selena in the movie of the same name, Gloria is scheduled to play Connie Francis in a 2009 biopic titled *Who's Sorry Now?*

Then there is the brand-new study out that finds 38 percent of Hispanics are NASCAR fans. The study is called "Hispanic NASCAR Fans:

Breaking through to Deeper Engagement." "This was an extremely valuable and informative quantitative study for us," said Brian Moyer, NASCAR's managing director of market and media research. "There were a number of critical learnings that will inform our multicultural strategy and stakeholders going forward."

If NASCAR sees the future, every other potential business that craves success had better get on board this powerful gravy train before it leaves the station. The impressive U.S. Hispanic parade is moving. America doesn't just look different than it did for most of the last two centuries; it also shops, eats out, and is entertained differently. The nation's Great Progression is a two-way street. America offers opportunity; the new Americans offer their blood, sweat, tears, toil and money. A vast new market has opened, one that offers a powerful antidote to decline and recession. Commerce will be the lubricant to ease inevitable integration. It has always been so in a free country.

★ 13 ★

THE SPANISH REPUBLICANS
The Party of Lost Opportunity

"Y yo tambien voy a hablar un poquito en español." ("And I'm also going to speak a little Spanish.")

> —George W. Bush at a January 2000 press conference

"Neither in French nor in English nor in Mexican."

> —George W. Bush, declining to take reporters' questions during a photo op with Canadian Prime Minister Jean Chrétien, April 2001

"¿Mamá, por qué es el mentiroso todavía a cargo de la ley?" ("Mommy, why is the liar still in charge of the law?")

> —The testimony of Alberto Gonzalez before Congress, recast as a cheap *telenovela* set in Mexico City by Jon Stewart's *Daily Show*, July 2007

When former Maryland lieutenant governor and FOX News contributor Michael Steele became the first African-American chairman of the Republican National Committee, in February 2009 we joked on-the-air on *Geraldo at Large* that "now there are two of you [black Republicans], if you include your wife." Ha.

Fresh off their pounding in the November elections, in which the GOP received just 5 percent of the black vote and about 30 percent of the brown, Steele's election to head the RNC seemed a great first step toward reopening the Reagan/Bush GOP "big tent" that everyone from Karl Rove to the late Jack Kemp said they needed to have a shot at again becoming America's majority party.

Steele's political vision was a departure from the harshly conservative view that had cost the Republicans the presidential election by alienating Hispanics and other voters. And days after his election, Chairman Steele really showed his mettle when he went on CNN's now-defunct D. L. Hughley weekend show (it is defunct because CNN foolishly ran it opposite my show on FNC). Whether or not it was his intended purpose, Steele admonished, however mildly, no less a conservative luminary than talk show titan Rush Limbaugh. Steele was especially critical of Limbaugh's apocalyptic remark about the new president's prospects, Rush saying that he wished President Obama would fail, which seemed to sum up the sour old GOP's vision of life.

"Rush Limbaugh is an entertainer," Steele told Hughley in one of the frankest statements out of the mouth of a politician in a long time, not unlike an Italian prime minister criticizing the pope. "Rush Limbaugh— his whole thing is entertainment. He has this incendiary—yes, it's ugly. . . ." Steele's voice trailed off as if he understood that he had stepped off a bridge. Stop the presses. Go to confession. That was huge. While Steele's statement might not sound like a real ass-kicking, it was an unprecedented critique, given Limbaugh's fervent following among right-wingers. However they all worked to minimize it, it was major and will be long remembered.

When I watched the clip of Steele at his televised Thermopylae on YouTube, I applauded his courage, particularly since the statement followed similar remarks by other Republican critics of Limbaugh, who had later cravenly apologized when battered by conservative supporters of Rush. Then I was disappointed to hear that Steele too had peed his pants after Limbaugh rallied the old guard troops against him, the chairman telling the influential Politico.com Web site that he had telephoned Limbaugh to apologize on the air and that:

"My intent was not to go after Rush—I have enormous respect for Rush Limbaugh," Steele said in the telephone interview. "I was maybe a little bit inarticulate. . . . There was no attempt on my part to diminish his voice or his leadership. I went back at that tape and I realized words that I said weren't what I was thinking," Steele said. "It was one of those things where I was thinking I was saying one thing and it came out differently.

What I was trying to say was a lot of people . . . want to make Rush the scapegoat, the bogeyman, and he's not.

"I'm not going to engage these guys and sit back and provide them the popcorn for a fight between me and Rush Limbaugh," Steele added. "No such thing is going to happen. . . . I wasn't trying to slam him or anything."

It was sad. He was saying one thing while thinking the opposite. That may be why I got married all those times. And talk about your incredibly shrinking backbone. I think Limbaugh is a great talent. There are no accidents in his level of success. You make it that big because you have something going on. But as I said live on Sean Hannity's show in the fall of 2008, much to Sean's dismay, "Rush Limbaugh is like MoveOn.org. He is an ideologue. I don't believe anything either of them says."

I met him at a holiday party, and he's very charismatic. But he is the man who in May 2007 laid down "the Limbaugh Laws" on immigration, which included, "You have to be a professional or an investor, no unskilled workers allowed. If you're in our country, you cannot be a burden to taxpayers. And another thing: You don't have the right to protest. You are a foreigner: Shut your mouth or get out."

In May 2008, Limbaugh further estranged himself and fellow Republicans from Hispanics when he referred to Los Angeles mayor Antonio Villaraigosa as "a shoeshine guy," a reference to the mayor's rags-to-riches climb out of the barrio to city hall. As a lame statement it rates right up there with Limbaugh's wish that Obama fails. I shudder to think how he would describe me—although I usually don't shudder; I bite back.

"It was really, really ugly stuff that was out there," Danny Vargas, chairman of the Republican National Hispanic Assembly, told HispanicBusiness.com in the wake of the 2008 presidential elections. "It was just the ugliest side of bigotry and xenophobia and racism in our society, by a very, very small percentage of Republicans." And while Vargas specifically excluded Limbaugh from the ugly ones, he added that the things Limbaugh said "weren't necessarily helpful to the debate." Yeah, Danny, you might say that.

The assembly that Vargas heads, which had a much easier time under the administration of George W. Bush, has an informational Web site. To dispel doubts that the words *Republican* and *Hispanic* can coexist in the same sentence, the Web site has a charming category called "I am a Republican because . . . " ("*Soy Republicano porque . . .*").

The first platform reads, "I believe the strength of our nation lies with the individual and that each person's dignity, freedom, ability and responsibility must be honored." ("*Creo que la forteleza de nuestra nación yace en el individuo, y que la dignidad, libertad, habilidad y responsabilidad de cada persona deben ser honoradas.*")

It sounds better in Spanish, less hokey. At the risk of sounding disingenuous, though, because I'm not disingenuous, the pledge goes on to talk about equal rights, free enterprise, fiscal responsibility, limited government, innovation and values. But it doesn't mention immigration rights. Hello? Twelve million Hispanics and you don't mention the issue at all in your "Why I Am a Republican" section? That's like not telling where you went when you talk to your class about what you did on your Christmas vacation. It is not just changing the subject. It is rather a willful evasion of particular personal responsibility. There is no permissible reason for failing to pick a lane. For every Spanish person, Republican, Democrat, Independent or vegan, this is the defining issue. Firm, compassionate, friendly, patriotic immigration reform must be the goal. The site also doesn't mention gay marriage or abortion, but on those hot-button topics, Hispanics are as sincerely divided as Reagan Democrats. That's what the Great Communicator meant in 1979 when he said, "Hispanics voters are Republicans. They just don't know it yet."

Ahhh, the good old days before the Minutemen, the wall and the raids made people lose sight of the fact that our nation was built by immigrant entrepreneurs of all sorts. Those were the days when Bush came close to scooping Obama by four years and becoming the nation's first honorary Hispanic president. In 2004, after reaping almost 44 percent of the Latino vote, which for a Republican amounted to unprecedented support, the former Texas governor let the Latino community know he appreciated the favor by making several high-level appointments.

I've spoken earlier about Commerce Secretary Carlos Gutierrez, who turned out to be among Bush's most competent, enduring and least controversial appointments. Among the most important, though, was the elevation of Alberto Gonzales from White House Counsel to the Justice Department as the attorney general of the United States, the first Hispanic to be so honored.

Unfortunately, the appointment turned out disastrously, with Gonzales assuming in the public eye the role of torturer in chief, whose seemingly stubborn, evasive defense of warrantless surveillance, waterboarding and similar harsh interrogation techniques—among other, more political scandals—made him seem devoid of conscience or independence.

Still, in April 2007, amid a growing chorus calling for Gonzales's resignation, then Democratic presidential candidate and New Mexico governor Bill Richardson resisted, saying bluntly, "The only reason I'm not there is because he's Hispanic, and I know him and like him. . . . It's because he's Hispanic. I'm honest . . . I want to give him the benefit of the doubt."

Richardson's action at the time struck me as not only harmful to his own presidential aspirations, but also charming and naive. He was rooting for the ethnic home team and I appreciated the sentimentality of that. It was also a reminder of Richardson's more logical calls for Latino political and ethnic unity following the 1995 passage in California of noxious Prop 187, which denied public assistance and education to the children of undocumented immigrants, most of whom are Latino in the Golden State.

"We have to band together," Richardson said at the time. "And that means Latinos in Florida, Cuban-Americans, Mexican-Americans, Puerto Ricans, and South Americans. We have to network better. We have to be more politically minded. We have to put aside party and think of ourselves as Latinos, as Hispanics, more than in the past."

While I agree with the general need for the Latino community to coalesce to advance our shared priorities, backing Gonzales was a hard sell in summer 2007, as the Comedy Central show quoted above makes obvious. How can you support an attorney general who can be mocked with, "*¿Mamá, por qué es el mentiroso todavía a cargo de la ley?*" ("Mommy, why is the liar still in charge of the law?")

The wars in Iraq and Afghanistan were both going badly, weakening his boss politically. Worse, the attorney general's testimony that July before Congress about the apparent excesses of the Bush War on Terror seemed evasive and untruthful.

Just a week after his kind words of support, even Governor Richardson decided to cut him loose, saying, "I believe he should resign. I like the guy . . . he's a fellow Hispanic. He came up from very humble means. He's an able guy, but it's obvious that he wasn't engaged in his department and he couldn't answer the testimony in the Senate, and I waited until the Senate to make any view that he should or shouldn't resign. The Justice Department should be above politics."

So who is Alberto Gonzales? Once touted by myself and others as potentially the best candidate to become the first Hispanic-American justice on the United States Supreme Court, former attorney general Alberto Gonzales has instead seen his reputation in tatters, his career in shambles.

A victim particularly of the scandal concerning his role in firing several federal prosecutors, allegedly for political reasons, and the truthfulness or lack of it of his testimony about the role he played in instituting the government's secret eavesdropping program, General Gonzales could not find a job with a major law firm in Washington, D.C., at the time we spoke in January 2009. And he couldn't find a publisher for his memoirs. And as if he needed any more heartache, he had just stirred up another hornet's nest of criticism by telling the *Wall Street Journal* that he too was "a victim of the war on terror."

To add injury to insult, on the Saturday morning we were supposed to do a face-to-face interview, the former attorney general instead had to join me on the phone because he got whacked in the eye playing squash. At first I didn't believe him and thought he had concocted a bizarre excuse to evade the scheduled grilling; I asked him, "What's a Mexican doing playing squash anyway?" He didn't laugh, but since he apparently felt bad about my traveling down to the nation's capital from New York on a wild-goose chase, he agreed to do the interview over the telephone. I began kindly enough.

"So, how are you feeling, General?"

"Well, my eye is uh, swollen, and my face is a little sore, Geraldo. But I'm happy to be here with you."

Then it was time to get to the issues. "Let's start right off the top with your explanation of this kind of bizarre statement that you too are a victim of the War on Terror."

"I never said that I was a victim," he said, sounding exasperated and defensive. "What I was saying was that the criticism, the attacks, the bumps and bruises, however you want to describe it, that I took in connection with our efforts to secure America from further attack, really, it came with the job that I had. It's gonna invite criticism. And I accept that. I don't admire those who play politics with public safety or with national security issues, and to the extent that I got caught up in the political cross fire on these kinds of issues, I think that was unfair to me."

"But you have said, General, that mistakes were made. What mistakes did you make?"

"Wouldn't it be great, Geraldo, if we could all take back the mistakes that we made? I have testified to the mistakes that I have made, and all I will say with respect to those is that I learn from them, and my goal is to simply help others make sure that those kinds of mistakes don't happen again."

"But, General, was it a mistake specifically to fire those nine U.S. attorneys, specifically David Iglesias of New Mexico?"

"No, there was nothing improper from my perspective, and if you'd study the report that came out, they found no criminal wrongdoing by me."

That was true. The inspector general was critical of Gonzales, but stopped well short of saying that his conduct was criminal.

The former attorney general continued, "These are political appointees who serve their full four-year statutory time. They serve at the pleasure of the president so long as their removal is not for improper partisan reasons, for example, to interfere with an ongoing investigation. And there's nothing improper about the removal of these U.S. attorneys, and if you study the report carefully by the inspector general at the Department of Justice, it will confirm that I did not engage in any criminal wrongdoing with respect to either the removal or with respect to my testimony to the Congress."

"Let me ask you how you feel about the apparent, at least from the outside in, wreck of your public career," I asked, trying not to sound cruel.

"The criticism comes with this kind of position. You're gonna make mistakes, and if you think that the Obama administration and the next attorney general is not gonna make a mistake, then you're living in a fairytale land. It just happens at this level."

"Do you feel that you are a scapegoat? That you have been singled out as the one person to bear the brunt of the public responsibility for any excesses committed during the Bush administration?" I asked, giving him a way to put his plight in a historic perspective.

"What I will say is I accept full responsibility for the actions that I took. I don't think that I deserve some of the criticism and some of the treatment that I have received. I do deserve my good name back. I've worked hard in public service for thirteen years. I've done my very, very best to serve our country. And I take heart in the fact that, because in part, a very small part, because of my service, America has remained safe since 9/11."

But then I had to sum up the feeling of so many Americans, Hispanics particularly, who saw in Alberto Gonzales the wreck of promise.

"Coming from a dirt-poor Tex-Mex migrant family, you worked your way up all the way to Harvard, all the way to the Texas supreme court. There you were. You became an assistant to Governor Bush, then President Bush. People allege or maintain that rather than being an independent attorney general, a constitutional figure who heads the Justice Department, you became or continued in your role as consigliere to George Bush. His lapdog, his gofer guy that just did whatever political thing that was expedient for your boss, the president."

"I categorically reject that characterization. People conveniently forget that as attorney general, you wear two hats. You're the chief law enforcement officer of the country, and obviously you have to make sure that the laws are followed, and you have to prosecute wrongdoing, no matter if that wrongdoing is in the White House or in Congress or in the state house. But you're also a cabinet official. You're on the president's team. You have an obligation to support the president's policies and the president's priorities."

I persisted. "Yet, the reality is, you can't get a job with a major law firm. No big publisher will accept your memoirs. You are stained by the taint of these alleged excesses. And now a life once so promising appears, to put it mildly, to be without specific direction."

"As long as this kind of investigation sort of hangs over my reputation, it's sort of unrealistic to expect that I would assume a position in my other life.

"When it's all said and done, I think that everything will work itself out."

I hope things do work out for him. Call me crazy, but I believe that anyone who was in government on September 11, 2001, when the attacks came, lived in an altered state where responsibility for failing to keep the nation safe from Osama bin Laden weighed heavily. More personally, he was also caught in a grinder by loyalty to his longtime boss, which overwhelmed the objections he could have or should have made concerning Bush/Cheney policies regarding surveillance, torture, warrantless searches, habeas corpus and the politicization of the Justice Department.

But while most everyone else involved at the top of the Bush administration has moved on to comfortable political and economic afterlives, why is it only the Mexican guy who got left holding the bag?

That's the definition of a scapegoat, and because I believe that sincerely, I'm involved in rehabilitating his once promising career. Look for the former attorney general as a frequent guest commentator on *Geraldo at Large*. And remember Gonzales wasn't the only high-ranking Hispanic to take the fall for the team during the Bush years, or the last Latino to gain my perhaps misguided affection and loyalty based on his roots and family background. Remember Lt. Gen. Ricardo Sanchez, the scapegoat for everything that went wrong in Iraq? If I don't give these guys a break, who will?

But there's a cautionary tale in the stories of generals Sanchez and

Gonzales, a line that we Hispanics who get jobs from unlikely patrons must never cross, regardless of party affiliation or ideology. As with stories that affect national security, when issues impact *la raza*, the race, *la familia*, the *mishpokhe* (remember I'm half Jewish), we have the responsibility to be absolutely certain we believe what we are saying beyond even our usual professional level of candor, specificity, fairness and accuracy.

We must never take a position we don't believe, as a function of loyalty or gratitude to the boss, above personal principles. Yes, we are like other Americans, in that we appreciate those who respect and appreciate us, particularly if they put our family's meals on the table. But we can never say or do something we don't believe is responsible and accurate, just to please powerful friends or patrons. I'm not saying that either Sanchez or Gonzales did that; I'm just saying that in these difficult times accommodation is not what Hispanics need from their role models.

Also, there are some issues that, while not requiring a litmus test, do require deep, nonprejudgmental consideration by Republicans or others seeking Hispanic votes:

1. Discrimination and immigration are big deals to us. For fear of becoming tiresome and ineffective, we don't bring those issues up every day, but as with Jews and Israel, Italians and Italy, the Irish and Ireland, there is extreme sensitivity. There is also scorn for those who cavalierly talk trash about our home countries or even about undocumented workers from those countries whose names sound just like ours and who have mustaches similar to our own.

2. Even in these tumultuous times along the Mexican border, anyone whose idea of immigration reform is "enforcement only" has zero chance of winning our approval, ever. Zero chance, Democrat or Republican. Think devout Catholics and abortion. That is why the GOP lost. That is why the GOP will never win again in the current political era. Rush is wrong about Hispanics. If your idea of immigration reform or securing

the borders is sending the 82nd Airborne to El Paso or Nogales, don't even bother asking for our vote. You are looking for *Tío Tomás*—you're looking for Uncle Tom.

3. Hispanic-American citizens love this country and respect her institutions. And even in tough times, 91 percent of Latino immigrants still here despite the crippled opportunities of the Great Recession say there is much greater opportunity and optimism here than home. We love the military, the church, our parents, grandparents, children and grandchildren.

4. We are flamboyant and spontaneous but, at some level, instinctively conservative and traditional. Despite the phenomenal evolution of the thoroughly modern Latina, machismo is around, an unfortunate vestigial social throwback. That sometimes makes the male-female dynamic peculiar and slightly different from the mainstream, especially among newer arrivals, although not as different from the Anglo mainstream as, say, Muslims are, not that there's anything wrong with that. Furthermore, with acculturation and assimilation the cultural and civic differences eventually even out.

5. However much we are loyal and true Americans, like all immigrants—which really means all of us Americans, including descendants of the founding families—we miss "home" even if we never saw it. And as with all those who identify themselves as Irish-, Italian-, Japanese-, or whichever hyphenated American, we are sensitive to slights. Even in the case of Mexico's recent travails, we find exaggeratedly negative stories about these ancestral homelands to be unnecessary, inappropriate and enduring slights.

6. We are different from one another, but in nuanced ways. An advertisement or political pitch designed for, say, a Puerto Rican doesn't necessarily play among immigrants from the Dominican Republic or Cuba or Mexico, despite the fact those nations are relatively right next door to one another. But we won't hold it against you for trying to communicate. Unlike the stereotypical

French or snobby English or isolationist Americans or the Royal Spanish Academy, most Hispanic people are charmed when non-Spanish-fluent speakers try to *hablar español*. Spanish speakers treat non–Spanish speakers who try with affection and respect. We love you for trying.

7. Despite our regional or national differences, we are forging a common identity, and however far removed geographically or even racially we were when we began our American odyssey, we consider ourselves more alike than not. Moreover, that is an irreversible trend. There is a growing feeling, especially among the young, that we are on a common voyage. Politicians who try to make a narrow political calculation to appeal to, say, just first-generation Cuban exiles in south Florida are treading a dangerous path. Remember former presidential candidate Mitt Romney? He had it going until he decided that bashing illegal immigrants was his ticket to success in the race for the GOP nomination.

Those south Florida Cubans voted five to one for John McCain in the GOP primary. Those Latinos are why McCain was the Republican nominee, just as, nationwide, they are the biggest reason why Barack Obama is president.

Republicans can be angry and exclusionary, or they can be back on top. Remember what I proposed at the beginning of the book? Given the demographic realities of the United States, no party can succeed nationally if it attracts just a third of Latino voters. That is also specifically true on a state-by-state basis in a dozen crucial battlegrounds. Political sanity and self-preservation demand that those who would lead us understand that the world has changed—in a good way.

★ 14 ★

AFTER CASTRO

Relations with Cuba and Latin America in the Twenty-first Century

"I find capitalism repugnant. It is filthy, it is gross, it is alienating . . . because it causes war."

—Fidel Castro

"Condemn me. It does not matter. History will absolve me." (*"La historia me absolverá."*)

—Fidel Castro's reconstructed testimony at his trial for the raid on Moncada Barracks, October 16, 1953

"With what morality can the [U.S.] leaders talk of human rights in a country where there are millionaires and beggars, where blacks face discrimination, women are prostituted, and great masses of Chicanos, Puerto Ricans and Latin Americans are deprecated, exploited and humiliated?"

—Castro, World Communist Youth conference, July 26, 1978

"He's done some good things for his people."

—U.S. Secretary of State Colin Powell, April 26, 2001

W̲e waited for hours. The president had scheduled the dinner for around eight, and as was his custom Fidel Castro made his appearance well after midnight. When he came in he lit up the room. Though he was fifty-one years old, his sails were full of swagger and personality. In that incandescent moment I will never forget, I realized this guy was bigger than the Stones or the Beatles, all of whom I had already met and interviewed. Meeting Fidel helped me understand why the people still living on the island of Cuba tolerated hardship and diaspora. It was

July 1977, and as an ABC News reporter I got assigned to cover the return of Mary Walsh Hemingway to the home she shared with her late husband, Ernest, the writer and adventurer against whom we all measure our writing and our adventures.

Built in 1886 and set on twenty-two still-preserved acres of a former sugarcane plantation on a hill overlooking Havana, the ranch is called Finca Vigía ("Lookout Farm"). It is located just down the north coast from the town of Cojímar, Cuba, where Papa moored *El Pilar*, the legendary fishing boat he used to bring in tuna and swordfish. Historically more significant, it was where in 1951 he wrote *The Old Man and the Sea*, the little book about chance, character, death and glory, not to mention fishing.

Mary, his fourth wife, was determined to make a film about the joyously tumultuous time she spent there with her sporting genius, who wrote her when she was his new lover and just arriving for the first time: "When you come in by plane from Miami, I will be waiting at Rancho Boyeros airport . . . and we will go in the car across this beautiful country to our home."

El Comandante agreed to meet the woman who was Papa Hemingway's lover and, later, wife. Almost seventy, she seemed a historic figure herself to me then, and the dashing Castro could not have been more charming, either to her or to the rest of the room. He spent enough time speaking with my wife, Sheri, and me that I asked a couple of questions about what impact Jimmy Carter's bold move in giving the canal back to Panama would have on future U.S.–Cuban relations.

He essentially said it wouldn't hurt, and might even help if followed by a more rational policy toward his embargoed nation. I reported the statement on my show, and ABC's *World News Tonight* anchor Peter Jennings complimented me on getting the scoop, the first and only time Jennings did that in the fifteen years we worked together.

I returned to Cuba eight years later, sailing the *New Wave*, my old forty-four-foot Gulfstar ketch, there after parting company with ABC News in 1985. Otherwise out of work, I was making a self-funded documentary about sailing from New York to Los Angeles, and our first foreign port of call was to be Havana. As we were journalists, obtaining visas was a fairly straightforward process, even in those days long before President Obama's dramatic easing of travel restrictions against the Western Hemisphere's last communist nation. Relying on contacts made during our 1977 visit, we also managed to arrange the more complicated permissions necessary, both from U.S. security agencies like the Coast Guard and from the Cuban navy, to arrive by sailboat.

As we were departing Key West, I had one last conversation with our New York UN-based Cuban contact and at that point was given a specific offshore rendezvous point and an exact arrival time. Then I was given the even sterner admonition that we "had better be where you are supposed to be, when you are supposed to be there," and that we "had better have exactly who you said was going to be on board, on board."

After a stormy passage across the ninety-mile-wide Straits of Florida, which are still constantly being crossed in the opposite direction by so many Cuban refugees fleeing Castro in far less seaworthy vessels, we arrived at the offshore location in the early morning. Cuba was barely a smudge on the horizon, which was otherwise empty. Finally, after a wait of no more than thirty minutes, a fast patrol boat appeared over the horizon, charging toward us. On its foredeck a skinny young sailor who seemed about fifteen years old was nervously pointing what looked like a gigantic .50-caliber machine gun right at us.

The vessel slowed, and we were commanded over loudspeaker to follow ("*sígueme*"), and they escorted us into Marina Hemingway, the big public works project constructed by Castro's East German allies to attract sailing tourists. Built in the 1970s, it was already shabby and essentially deserted. We docked and, after a thorough search of our boat, were assigned a minder, an intelligence officer who stayed with us for the entire trip, almost never letting us out of his sight, and permitting filming only when he said we could.

What struck me on that second journey was how much shabbier everything seemed, from the obvious infrastructure stuff, like roads and bridges, to the seaside apartment buildings and high-rise hotels, even the famous show at the Tropicana Cabaret. It all looked worn out. Communism was like a melancholy dust lying heavily on everything and everyone, except maybe the party apparatchiks.

It was not just that the 1959 Chevys and Fords were that much older; it just looked like everything, including Castro himself, was fading under the press of years, the crushing U.S. embargo on spare parts, and lack of maintenance. Cuba wasn't just frozen in time; it was wearing out. What continued to impress me, though, was the pride expressed by the average Cuban in their health and education systems. Despite all that the country had endured internally and externally, Cuba's health care system was providing impressive universal care for even the poorest resident. It wasn't as brilliant as filmmaker Michael Moore protested in *Sicko*, his polemic on health care in which he had the audacity to drag ailing 9/11 Ground Zero rescue workers to Cuba to be cared for on camera, but it was exceptional, given the nation's poverty.

More than twenty years later, London's mayor, Ken Livingstone ("Red Ken"), was even more impressed. "What's amazing here is you've got a country that's suffered an illegal economic blockade by the United States for almost half a century and yet it's been able to give its people the best standard of health care, brilliant education . . . to do this in the teeth of an almost economic war I think is a tribute to Fidel Castro."

To see it is to understand the irrational and vindictive impact on the lives of ordinary people of the hard-line U.S.-Cuba policy, which, if anything, became harsher and more rigid under President George W. Bush, not that Bill Clinton did anything about Cuba that could be regarded as open-minded or helpful. In 2002 the United Nations' General Assembly—granted, a left-leaning organization—nevertheless voted to condemn the embargo by a vote of 173 to 3.

The dirty semisecret of this anomalous foreign policy is that it was not crafted by the White House, but by politicians catering to what used to be called the "Cuban exile" community in south Florida. The good news is that the political clout this group once wielded has been dramatically eroded in recent years. The hope is that the coming-of-age of a new generation of Cuban-Americans will advocate a more moderate position with a new president eager to break the policy of mutual unremitting hostility.

One of the old policy's new faces is Miami's conservative Republican congressman Lincoln Diaz-Balart, who was at the Latino Inaugural Gala in January 2009. He gave me a nervous but pleasant nod and then hurried away from my at-the-time live camera position, perhaps not wanting to complicate a gala evening with sticky questions about how and why the Sunshine State's Latino voters had rushed from the red side of the aisle to the blue, delivering Florida's twenty-seven electoral votes to Barack Obama.

Like his brother Mario, also a South Florida Republican congressman, Lincoln Diaz-Balart is a nice guy and an effective legislator whose family of patriotic public servants has done a noble job representing their community. But his presence at the gala reminded me of the new president's gutsy pledge to reassess U.S.-Cuban relations,

The tentative thawing of relations between the two archenemies brings the fascinating possibility that we will finally move into line with the rest of the world and recognize that no government is perfect, certainly not Castro's, and that if we can do business with countries like Russia and China, not to mention Kyrgyzstan, Tajikistan and virtually every other dictatorship in Asia and Africa, then we should be able to alter our onerous and antiquated Cuban embargo almost a half-century after it was imposed.

When President Obama specifically put lifting restrictions on travel and remittances for Cuban-Americans on the table, it brought into focus a central question. What, after all, is the reason to restrict travel to the island by U.S. citizens to begin with? We can go freely to Beijing or Moscow but not to Havana? Why, because a powerful lobby group is dictating our nation's foreign policy? Why were there caps on family members' financial remittances being sent back to the impoverished island when there are no similar caps on remittances by any other group to any other country, however repressive or totalitarian that country may be?

Erica and I also attended a second Latino-themed inaugural celebration of Obama's election, this one held at the ornate and historic (1910) Organization of American States Building near the White House, and hosted by a coalition of grassroots Latino community organizations and the U.S. Hispanic Leadership Institute. I had the opportunity to speak with numerous dignitaries and officials from various Latin American countries that night. Aside from celebrating the hope that Obama's election signified a change in America's herky-jerky policy toward Latin America, the sentiment was unanimous that the time had finally arrived for the United States to reassess its position vis-à-vis Cuba.

The new administration telegraphed its intention to at least move in that direction when during her confirmation process, the designated Secretary of State, Hillary Clinton, told Senator Richard Lugar (R-In.) in writing that "President-elect Obama believes that Cuban-Americans especially can be important ambassadors for change in Cuba." But when Senator Richard Lugar asked the secretary-designate about the possibility of taking Cuba off the State Department's "State Sponsors of Terrorism" list; of increasing cooperation with Cuba in fighting drug trafficking; and of developing cooperation around "energy security and environmentally sustainable resource management," Mrs. Clinton wouldn't go beyond indicating vaguely in her letter to the senator that "the new administration anticipates a review of U.S. policy regarding Cuba."

As you might expect, the old-guard hard-liners object to any easing of restrictions, but history finally seems to be passing them by. One bold step into the future would be the closing of the odious prison camp at Guantánamo Bay. If it gets done, as the president promises it will, the move would be a symbolic beginning for a new era between the United States and Latin America. Despite scaremongers who warn ridiculously of freed terrorists from "Gitmo" being dumped in American neighborhoods or malls near you, its creation was as big a mistake as turning a blind eye to the sadistic Abu Ghraib prison practices in Iraq.

Putting our POW camp in Cuba was an obvious shyster's ploy to circumvent the U.S. Constitution: an unseemly trick to negate the prisoners' right of habeus corpus—the right to a fair hearing on why you are incarcerated—which dates back to sixteenth-century England, and which became one of the pillars of our Republic. As Senator John McCain has often said, Guantánamo helps disparage our nation's international reputation and makes us look like "do as I say, not as I do" hypocrites and worse.

Despite the howls of protests from hard-liners, President Obama still seems committed to closing America's Devil's Island, although he has slowed the process to appreciate fully the alternatives for dealing with inmates who are considered threats to the United States or its interests. On a pragmatic level, now that Florida's Hispanic community has been leavened by non-Cubans, the new president is no longer beholden, as his predecessors thought they were, to that virulently anti-Castro exile/immigrant community, which has dictated and distorted U.S. foreign policy since the 1959 revolution destroyed life there as they knew it.

The prospect of shutting Guantánamo down and modernizing U.S.-Cuba relations was well—but cautiously—received even by the aged and infirm old lion himself. Castro wrote in his January 2009 *"Reflexiones"* column, "I expressed that personally I had not the least doubt of the honesty with which Obama, the 11th president since January 1, 1959, expressed his ideas but in spite of his noble intentions there remained many questions to answer."

Congress began the process of answering one of Fidel's questions when at the end of March 2009, Senator Byron Dorgan (D-ND) introduced a bill to end most travel restrictions on Americans visiting Cuba. A House version of the same bill had 120 cosponsors. According to the AP, Senator Dorgan said the embargo was a "failed policy that has failed for 50 years."

Calling President George W. Bush's policy toward Cuba a "humanitarian and strategic blunder," President Obama promised a new era of U.S.-Cuban relations when he pulled the trigger on ending travel restrictions in early April 2009. "I will immediately allow unlimited family travel and remittances to the island. It's time to let Cuban Americans see their mothers and fathers, their sisters and brothers. It's time to let Cuban American money make their families less dependent upon the Castro regime."

The common hope among at least those U.S.-based Latinos under the age of sixty is that Obama is unemotional and smart enough to know that punitive isolation is spite not policy. "If Obama were to cease the outdated strategic stalemate with Cuba that has locked U.S. bilateral policy toward the island in an obsolete time capsule, it would help herald a new dawn for U.S.–Latin American relations as well as improving badly frayed hemispheric ties," says the nonpartisan Council on Hemispheric Affairs (COHA).

A week after the president's announcement of lifting the travel and other restrictions and opening the door to telecommunications links with the island, in April 2009 it looked as if that "new dawn" was on the horizon. The apparent breakthrough came during the Fifth Summit of the Americas held in the Caribbean nation of Trinidad and Tobago, when there was a stunning, long-distance reaction to the Obama moves from the Cuban government.

As an unelected dictatorship, alone among the 35 nations in the Western Hemisphere, Cuba is not a member of the Organization of American States (OAS), and has therefore not been permitted to attend the summit since 1962. Nevertheless Cuban leader Raúl Castro, who took over for his brother in 2006, replied to the Obama initiative making an, exciting offer to sit down with the United States and to discuss "everything, everything, everything, including human rights, freedom of expression and political prisoners."

"That's a sign of progress," Mr. Obama said at a subsequent news conference, "and so we're going to explore and see if we can make some further steps."

But even as the Obama administration and Raúl Castro's government looked poised to start that exploration immediately, Papa Lion emerged from his den to growl his disapproval. Although always described as "ailing" and "infirm" 82-year old Fidel Castro had no trouble saying soon after the summit that President Obama had "misinterpreted his 77-year old kid brother Raúl's remarks. Fidel reminded everyone how difficult rapprochement will be when he wrote: "When the President of Cuba [Rául] said he was ready to discuss any topic with the U.S. President, he meant he was not afraid of addressing any issue. That shows his courage and confidence in the principles of the Revolution."

Fidel also seemed to go out of his way to insult the new president. Having previously said some positive things about Obama, now Castro accused him of "superficiality," and called on him to do more than the "positive, although minimal" changes announced, adding, "we need many others." In a later column posted online, he wrote, "Of the blockade, which is the cruelest of measures, not a word was uttered."

That sounded to me like Fidel was taking the whole process back to the Cold War freezer, but then Secretary of State Hillary Clinton put a positive spin on it when she spoke about our evolving Cuban policy a couple of days later with the House Foreign Affairs Committee. After first accusing Fidel of "contradicting" his brother Raúl's seeming openness, Secretary Clinton added that it shows "there is beginning to be a debate" inside Cuba about how to move forward with the new U.S. relations.

If that debate opens Cuba to the U.S. market, the economic system that Castro professes to loathe will help remake his tired nation. It will lead first to an open-closed mixed system like the Vietnamese and Chinese have now. That will gradually open under the press of capital and new ideas, and the process will accelerate after the Castros inevitably depart the stage. Cuba is a sleeping giant. It was long the Pearl of the Antilles for a reason. Cuba is huge; at 44,164 square miles it is about the size of Pennsylvania and more than ten times the size of my beloved Puerto Rico. There are 11.5 million Cubans (plus almost 2 million already here), and they are one of the world's most enterprising and competent people. Just look how they managed to survive the bungling Soviets, their own broken hearts caused by economic hardship and divided families separated by the Florida Straits and the ironhanded American blockade. It has vast potential for agriculture, tourism and commerce. On the other hand, there are things that we could learn from them, like how to make sure all people get the health care they need.

How President Obama handles our relations with Cuba and the rest of Latin America will be one of his biggest tests. It was not by chance that the first foreign leader to meet with President Obama was Mexico's Calderón, who came to Washington to press not only for assistance in battling border violence and critically needed immigration reform, but also the need for the United States to be engaged, if only for our own self-interest, in Latin America. "The more secure Mexico finds itself, the more secure [the] U.S. will be," said the embattled Mexican president.

As the Woodrow Wilson International Center for Scholars' Mexico Institute put it, "There are few countries, if any, which are as important to the United States as Mexico. We share more than just a two-thousand-mile border. Our economies and societies are deeply interwoven and what happens on one side of our shared border inevitably affects the other side." The institute points out that "over a tenth of Mexico's population now lives in the United States, and three percent of the U.S. population was born in Mexico." Mexico is also our third-largest trading partner, and the second destination of exports, accounting for roughly one-eighth of all U.S. exports.

Mexico needs an advocate in Washington. Under the Bush administration, the only legislation anyone in D.C. cared about was laws designed to keep Mexicans out of the country. Those cries were amplified in April 2009 when Mexico fell into the grips of the deadly swine flu epidemic that infected visiting Americans with the virus, spreading it here. Calls were raised to quarantine the entire country! Assuming the epidemic is contained with minimal global damage, the harsh focus will again be on immigration. It is so raw an issue that until Mexico's border violence erupted into a full-scale war it overshadowed the malignant trade that sends Latin American drugs, principally cocaine, heroin, methamphetamines and marijuana, into the United States in exchange for roughly $15 to $25 billion in cash per year and all the heavy weapons Mexican cartels need to massacre one another, not to mention the cops and soldiers trying to control them.

Hopefully the new president will follow through on his promise to readdress failed immigration reform, because, according to the institute, "no single issue would serve to create goodwill between the two countries than a comprehensive immigration reform in the United States, which would allow for the two governments to engage in discussions on a range of issues that are currently off the table including enhanced forms of security cooperation."

But with the still-weakened U.S. economy teetering on the brink of depression, immigration reform will prove to be a difficult proposition for the forty-fourth president. Indeed, by late June 2009 President Obama was putting the brakes on his campaign promise to make the creation of a pathway to citizenship for illegal immigrants "a top priority in my first year as president." While reiterating his eventual intention to pass some type of reform, it won't be a general amnesty, and it won't happen right away. He told a Latino prayer breakfast, "For those who wish to become citizens, we should require them to pay a penalty and pay taxes, learn English, go to the back of the line behind those who played by the rules." If I was a betting man, I would put the probable time for putting immigration reform back on Washington's front burner at 2011, when the president will again be looking to secure Latino votes ahead of the 2012 national elections, and, hopefully, after the economy has recovered from its current swoon. Even I can't blame the average Joe (not that plumber douche bag from Ohio, but a real working-class hero) who feels that this is not the time to add workers to the U.S. labor pool. Patient explanation that the immigrants enhance the economy sounds flat to folks who are recently unemployed. The new president has to explain how they are almost invariably taking the dirty jobs that Americans don't want. But if those dirty jobs prove to be the only jobs out there, the argument will not resonate.

And our hard times also encourage talk of rejecting the NAFTA treaty and embracing other protectionist trade policies that are sure to aggravate our strained relations with the continent, which already feels estranged and ignored. Hopefully, the tone changed following President Obama's bravura performance at the summit, which drew generally high praise from his fellow leaders, including Brazil's Luiz Inácio da Silva who said the meeting could mark the beginning of a new era between the U.S. and the rest of the hemisphere.

We have a lot of ground to make up. Our shunning of our neighbors to the south during our nation's late, lamented economic boom did not help. Over the Bush years, an unmistakable trend toward left-leaning governments in Nicaragua, Honduras, Bolivia and most notably in Venezuela has profoundly eroded our influence and ability to affect events, and is even undermining the legitimate commerce that should be encouraged to the mutual benefit of all of us in the New World.

Aside from Mexico, the dope trade is also severely undermining stability in crucial nations like Guatemala, Honduras and the traditional drug-producing Andean nations of Ecuador and more notably Colombia, the latter still the world's biggest cocaine producer despite a decade of intensive U.S. military aid. The danger of destabilization and anarchy in these countries is real, the violence primitive and widespread, and the negative impact on the United States is inevitable.

On issues from coordinating that fight to regulating migration and bolstering trade and tourism, Obama has a chance to stop South America from spinning out of the orbit of the United States and into the hands of radicals like Hugo Chávez.

Having spent a lot of time in Venezuela, from Angel Falls to the Margarita Islands, I can report that the nation's virulently anti-American president, Hugo Chávez, is an agitator who will take actions that do not benefit his own needy people, so long as what he does tweaks and undermines the United States. How else to explain his open invitation to the Russian navy to use of his country's ports and air bases? Why would he sign multiple arms deals with Russia worth nearly $5 billion at the same time his countrymen don't have enough to eat? And when it comes to the 1823 Monroe Doctrine, the principle that the United States will not condone any European country becoming strategically involved in the New World, Chávez has become a one-man wrecking crew.

"Chávez has been a force that has interrupted progress in the region," Obama said during the presidential campaign, although he added that he was willing to meet with both the Venezuelan and his Castro soul brothers. Chávez responded with typical bluster, saying, according to COHA, "Hopefully I am wrong, but I think Obama will be the same harmful influence as Bush."

But even the militant and paranoid Chávez provided a glimpse of something promising: that the exuberant optimism of U.S. Latinos so much in evidence during the president's inauguration also grips South and Central America.

"He is a man with good intentions; he has immediately eliminated Guantánamo prison, and that should be applauded," said the Venezuelan president, according to COHA. "I am very happy and the world is happy that this young president has arrived . . . [we] welcome the new government and we are filled with hope."

The ebulliently left-wing Venezuelan president finally met ours face-to-face at the April 2009 Summit of the Americas as the two men were lining up for their ceremonial entrance to begin the proceedings. Obama strode over to Chávez and introduced himself. Chávez seemed genuinely pleased, saying enthusiastically as they were shaking hands, "With this same hand eight years ago I greeted Bush. I want to be your friend."

"They shook hands in an historic greeting after several years of tension during the Bush administration, when relations between Washington and Caracas had deteriorated," said a release from the Venezuelan Communications and Information Ministry. Later that night President Obama joked to reporters that his reply to Chávez's greeting had been *"¿Cómo estás?"*

In a later, even more flamboyant gesture by Chávez captured by photographers and cameramen from around the world, the Venezuela president presented ours' with a copy of the book *Las Venas Abiertas de America Latina* (*The Open Veins of Latin America: Five Centuries of the Pillage of a Continent*). It was inscribed, "For Obama, with affection."

Written in 1971, the work by leftist Uruguayan author Eduardo Galeano essentially accuses the United States and other big powers of colonial exploitation of the region. But since it is written in Spanish, the new president didn't immediately grasp its content or what the gift was intended to mean. Saying that it was "a nice gesture. I am a reader," Obama later joked with reporters, "I thought it was one of Chávez's books. I was going to give him one of mine." But the man who got the last laugh was probably Mr. Galeano, the book's 69-year old author. The English version of *The Open Veins* shot from about 54,000th on Amazon.com to second place within 24 hours.

Shortly after giving Obama the book, Chávez took a more substantive, conciliatory step when he announced that he was naming Roy Chaderton, his nation's current representative to the OAS, to be his new ambassador to Washington. The post had been vacant since the mercurial Chávez kicked out the U.S. ambassador Patrick Duddy in September 2008. Giving Duddy just 72 hours to leave Venezuela, Chávez claimed to have discovered an American-supported plot by Venezuelan military officers to topple him. The Bush administration responded by immediately expelling Venezuela's ambassador to the United States.

Despite the possibility of restored, full diplomatic relations with Venezuela, conservative critics jumped all over Obama for what they perceived to be his fawning over Chávez during the summit. Former House Speaker Newt Gingrich tore into the president for bolstering the "enemies of America." Gingrich added on *Fox and Friends* the next day, "Frankly, this does look a lot like Jimmy Carter. Carter tried weakness, and the world got tougher and tougher, because the predators, the aggressors, the anti-Americans, the dictators—when they sense weakness, they all start pushing ahead."

I ran President Obama's reaction to the critics that Saturday night on *Geraldo at Large*, when with his customary cool during the press conference that capped the three-day summit, he said, "Venezuela is a country whose defense budget is probably 1/600 of the United States. They own Citgo. It's unlikely that as a consequence of me shaking hands or having a polite conversation with Mr. Chávez that we are endangering the strategic interest of the United States."

Even relatively hawkish Hillary Clinton understands the crucial need to reach out to Venezuela, Cuba and the rest of Latin America, saying on the eve of her own mission to the region in spring 2009, "We share common political, economic and strategic interests with our friends to the south, as well as many of our citizens who share ancestral and cultural legacies."

The former first lady is obviously a well-qualified, well-regarded person to be America's chief diplomat, and one who gets it when it comes to Hispanics, having just represented New York State in the U.S. Senate. But it is also true that most of the Latin American officials I spoke with during the inaugural festivities and later worry that Secretary Clinton will pay scant attention to the tumultuous region because she has her hands full with crises in more traditionally chaotic regions, like the Middle East, the Persian Gulf and South Asia.

There is also a sense of regret at the loss of New Mexico's effervescent governor Bill Richardson, whose nomination to be Barack Obama's Commerce Secretary was withdrawn after embarrassing disclosures concerning a state grand jury investigating whether Richardson's state administration improperly took campaign contributions from contractors who later got state work.

Had he been confirmed, Richardson would have been Obama's highest-level and most visible Hispanic appointee. As COHA noted, Richardson is a staunch advocate of free trade, who would have brought to the Obama administration "a wealth of knowledge and experience on Latin American issues." As COHA noted in its original (December 2008) response to his nomination, "Richardson is in touch with . . . hemispheric trends and could be of inestimable value to the new administration, in presenting a new face to the region and a definitive end to the fallow relations that Washington has had towards the region."

COHA went on to note that the appointment of our highest-profile Latino politician "certainly is good news for the region's self-esteem."

He was widely regarded as the U.S.'s informal Hispanic in chief, and no one has ever said Governor William Blaine Richardson III was shy or self-effacing. In his 2005 book *Between Worlds: The Making of an American Life*, he wrote, "I choose bold. I choose action. I choose what's right for the people. I choose to make a difference."

One of the most likable, larger-than-life figures in modern Latino history, the gregarious and deeply experienced Richardson possesses an undeniably impressive résumé. He served in the Clinton administration as both UN ambassador and Energy Secretary; he is a seven-term former congressman, who has often been called upon to represent this nation in tough negotiations with difficult-to-deal-with countries like nuclear North Korea. And when President Obama said he would make an "excellent economic ambassador for America in these difficult times," almost everyone agreed.

Richardson, whose mom is of Mexican descent, and whose Boston-bred dad was born in Nicaragua, shocked the political world when he abandoned the candidacy of Hillary Clinton to favor Barack Obama in the race for the Democratic nomination. That surprise move caused outspoken Clinton loyalist James Carville to label him a Judas. Since the job Richardson really wanted, Secretary of State, went to Hillary anyway, what went around came around for the New Mexico governor, even before the grand jury indicted anyone for anything in his home state.

The feeling was that Richardson's portfolio as Commerce Secretary would have included the specific brief that he would be in charge of our relationships in Latin America. With him out of the picture, the fear is that Obama's cabinet is "devoid of anyone with a strong focus on Latin America," as the Council on Hemispheric Affairs put it.

The man first named as Richardson's replacement at Commerce didn't go over too well. Vermont's Republican senator, Judd Gregg, was thought to be a fine man, but one who probably wouldn't know the difference between a taco and a tortilla. The person finally confirmed as Commerce Secretary by the U.S. Senate was former Washington governor Gary Locke, the first-ever Chinese-American to be chief executive of an American state. His appointment went virtually unnoted in Latin America.

The one Obama administration official the regional leaders believe could help by being "the right man to revive deeply flawed U.S.-Latin American relations" is White House counsel Greg Craig, who "has espoused the adoption of a multilateral approach toward Latin America and has spoken out in his calling for respecting sovereign regional governments of varying political orientation, an approach which could prove to be highly promising," said the authoritative Council on Hemispheric Affairs.

It is incumbent upon Hispanic American leaders and those of us in the media to remind Washington that the other nations of the New World will not automatically follow America's lead in issues regarding trade or security. It doesn't make much sense to foster democracy in Iraq when, through paranoia, arrogance or ignorance, we allow our neighbors to slide into an anti-American mind-set that pushes them into the willing arms of our enemies.

In a March 2009 interview on the grounds of La Fortaleza, the 476-year-old official residence in Old San Juan, the island's popular young Republican governor, Luis Fortuño, talked about how Puerto Rico could help moderate the current crisis with Mexico and help heal relations with the rest of Latin America.

"We are the third border, as I call it, because when you come to Puerto Rico, you're in Iowa the next day. So it is an important issue here as well. We need to reach out so that we can contribute and collaborate with our friends, and they are friends, in the region. There are others who are not so friendly. And we have national security issues that have to be addressed aggressively. We Puerto Ricans as U.S. citizens have a unique situation where we can be helpful to the nation to bridge the gaps" with Latin America. "To a great degree, I think we can do more and we should do more in the sense of partnering with Mexico to secure the border, to make sure that our economies are stronger and do better on both sides of the border."

Right now, our biggest enemy in the region is neither Chávez nor Castro but the drug traffickers whose violence has alarmed the United States to such an extent that calls for enhanced border security up to and including military deployment along our southern border will probably prove irresistible, however ridiculous. Secretary Clinton tried to soothe Mexican fears that we were militarizing the border when, for the first time for a high-ranking American official, she acknowledged that the United States' insatiable appetite for drugs was fueling the traffic and that America was the principal supplier of the heavy weapons Mexicans were using to murder one another and whatever innocent person was in their path. Her point was that there is enough blame and responsibility to go around.

"The criminals and kingpins spreading violence are trying to corrode the foundations of law, order, friendship and trust between us that support our continent. They will fail," Hillary told Mexican Foreign Relations Secretary Patricia Espinoza during her spring 2009 visit. "We will stand shoulder to shoulder with you."

To borrow from Franklin Roosevelt, what I fear is fear itself; that the legitimate as well as the exaggerated concerns about spreading border violence will infect every other aspect of America's relations with our neighbors to the south. Even legislators who were open to the idea of modernizing immigration reform and easing cross-border life are caught up in the sound and fury of the war next door.

"I don't think it's enough," said Connecticut's Senator Joe Lieberman, loudly declaring an Obama plan to send more federal agents to the Mexican border inadequate. "The danger here is clear and present. It threatens to get worse."

Say it ain't so, Joe.

★ 15 ★

BÉISBOL

How Latinos Took over America's Favorite Pastime

"Pitch me inside, I will hit .400. Pitch me outside, and you will not find the ball."

—Roberto Clemente

"*Béisbol* has been berry, berry good to me."

—Garrett Morris, *Saturday Night Live*

The body had still not been recovered when I got to Puerto Rico on January 2, 1973, on assignment for *Eyewitness News*. In fact, frantic searchers never found the remains of Pittsburgh Pirates All-Star right-fielder Roberto Clemente, whose mercy mission to earthquake-ravaged Nicaragua had ended tragically two days earlier, when his charter DC-7 crashed off Isla Verde beach on New Year's Eve. The most famous is-land athlete ever, maybe the most famous Puerto Rican ever, the beloved Clemente perished along with four other men when their overloaded and outmoded prop cargo plane went down, plunging sharply nose-first into the ocean shortly after takeoff from adjacent Luis Muñoz Marín Airport. It is just a tiny measure of the popularity of this native son, and his revered importance to New York's huge Puerto Rican community, that a local reporter was sent to cover the death of an out-of-town ballplayer. I think it was my first overseas assignment.

The beach closest to the presumed crash point was still crowded with mourners bearing black-and-gold replica Pittsburgh Pirate jerseys or holding aloft pictures or signs bearing the Great One's name. Like Pitts-burgh, storefronts and balconies in stricken San Juan were also draped in black wreaths adorned with the number 21. Candlelit vigils had been staged both previous nights, and the island's brand-new governor, Rafael Hernández Colón, declared the commonwealth officially in mourning.

Charismatic and highly regarded by everyone, perennial MVP Clemente had led the Bucs to their 1971 World Series victory over Frank Robinson's powerful Baltimore Orioles just fourteen months before. Facing four different Orioles twenty-game winners, the electric outfielder from nearby Carolina, Puerto Rico, batted twelve for twenty-nine in the Series, a .414 percentage, including a monstrous fourth-inning home run over the wall in left center, which broke a scoreless game-seven tie. In his last regular-season at bat in September 1972, he doubled, the hit being the milestone three thousandth of his career.

Clemente's self-arranged rescue mission had an urgency born of reports of dire need made worse by anarchy in ravaged Managua. Only relatively meager relief supplies had so far arrived, and much was being looted. "Nobody steals from Roberto Clemente," he said, explaining to his wife, Vera, and others why he was going along with the relief supplies he had organized and, in doing so, ignoring warnings of risks about unstable weather and an old airplane not up to the task.

But, already delayed eighteen hours, the aircraft was the only one available. So it took off, crammed with sixteen thousand pounds of supplies for the stricken Central American nation, whose capital city of Managua was still in smoldering and chaotic disarray following a magnitude-6.2 earthquake that killed five thousand, wrecking the poorly built town and leaving 250,000 homeless. FAA officials would later blame poor aircraft maintenance and shifting cargo, as well as overloading, for the disaster that claimed our greatest sports hero. Clemente was the first Latino player inducted into the Hall of Fame, and he obtained the honor faster than any other ballplayer ever had.

While Latinos had been playing Abner Doubleday's game for a century, in life and certainly in heroic death Roberto Clemente is our Jackie Robinson. In fact, there is even a movement to have his number, 21, retired by all teams the way major-league baseball did singularly for Jackie Robinson's number, 42, on the fiftieth anniversary of his 1947 debut. Clemente won four batting titles, led the Pirates to championships in 1960 and 1971, and was one of the first big-time jocks to believe that if you could help someone else and chose not to, you were wasting your time on earth.

He may not have broken any color lines, like the all-time Dodgers great, but Clemente was an amazing role model during his magnificent eighteen-year career, especially for fellow Latinos, who now make up 30 percent of the Major Leagues' ballplayers. That represents a sea change that needs context. Blacks, who dominated baseball for decades after Jackie Robinson, are now just 8.4 percent of professional baseball, down from a high of 19 percent in 1995.

Latino roots run deep into baseball's history. Beginning in 1871 a Cuban named Esteban Bellan played for the Troy Haymakers in what was the predecessor of the National League. And that was even before the convulsions of the Spanish-American War wrested control of Cuba from Spain. A Colombian named Luis Castro from the inland city of Medellín played for the American League Philadelphia Athletics starting in 1902.

As their presence continued gradually to expand, it wasn't until the post–World War I era that the pace of Latino recruitment quickened. From one or two players per team, though, today at least a quarter or more, depending on the team, is Latino. They are by now so dominant in the Major Leagues that their ethnicity is really most noteworthy during events like the World Baseball Classic, when they surprise us by lining up in the unfamiliar colors of their home or their parents' home countries. Hispanic ballplayers have become as dominant in baseball as African-Americans are in professional basketball, so essential to the sport that it would not exist in its current form without them.

Without the Dominicans like José Reyes, Alfonso Soriano, Cardinals slugger Albert Pujols, Alex "A-Rod" Rodriguez (with or without tabloid rub-downs), the Red Sox' David "Big Papi" Ortiz, Angels slugger Vladimir Guerrero, or the once best pitcher in the "bigs," Pedro Martinez, professional baseball today would be unrecognizable; or without the Panamanians, like Astros outfielder Carlos Lee, Phillies catcher Carlos Ruiz, the

Rockies' Manny Corpas and the incomparable Yankee closer Mariano Rivera; or how about those Puerto Ricans, like the twin powerhouses Carlos Beltran and Carlos Delgado of the Mets, the incomparable Iván "Pudge" Rodriguez, Pedro Feliciano, who works out of the bullpen and ex-Yankee Bernie Williams.

In a town like Los Angeles, as one example, Mexican-born pitcher Fernando Valenzuela, with his startling windup and wicked corkscrew pitches, filled Dodger Stadium with a whole new cadre of Hispanic fans back in the 1980s, just as Dominican-born Manuel Aristides Ramirez Onelcida, better known as Manny Ramirez, with his trademark baggy pants, cascading dreads and lethal bat, is doing today (following a fifty-game 2009 suspension for violating drug policy).

According to Scarborough Research, 62 percent of all U.S. Hispanics are fans of major-league baseball, compared to 59 percent of the total population. Founded in 2001, the Spanish Beisbol Network broadcasts games of the Oakland A's, the Boston Red Sox, the Philadelphia Phillies and the Washington Nationals on the radio. Both New York teams, the Mets and the Yankees, broadcast in Spanish. The Yankees' Spanish play-by-play man, Venezuelan Beto Villa, is an expert in the most mundane details of Latino baseball life. "Latinos have overcome many obstacles and continue moving forward in this game," Villa told MLB.com's Jesse Sanchez. "The future is going to be more and more about Latino baseball players. That's more work for me to keep the stats updated, and then you have to see how they compare to the past. But it's a pleasure to do it."

Bésbol Mundial, which launched in 2005, is a Spanish-language magazine that focuses on the dominance of Latino players in baseball. Perhaps surprisingly, it claims 26 percent of its readers are women. In ballparks throughout the majors, teams routinely have departments devoted to Latino relations. You can call 1-800-BEISBOL for updates on statistics, personalities, and special events. The San Diego Padres market to fans on both sides of the nearby Mexican border, with celebrations of Hispanic Heritage Month, Mexican Opening Day, Fiesta con Los Padres, Padres Caravana, youth clinics and FanFest.

Fantasy baseball, with its virtual big leagues, has an all-Latino version of the game, and adherents find it shockingly easy to fill the nine positions on the field and in the batter's box with the best of the best. It is as easy to field an all-Latino dream baseball team as it would be to put an all-black NBA team on a basketball court (many actual teams already do), or NFL pro-football field (some teams are close), or an all-white team on the NHL ice.

Latinos dominate big-league baseball. There is a certain grace to these players, a blend of power, skill, speed and a love of the game that is born and bred of a century-old tradition. The fever for baseball began deep in the nineteenth century, but our first superstar was a Cuban-born pitcher named Adolfo "Dolf" Luque, who in 1923 compiled an awesome National League–best 27–8 record for the Cincinnati Reds; and he did it while handcuffing batters in six shutout games and with an ERA of just 1.93. As a perhaps unfair comparison, George Herman Ruth had a 9–5 record and a 2.97 ERA in 1919, his last full year pitching for the Boston Red Sox, before going to the Yankees (and home run hitting immortality) as Babe Ruth.

Lucky Luque's overpowering success sent a message south of the border and across the Caribbean basin that "we can play this game. We can win." And having happily caught baseball fever, dads throughout the region began giving their kids homemade gloves, bats and balls as rough, dusty baseball diamonds were scratched out of flat fields and lots everywhere, there as intensely as here. Throughout that arch of Latin countries nearest the United States, baseball clinics, Little Leagues, junior leagues, school teams, amateur, semipro and professional leagues were created. *Béisbol* became as Latino a passion as sex and politics.

As radio became gradually available, U.S. game broadcasts were followed religiously, especially *los Yanquis*. Remember how Santiago, in Hemingway's classic *Old Man and the Sea*, followed the Yankees with hand-me-down newspapers and scratchy radio broadcasts from far-off Miami? Santiago idolized the immortal Joe DiMaggio, whose father, according to Santiago, was a fisherman like him, and who had himself overcome adversity to become one of baseball's premier players.

Baseball success was early on seen as a Latino ticket to social mobility. In 1933, fourteen years before another legend, Jackie Robinson, shattered the color barrier with Branch Rickey's Brooklyn Dodgers, the Boston Red Sox signed an outfielder named Mel Almada, the first Mexican-born player in the Major Leagues. Cuban-born catcher Miguel Ángel González became the first Latino to manage a big-league team, helming the St. Louis Cardinals in 1938 and 1940. In 1939, pitcher Alejandro Carrasquel of the Washington Senators became the first of a long line of Venezuelans in the bigs. In 1942, Hiram Bithorn became the first Puerto Rican pitcher when he threw for the Chicago Cubs.

As baseball boomed in the postwar era, major-league scouts had spread throughout the region. White Sox shortstop Alfonso "Chico" Carrasquel (Alejandro's nephew) in 1951 became the first Latino All-Star. Chico then turned the Cleveland Indians on to another Venezuelan and future Hall of Fame base-stealing master, Luis Aparicio, who was the first Latino to be selected Rookie of the Year. Mexican-born Beto "the Aztec" Avila helped make the Cleveland Indians champions in 1954 when he hit .341 and became the first Hispanic to win the American League batting crown. The scouts signed the first Panamanians in 1955, Hector Lopez to the Kansas City Athletics and pitcher Humberto Robinson to the Milwaukee Braves. The mighty Dominicans came next in 1956, when the New York Giants signed infielder Osvaldo Virgil.

With the odious color line finally broken, the big leagues could recruit Latinos of all races. One of the best was Cuban-born former Negro League standout Saturnino Orestes Armas Miñoso Arrieta, a.k.a. "Minnie" Miñoso, a.k.a. "the Cuban Comet," a.k.a. "*el Charro Negro*" (when he was playing in Mexico) and finally "the Black Cowboy." When he donned his Chicago White Sox uniform after a stint with the Cleveland Indians, he was considered the first black ever to do so. Minnie later endeared himself to White Sox fans when he went eight seasons in a row in which he batted over .300 and stole over thirty bases, both stats considered the benchmarks of excellence. As an ancient reporter who relies heavily on resilience, I most admire Minnie for being the only player in baseball history to have played professionally in seven different decades. My claim to fame is that I have been made fun of by *Saturday Night Live* in four different decades, but that is a story for another day.

In the 1970s and 1980s the steady stream of Latino recruits became a gusher. Hall of Fame pitcher Juan Marichal of the Dominican Republic intimidated batters with his high kick before delivering. Brothers Matty, Felipe and Jesús Alou, also from the D.R., once batted in consecutive order in a game at the old Polo Grounds. Cubans Luis Tiant and Miguel Cuellar each had four twenty-win seasons. Panamanian-born mighty Rod Carew won seven batting titles, had perennial starts as an All-Star and has a place in the Hall of Fame. And then came Venezuelan David Concepción, Dominican Manny Mota, and Tony Perez, the latter the heavy hitter and big cog in the scary Cincinnati Reds' "Big Red Machine."

By the end of the 1999 season, nine of the top ten hitters in the American League were Latino. They were 25 percent of all major leaguers and growing, and according to Marcos Bretón, author of "Fields of Broken Dreams: Latinos and Baseball" in *Colorlines* magazine, most of them "come from overwhelming poverty, a reality that Major League Baseball avidly exploits." Bretón goes on to describe how many All-Star players from Latin America—he profiles Oakland A's shortstop Miguel Tejada—were coming out of destitute barrios, where baseball is the only ticket out of Dodge, and how they were being signed for bargain-basement rates. In Tejada's case, he was acquired by the Athletics for just two thousand dollars.

By comparison, "Tejada's white American teammate, Ben Grieve, received a $1.2 million signing bonus." Bretón's point is that there is no equity in baseball recruiting, which reminds me of Tom Hanks playing a baseball manager in *A League of Their Own* telling his shaken female ballplayer that there is no crying in baseball.

Breton's main point is that MLB has a "boatload mentality." The scouts sweep into towns and villages and buy up all the available Latino talent, pay them next to nothing, like two or three thousand dollars, and have them tied up for low pay during their first years of contract life. Like Sammy Sosa, the man who battled for the championship in one of the most epic

Home Run Derbys ever—Sosa eventually lost to Mark McGwire. But Sammy was the first major leaguer to hit sixty-five home runs, although McGwire later passed him, en route to seventy. Barry Bonds would soon steal their pyrrhic honor with seventy-three before they were all tarnished by the spreading steroid scandal. In any case Sosa had been signed into the bigs in 1986 for just thirty-five hundred dollars, which Bretón points out was the exactly the same amount the Dodgers paid in 1946 to sign Jackie Robinson.

There is also the fact that most of those poor chumps who signed for the short money were left stranded and unemployed, never having been signed by the majors. So what? At least they had some time out of the purgatory Bretón describes. They had a shot at the big time, and that is special, and Miguel Tejada makes a lot more now than any other resident of the "destitute barrio" described in *Colorlines* magazine. And dreams are good things to have for would-be major leaguers everywhere.

By the way, in March 2009, the Houston Astros shortstop was sentenced to a year of probation for misleading Congress about the use of performance-enhancing drugs. Standing before the federal judge he said that he took "full responsibility for not answering the question," and apologized to Congress, fans of his sport, "and especially the kids." The five-time All-Star and 2002 American League MVP became the first high-profile player to be convicted of a crime stemming from baseball's steroid era. According to the Associated Press, "He was sentenced at the same federal courthouse where a grand jury has been meeting to determine whether seven-time Cy Young Award winner Roger Clemens should be indicted on charges of lying to Congress about whether he used steroids and human growth hormone."

Whether it was from "boatload mentality" among recruiters or the sheer skill of the players, by 2003, Latinos were the biggest thing in baseball. Alex Rodriguez ruled the world. He hit forty-seven homers, won the league MVP and was about to become a New York Yankee for about one quarter of a billion dollars. Albert Pujols of the St. Louis Cardinals was RBI king and player of the year. Sammy Sosa and Rafael Palmeiro reached and passed the five-hundred-career-home-run mark; not to mention

Pedro Martinez, and Mariano Rivera, the latter of whom was and is the best reliever of the modern era, and about 270 other Latino ballplayers from Puerto Rico, the Dominican Republic, Mexico, Cuba, Colombia, Nicaragua and Venezuela.

Imagine: If they signed 275 ballplayers, how many in total did they recruit and ship to the States to be evaluated? They must be emptying whole villages. Whatever, I think it is great and I wish them all the best. I also wish the word *steroid* had never entered the sports lexicon. Then you wouldn't have it on your mind every time you talked baseball.

As the number of Latino players continued to climb, there was some friction in the clubhouses, not to mention other funny business, but young men are especially designed for that funny business, so most of their antics go unjudged. When he wrote *Ball Four* in 1970, my old *Eyewitness News* colleague Jim Bouton made us immune to all scandal except chemical.

Except if it's A-Rod. Alex has had an exceptionally bad time since he got ratted out by fellow baseball great José Canseco, who, before Danny Bonaduce fought him to a draw in a celebrity boxing match, really was a terrific baseball slugger during those years with the powerful Oakland Athletics. To promote his radioactive 2005 book, *Juiced: Wild Times, Rampant 'Roids, Smash Hits and How Baseball Got Big*, Canseco hinted that he was going to give up A-Rod for steroid use. Then A-Rod lied to Katie Couric, and took the plunge into the tabloid world with the hooker in Canada, and Madonna, and the divorce and all the rest, ultimately confessing to steroid use, which I'm sure was a total pain in the butt, but, at $28 million per year, not as bad as it could be.

The perils of celebrity notwithstanding, the rise and dominance of Latinos in the majors set off some deep feelings among some of the other players. I always liked Gary Sheffield when he was with the Yankees. I'm delighted that the Mets signed him for 2009 and I cheered wildly when he hit his 500th home run, only the twenty-fifth major leaguer to reach that plateau. But Gary set off a bomb when he was still in Detroit when he suggested to a reporter for *GQ* that the reason there were more Latinos than blacks in baseball these days is because Latinos are easier to control.

"I called it years ago. What I called is that you're going to see more black faces, but there ain't no English going to be coming out . . . [It's about] being able to tell [Latino players] what to do—being able to control them," Sheffield told *GQ*.

"Where I'm from, you can't control us. You might get a guy to do it that way for a while because he wants to benefit, but in the end, he is going to go back to being who he is. And that's a person that you're going to talk to with respect, you're going to talk to like a man. These are the things my race demands. So, if you're equally good as this Latin player, guess who's going to get sent home? I know a lot of players that are home now can outplay a lot of these guys."

That surly shot summed up the worst of the reaction to the Latino surge in baseball. Ozzie Guillen, the razor-sharp, ever-hustling Venezuelan shortstop who went on to become the first Latino manager to win a World Championship, with the Chicago White Sox in 2005, and who can be volatile to say the least, answered Sheffield with a theory of his own, telling the *New York Daily News* that "I guarantee that Latin American people play more baseball than any people, because that's all we have. You have more people playing baseball in Venezuela or the Dominican than anywhere, so there are going to be more players from there.

"It's not that they can control us; maybe when we come to this country, we're hungry," he told the paper, which reported that blacks were only 8.5 percent of major leaguers, the lowest in twenty years. "We're trying to survive. Those guys sign for $500,000 or $1 million and they're made. We have a couple of dollars. You can sign one African-American player for the price of 30 Latin players. Look at how many Latin players have won Cy Young or MVP awards the last couple of years, how many Latin players have been in the All-Star Game; it's quantity and quality."

I don't know if Sheffield was all right, part right or flat wrong. But it seems that Ozzie laid it out in sensible terms. There is an enormous amount of human capital in Latin America: talent, energy, ambition, commitment. That's why Latinos have been berry, berry good for baseball. It is an industry that has treated at least the Latinos who make it with respect. And importantly, it has given Latinos opportunities—even to become general managers, as with Omar Minaya, first of the Expos and now of the Mets, and owners, like Mexican-bon Arturo Moreno, owner of the Anaheim Angels.

The bottom line is that as owners, managers, coaches, players and fans, Latinos are playing an essential role in this multibillion-dollar industry. With so much focus on Hispanic gaps and deficiencies, it is comforting to have an area in which Latinos already so clearly excel and rank among the best in the world. I wish baseball were peanut butter that I could spread around to every other aspect of community life.

★ 16 ★

MUTTS LIKE US

The Impact of Intermarriage on Latino Political Power

"When are you going to start popping out some Sorta-Ricans?"

—Asked of Debra Messing, a high-powered Jewish executive married to the equally high-powered Latino lawyer played by John Leguizamo in *Nothing like the Holidays,* 2009

For me the really funny thing about that line in John Leguizamo's charming holiday movie is that it is followed by an actor who uses me as a precedent-setting "Sorta-Rican." An uncomfortable afternoon speaking engagement can illustrate the complication that reality, "Sorta-Rican," represents.

There was a good crowd at the midday seminar sponsored by the Hispanic Ad Council in November 2008 at the Museum of Broadcasting in Manhattan. The topic was the media and Hispanics, the audience was scores of mostly Latino twenty- or thirty-something ad company executives, and I had accepted the invitation as part of a personal crusade to enlist as many fellow-thinkers as possible in a campaign to keep the issue of immigration reform alive.

There were two specific goals I had in mind. First and more immediate was to pressure the federal government into stopping its obnoxious workplace raids by immigration authorities. In the year since the Kennedy/McCain reform legislation died in Congress, the raids had been spreading terror in the migrant community and were impacting the Hispanic community disproportionately.

Families were torn apart, allegations of abuse against incarcerated

233

deportees became widespread, and for the first time in a long time, entire towns were feeling the tremors of being targeted by the immensely powerful apparatus of federal government or hypereager local sheriffs like Phoenix's notorious hard-ass Joe Arpaio.

My second and obviously more sophomoric goal in doing a round of speeches at that time, during the last days of outgoing president George W. Bush, was to help convince him to pardon every immigrant here illegally, if their only crime was their mere presence in the United States. It would have been a parting gift to Latinos, a group that had given him extraordinary political support, and the move would have helped burnish his tarnished exit image among liberals.

It never happened. The deeply unpopular forty-third president chose to ignore immigration reform, once his old favorite issue, leaving office instead as the man who presided over America's economic collapse.

But that afternoon of the media seminar in October 2008, Bush was still president and the election was not yet decided. I spoke emotionally about the need for the community to come together in November and punish the candidates at the federal, state and local levels who created an odious anti-immigrant climate so potent it bent John McCain's principled position and even scared the lame-duck president away from his own previously stated preference.

I clenched my fists and exhorted the audience to get up and do something. Following up, and feigning innocence, the female moderator, who had the charisma of a lemon, asked what she obviously had prepared as her ambush question.

"Geraldo, are you even Hispanic?"

I don't want to sound like an asshole, but I was steamed. My response was to turn to the audience and essentially ask them, "How dare she?" indicating the woman with a contemptuous nod of my head. Then, after briefly chronicling the history of my family's unique blend, I went on, getting angrier about being a Latino community icon blah, blah, and about the need to close ranks against those who would divide us by some test of racial/ethnic purity.

There was a time when the question would have hurt instead of infuriated me; when the charge of not being Puerto Rican enough would have set me back on my heels. Every half-breed suffers that insecurity at some time in his or her life. Barack Obama did, as he writes eloquently about not being black enough for some South Side Chicago activists. His was an experience similar to my own back in 1968 through 1970, when I had to convince the activist Young Lords that I was Puerto Rican enough to be their lawyer and mouthpiece back in the days of demonstrations and sit-ins.

The insecurity of mutts like us is the classic consequence of intermarriage. At some point in almost all our lives, we have to choose sides. For me that choosing came in 1968, when I grew my now forty-year-old mustache (winner of the 2008 ESPN "All-Time Great Mustache" contest), and forbade anyone to call me Gerry. Still, someone occasionally raises the issue of my Jewish mother as an attempt to undermine my bona fides as a spokesman for or representative of the Latino community.

My drama is acted out in public, but I am not unlike millions of other half-, quarter-, eighth-, and other fractional breeds in having to face the question of identity at times in our lives. More important, the question of whether someone is Hispanic has consequences now that Latinos are coalescing and becoming a community that votes its perceived interests on issues like immigration and the economy.

What answer do you give the census taker when he or she asks what your ethnicity is? If we remember that the two practical reasons for unambiguous ethnic identification are to identify discrimination or, its flip side, qualification for affirmative action, the question has real-world considerations on a host of issues ranging from school admissions to business preferences to tax credits.

Are we a distinct racial group, like African-Americans or Asians? Are we an ethnic group, like the Eastern Europeans? Or are we more like the Jews, a multiracial conglomerate, essentially an informal tribe united by common beliefs and a shared gene pool stretching back to the beginning of history?

Is an Irish-born man or an Italian-born woman transformed into a Hispanic if they live in Mexico? What if they lived in Mexico, but then moved here to the United States? And what about their children?

The fundamental truth about America is that we all came from someplace else. Even "Native Americans" trace their ancestors to the continent's first wave of immigrants, the hardy trekkers who crossed the land bridge from Siberia into Alaska fifteen thousand years ago.

These early birds segregated into evolving tribal cultures, eventually spreading throughout the hemisphere. The Europeans who showed up in more recent centuries usually sorted themselves by religion, the various Protestant sects to the areas now known as New England and the mid-Atlantic, the Catholics largely heading either north or south of them.

As the various civilizations clashed and coalesced, thanks largely to the unparalleled success of the British Empire worldwide, the Anglo-Protestant culture also became dominant in the northern hemisphere of the New World. Here, in an extraordinary run that rivals any empire of any place or time, ex-pat Brits and their descendants created our incredible democratic Republic.

True, half of them were guilty of what Lincoln later, in 1854, called "the monstrous injustice of slavery," which "deprives our republican example of its just influence in the world, enables the enemies of free institutions, with plausibility, to taunt us as hypocrites." But, unique in the world at the time, they established a system of government that still works four centuries after Plymouth Rock. Before you tell me to hold my horses and remind me of the countless contributions of this or that other racial, religious or ethnic group over the generations to the establishment of our great nation, remember what Barack Obama said about how different he looks from all those old white guys pictured on our currency.

Our first thirty-four presidents were all what we are now calling Anglo-Americans. That is, Caucasians whose religion is Protestant. Irish-Catholic John F. Kennedy interrupted the skein for a mere three years, 1961 to 1963, before Lyndon B. Johnson, another white Anglo-Saxon, in his case Texas Protestant, took over after the assassination of the young and gracious thirty-fifth president. The old-school white guys held that top job until the unprecedented triumph of the African-American, part-Protestant, part-Muslim junior senator from Illinois in 2008.

But even as they dominated the nation's cultural, social and financial power structure over the years since Jamestown circa 1607, a trick gene had been implanted in America's DNA. It was the integration time bomb that would ultimately alter the face of the nation. Remember Pocahontas.

The world's most-successful-free-country-ever offered something unheard of: societal mobility. Despite often draconian restrictions, sanctioned cruelty and institutionalized de jure racism, over time Americans gained relative freedom to move, marry and work our way out of bondage, poverty and serfdom, and, after centuries of blood, sweat and hardship, even the "great stain" itself, slavery, was abolished by Lincoln's 1863 Emancipation Proclamation.

Slavery's wicked younger brother, Jim Crow segregation, took another hundred years, but in Lyndon Johnson's Great Society, even segregation and laws prohibiting miscegenation fell into history's trash heap.

It took a while. Remember, until the U.S. Supreme Court struck down Virginia's Racial Integrity Act in 1967 it was illegal for an interracial couple to live together in the commonwealth and other states of the white supremacist Old Confederacy. Glad my parents never visited. I was twenty-four years old in 1967. Isn't it a trip that it took that long? Isn't it also wild that in 2008 a respectable majority of Virginians voted for Barack Obama, the son of an interracial marriage that would have been illegal when he was born?

As America acted out its harsh red-white-black-brown-yellow racial drama, each successive immigrant wave initially clung to its native identity. The age of the hyphenated identity was upon us, with its Irish-, German-, Italian-, Polish-, Asian-, Latino-, African-—and others too numerous to name—Americans.

But as freedoms expanded in chaos and conflict, or driven by conscience or personal commercial success, those imported cultures broke out of their locked boxes. They spread and blended as barriers between tribes gradually but inevitably eased. And the entire process of assimilation was hugely accelerated by social, racial, religious and romantic integration. Irish longshoreman married Italian girls. Greek sailors hooked up with Russians, Asian women with Jewish shopkeepers and so forth. For a time it seemed to me that every pretty Puerto Rican girl around New york was marrying an Irish cop or fireman. The mosaic began to melt, and there were increasingly ample immigrant ingredients to stir into the blender.

When in 1940 my second-generation-immigrant Eastern European Jewish mother met and married my first-generation-immigrant Puerto Rican Catholic father, her parents freaked, sitting shivah, the traditional mourning of the Jewish faith when a loved one passes away. In time things settled, the rough edges smoothed and the five children of Cruz Rivera and Lilly Friedman Rivera became double-hyphenated heirs to two gene pools that could not be more distinct.

But while my folks were intermarriage pioneers who bucked conventional mores back in dawn of the Jazz Age, they certainly have plenty of company now. That is especially true among Latinos, who, because of various important historic and aesthetic reasons, are of all races, far more multiracial than any other American ethnic grouping.

A DNA sample of the average Puerto Rican would yield quantities of European, Caribbean and African heritage, among others. A typical Mexican's DNA would be spiced with Aztec or Mayan blood at least. Many Japanese have settled in unlikely nations like Peru, bringing their unique DNA across the South Pacific to South America. And that stew has only been freshened by the Latino experience here in the United States.

These days, one out of every four Hispanics is married to a non-Hispanic white spouse. That rate of intermarriage is much lower among recently arrived immigrants. When only U.S.-born Hispanics (like me) are considered, fully one in three is married to a non-Hispanic spouse (as I am). And intermarriage is even more intense a trend than that in some parts of the land. Most recent immigrants are still concentrated in the South and Southwest. When you go outside that geographical region, fully half of all younger, native-born Hispanics are married to a non-Hispanic spouse. Every other one. It reminds me of the old rank about intermarriage killing more Jews than the Holocaust.

My family is a classic example of the intermarriage phenomenon.

After our parents' example, with one exception, we five Rivera children married—and, in some cases, remarried, and in my case re-re-re-remarried—non-Hispanics. Because of the subsequent spreading of our dearly beloved gene pool, the generation that follows my siblings and me can scarcely be identified by ethnicity; hyphens have become unwieldy, bordering on obsolete.

My five children are, in order of birth:

Gabriel Miguel, who is five-eighths Eastern European, one-quarter Puerto Rican and one-eighth Italian-American, is a handsome computer genius living in southern California whose religious preference, I think, is still Jewish, as is that of his beautiful bride Deb (a certified UCLA Ph.D. genius, and our first Dr. Rivera!), although they definitely have Buddhist tendencies.

My dashing twenty-one-year-old Cruz Grant is half-Mexican, one-quarter Puerto Rican and one-quarter Eastern European. He attends New York's Maritime College, looks great in uniform, and his religious preference has always been Catholic.

Isabella Holmes and Simone Cruikshank, my darling, accomplished, gorgeous teenage daughters, are half-Scottish, one-quarter Puerto Rican and one-quarter Eastern European, and their religious preference is Episcopalian, although Isabella loves Shabbat.

And, last but not least, my pearl, Sol Liliana, our precious and the pride of my stunning, fabulous wife, Erica's and my adoring eyes, is three-quarters Eastern European and one-quarter Puerto Rican. Her religious preference when she becomes old enough to express one will probably be Jewish, like her mommy and daddy.

What is a young person with an unmistakably Latino last name like ours to put down when asked for racial or ethnic identification on a college or job application? To what group or subgroup do we and they belong?

During the Nazi era, a single Jewish grandparent out of four was enough to doom a person as Jewish enough for the gas chamber. In the noxious 1896 *Plessy v. Ferguson* case, the United States Supreme Court ruled that it was constitutional for Louisiana to require Homer Plessy, who was one-eighth black and seven-eighths white, to be confined to sit in the "colored" car.

The awesomely intermarried Native Americans are said to be "Indian" enough to be considered among our original inhabitants if they have a single great-grandparent from a federally recognized tribe among their ancestors. In their case, the implications are practical and relevant to issues like tribal treaty rights, access to various programs and sometimes even economic windfalls like oil rights, cigarette sales or the right to build and operate a casino.

Recalling the dramatic statistics with which I began this essay, about the nation's coming Hispanic 25 percent plurality in 2040 and Hispanics' ultimate majority by the end of the twenty-first century, the question that must be asked is, what impact does intermarriage have on those demographic prospects?

If my children are all recorded as Hispanic on Census data, the grand total will be far greater than if some arbitrary test of racial or ethnic purity is imposed. And I'm sure they will, if asked, tell people they are proud to be Hispanic, in the same way Americans with even a drop of Irish blood claim to be heirs of Saint Patrick. In the case of the Irish, the proud claims far exceed actual intimate ties to the Emerald Isle by a mile, according to the experts.

"Hispanic intermarriage may have been a factor in the phenomenal growth of the U.S. Hispanic population in recent years, and it has important implications for future growth and characteristics of the Hispanic population," said a 2005 study on intermarriage by the Population Reference Bureau.

Demographers Sharon Lee and Barry Edmonston put it this way in their comprehensive study "Hispanic Intermarriage, Identification and U.S. Latino Population Change" published December 2006 in the *Social Science Quarterly*:

"Almost two-thirds of children of intermarried Hispanics are identified as Hispanic. The Hispanic population in 2025 is larger by almost one million when Hispanic intermarriage and identification rates are included in population projections. Intermarriage and the propensity of 'part-Hispanics' to identify as Hispanic will be significant contributors to future Hispanic population growth, with implications for the meaning of Hispanic ethnicity and ethnic-based public policies."

Despite our enormous pride in being Latino, those who believe that current immigrants from Asia, Latin America and the Caribbean are less able or willing to be assimilated than those from European countries "may be making two important errors," said Barry Edmonston in a separate article, "Statistics on U.S. Immigration."

First, they assume current racial categories are fixed and essential, when intermarriage means necessarily that the boundaries between groups may "blur in the future. Our ideas of what constitutes race or a racial difference are likely to be very different in a few decades just as they are now very different from what they were at the beginning of the twentieth century."

Clearly, intermarriage should be a major factor in the phasing out of race-based preferences of all sorts, business, academic and tax policy. At what point will Hispanic ethnicity become like Italian, Irish, German or Polish ethnicity have become today? Like those white ethnics before us, we have the ability to proclaim and celebrate our roots, our affinity, shared interests, values, and our position on various issues like immigration, and how profoundly irritating we find hateful rhetoric. But if anyone learned anything from the outcome of the 2008 presidential contest it's that even part-Latinos will never again allow to prevail race-based, race-baiting anti-immigration policies that are barely disguised bash-a-Mexican fests.

Remember, in the film *My Big Fat Greek Wedding*, when the Greek-born dad tells his daughter that he doesn't care who she marries; as long as their children go to Greek school the way their mom did, then Grandpa would be happy? That's the way it is with my children. All five of them have been educated in Spanish in school at one time or another; even the baby spent time in a Spanish-immersion preschool. My big boys have both studied Spanish abroad in Mexico and Spain, we have a home in Puerto Rico, we wrap ourselves in our mostly Hispanic-dominated family, we all love Spanish food, and we march proudly in New York's annual Puerto Rican Day parade, shouting, "*¡Viva la raza!*" or "*¡Viva Puerto Rico!*"

Of more practical effect, as a family, we are also in sympathy and in sync with Hispanics from the top to the bottom of the socioeconomic ladder. When Lou Dobbs insults a young Mexican immigrant, he insults us.

None of which minimizes another essential—perhaps *the* essential— truth: We are all patriotic and responsible American citizens who love our country, and identify with and for our nation first, foremost and without limit. But like most Americans, we are somebody more and different too.

When Barry Obama decided to define himself and declare his racial and ethnic roots to the world, he began using his given name, Barack Hussein Obama. But as happened in my own life, he encountered head-winds because some felt he was neither black nor white. Once he chose a racial side he struggled to be accepted as black enough. That quest is part of what led him to the South Side of Chicago and into the ultimately toxic embrace of the Reverend Jeremiah Wright. And it was the political firestorm created by the revelations of the reverend's sometimes-inflamed black-liberation theology that forced candidate Obama to retreat from his hard-earned blackness.

In his seminal speech on race Obama went to great lengths to remind mainstream white America that he was also part of their crowd, part Barry, just as Geraldo will always be part Gerry.

"I can no more disown him [Reverend Wright] than I can disown the black community," Mr. Obama said. "I can no more disown him than I can my white grandmother—a woman who helped raise me, a woman who sacrificed again and again for me, a woman who loves me as much as she loves anything in this world, but a woman who once confessed her fear of black men who passed by her on the street, and who on more than one occasion has uttered racial or ethnic stereotypes that made me cringe," he said, calming mainstream nerves that he had a secret Black Panther–like hidden racial agenda.

The bottom line is that Barack Obama is not the first black president. He is the first half-black, half-white president—a mixed-breed. Unless you want to apply that old *Plessy v. Ferguson* rule that a state can decide that one drop of black blood means a person is all-black.

Separate but equal, which *Plessy* was really about, was finally repudiated by the Supreme Court in *Brown v. Board of Education* in 1954. But that one-drop rule may actually be true in a good way. Sometimes I feel both all-Jewish and all-Latino. Sometimes I also feel all-Catholic, but that is for another book. As our brilliant young president said charmingly when talking about what breed of puppy he and first lady Michelle wanted for their adorable daughters in the White House, he answered maybe "a mutt like me."

SPANGLISH

The Rapid Spread of the World's Newest Language

"¡El roofo está leakiano!"
—Spanglish expression (The proper Spanish: *"Hay una gotera en el techo."*)

L ike the Irish, Italian, German and Jewish immigrants and others who came in great waves to the East Coast between 1850 and 1920, Hispanics are also blending into the dominant culture in America's great melting pot. We are assimilating, but even as we do there is something else going on.

Because there are so many Latinos concentrated particularly in the Southeast and Southwest, we are not disappearing as a distinctive ethnic group; we are acculturating, changing, even as we change the world around us. Acculturation is defined in the *American Heritage Dictionary of the English Language* as "the modification of the culture of a group or individual as a result of contact with a different culture." So even as what's been called "the Great American Assimilation Machine" chugs on, making U.S. Latino culture distinctive from Latino cultures in other countries, that blended culture is also changing and being changed by the ways of the non-Spanish-speaking population in the United States.

One example is the extraordinary explosion of perhaps history's most charming new language, one that has vast flexibility and few rules. It's an in-between lingo that varies from geographic location and nation of origin, an almost totally subjective combination whose linguistic emphasis depends on the competence of the speaker in either English or Spanish. A 2007 survey jointly conducted by the New Generation Latino Consortium (NGLC) and New American Dimensions (NAD) found that young Latinos were embracing a new hybrid culture.

"Many in the anti-immigration movement incorrectly characterize all Hispanics as rejecters of English who resist the impulse to become American," notes David Morse, president and CEO of NAD. "It's simply not true. Our study shows that young, U.S.-born Hispanics are submerging themselves into American culture wholesale. Although they may participate in the popular culture of two different languages, there is a clear preference for English—and 'Spanglish.'"

On the one pole, those who are essentially Spanish speakers, mostly the newer arrivals, flavor their speech with occasional words of English. *"Tengo que ir a* (I have to go to) school." "Don't *backupear* the car into the *yarda."* "Brenda is *pregneada"* (for pregnant, when the actual Spanish would be either *embarazada* or *encinta).* Or signs that warn Latino day workers *"No Hangear"*—"Don't hang out here." *Troca* is "truck," not the traditional word, *camión.*

On the other pole are the totally assimilated, who can barely order a burrito or enchilada at Taco Bell. "I'm not buying a drink for that *borracho* (drunk)." "That's *chévere* (cool)!" *"Serio, hombre* (Man, I'm serious)." *"¿Tiene chicle?"* ("Do you have gum?") "Let's sit on the *porche* (porch)." "He's a *mojado* (wetback/recent immigrant) or *tinto* (African-American)." *"¡Wachar!"* ("Watch it") *"Ya estuvo."* ("I'm done.") "Pedro *trabaja* (Pedro works) overtime."

Though it distresses both the Royal Academy of the Spanish Language in Madrid and English-only anti-immigration activists in the United States, to appreciate the almost stealthy penetration of Spanish words into the spoken American English language, consider the widespread adoption of the following words into everyday language in the United States: *amigo, armada, avocado, bodega, bonanza, burro, chipotle, chorizo, cigarro, desperado, El Niño, embarcadero, gringo, hacienda, hombre, incommunicado, iguana, jaguar, loco, macho, mojito, mole, mosquito, mustang, nacho, negro, olé, paella, peyote, piña colada, poncho, quesadilla, rancho, renegade, rumba, salsa, savvy, sierra, sombrero, taco, tequila, tomato, tortilla, turista,* and *vigilante.*

Given their almost universal adoption by English-only speakers, you can make a strong argument that Spanish is no longer a "foreign" language. The question, "*¿Qué está pasando?*" ("What's happening?") would be understood by most English-only speakers, as would, "*¡Yo estoy freziando!*" ("I'm freezing!") or "*¡No parquear!*" ("No parking," rather than the true Spanish "*No estacionar*") "*Voy a pagar con* (I'm going to pay with) cash." "*Puede* (can you) babysit?" "*Tengo que enviar un* (I have to send an) e-mail."

English has also altered U.S. spoken Spanish in a huge way, making the informal but widespread blending of the two a fresh and alternative way of communicating. Called Spanglish by some, or Cubonics (for Cubans in south Florida during the 1960s), it is perhaps the world's newest and fastest-growing language. Unlike pig latin, it is a real linguistic phenomenon whose impact ranges from practical to comical.

Whether it is labeled a fusion, a collage or a hybrid, there is no doubt but that millions of people, especially young people, flavor either their English or their Spanish with proper words from the other language or jury-rigged words that are true mishmash hodgepodges. "To change" becomes *changear* (not *cambiar*, the Spanish word). "Microwave" becomes *microonda. El machino* is used for "machine," not the Spanish *la máquina.*

There are no rules for Spanglish other than that it is a blend of both languages in varying degrees, usually depending on the specific fluency of the speaker or the region of the country. "*Tengo que estar* (I have to be) home *por* midnight." "*Se vende rins* (tires for sale)." "*Vamos al* (Let's go to the) movies." "*Quiero café y un* (I want coffee and a) sandwich." "*Ella es muy* (She's very) sexy!"

Without being overly technical, Spanglish is not the same as a truly bilingual person switching, as many of my cousins do, effortlessly from Spanish to English in the same sentence. "*Mami,* Bobby *está enfermo y no va a* school today." And it's not the same as the English words being adopted by Spanish speakers, like "*Ella es* cool" or "*tengo que parquear el* bus," "*necesito un klinex*" or "*¿puedo usar su laptopa?*"

Spanglish can also function as a lingua franca, a third language used by people who don't share one. It has the effect of allowing the huge, newly arrived Latino population to communicate in an overwhelmingly English-speaking environment. "*¿Puedo usar la* (Can I use the) Internet?" "*¿Á qué hora* (what time) do you work *mañana?*" "*Usa el* flash *para su foto.*" "*Me voy al* (I'm going to) school."

And it allows English speakers to order in restaurants, instruct their Spanish-speaking employees and associates, celebrate Cinco de Mayo, complete with piñatas, or find their way around those fabulous Spanish-speaking vacation resorts, especially to the *baño.*

When I'm on Spanish radio, or addressing a primarily Spanish-speaking audience, those English speakers listening almost always get the gist of my remarks. "*Estoy muy ocupado con la situación en el* Middle East." "*Si quiere hablar conmigo, enviarme un* e-mail." "*Me gusta salsa más que* rock and roll."

In the most comprehensive attempt to codify the lingo, Ilan Stavans, a Mexican-American professor at Amherst College, wrote *Spanglish: The Making of a New American Language* in 2003. In the book Professor Stavans attempts to translate Miguel de Cervantes's classic book *Don Quijote de La Mancha,* into Spanglish. It is pretty funny, but I'll bet you get the drift even if you don't command any Spanish.

"*In un placete de La Mancha of which nombre no quiero remembrearme, vivía, not so long ago, uno de esos gentlemen who always tienen una lanza in the rack, una buckler antigua, a skinny caballo, y un greyhound para el chase. A cazuela with más beef than mutón, carne choppeada para la dinner, un omelet pa' los Sábados, lentil pa' los Viernes, y algún pigeon como delicacy especial pa' los Domingos, con-sumían tres cuarers de su income. . . . Livin with él eran una housekeeper en sus forties, una sobrina not yet twenty y un ladino del field.*"

Professor Stavans also taught a course on Spanglish at Amherst. "The course spans almost five hundred years, from 1521 to the present," read the 2000 college catalog. "It starts with the Spanish explorers to Florida and ends with today's rappers and poets. . . . The various modalities of Spanglish, spoken by, among other groups, Nuyoricans, Chicanos, and Cuban-Americans, will be compared. The development of Spanglish as a street jargon will be compared to Yiddish, Ebonics, and other minority tongues."

Professor Stavans's efforts notwithstanding, Spanish-language purists loathe Spanglish. Several years ago, Yale University Spanish literature professor Roberto González said, "Spanglish is an invasion of Spanish by English. Spanglish treats Spanish as if the language of Cervantes, Lorca, García Márquez, Borges and Paz does not have an essence and dignity of its own."

Dude, *cálmate*. Most users are young, and to them Spanglish is really less about communicating and more about belonging. It's like a secret handshake, a poets' society, inside joke, wink or a nod. It is an announcement that "Hey, I'm cool too and, regardless of modest circumstance, proud to be part of the club."

Chévere.

CONCLUSION
The Shared Destiny of America and Her Latino Population

I n March 2009, all twenty-four members of the Congressional Hispanic Caucus met with President Barack Obama at his invitation in the White House. Aside from reminding the new, still popular, but already embattled chief executive that Latinos had essentially put him in office with their record turnout and two-to-one vote in his favor, the caucus had as its principal goal, as reported by Tyche Hendsicks in the San Francisco Chronicle, of "holding the president to his promise" to overhaul the nation's dysfunctional immigration system. Following the meeting, the Latino leaders professed that they were pleased with the results, because the president pledged that he would move forward with a plan for, as the White House statement had it, "comprehensive immigration reform."

The president called the meeting a "robust and strategic" conversation on immigration, but it was clear that the subject most on the mind of even that great supporter of reform was the security situation along the Mexican border. "During the meeting," read the White House statement, "the President announced that he will travel to Mexico [in April 2009] to meet with President Calderón to discuss the deep and comprehensive U.S.-Mexico relationship, including how the United States and Mexico can work together to support Mexico's fight against drug-related violence and work toward effective, comprehensive immigration reform."

The following day, I was on the panel of the 13th Annual U.S.-Mexico Border Issues Conference organized in Washington by the U.S.-Mexico Chamber of Commerce and Congressman Silvestre Reyes of El Paso, Texas. The room was packed with congressmen, businesspeople and various interest groups favoring immigration reform, including Congressman Xavier Becerra of California, who spoke glowingly of the meeting with President Obama and his reaffirmation of essential support for immigration reform.

When it was my turn to speak, I threw ice water on the celebratory rhetoric, suggesting that the representatives were burying the lead, and that the real headline out of the White House meeting was that the president had offered neither a commitment to support specific reform legislation nor a timetable within which his "support" would be implemented. I told the audience that if we cared about Mr. Obama, that vagueness was a good thing, because the last thing this president needed right now was to reignite the acidic debate over immigration. I also pointed out the polls showing in early 2009 that, given the current climate, the Latino community puts education and the economy ahead of immigration as issues it is concerned about.

Nobody knows where or when the Great Recession will end. But clearly, with 13 million Americans newly unemployed over the last two years, at this critical moment in history, most citizens would not make legalizing 12 million undocumented immigrants a priority. Perhaps by the time you read this, the economic crisis will have waned, and the country will be in a better, more generous mood. If so, immigration reform will again be on the front burner in Washington. As the sixty-five-year-old head of a huge extended family, which has lost a fortune in 401(k) money to the collapsed stock market, I deeply hope there is light at the end of this scary financial tunnel.

But that light may be a long time coming, and the evolution of the nation's Latino community cannot wait.

Our legislative agenda must be tailored to these tough times. If anyone needed evidence of that, witness the reaction from political conservatives to House Speaker Nancy Pelosi's address to a mostly Hispanic gathering at St. Anthony's Church in San Francisco two days before the White House Hispanic leadership meeting. Invited by Chicago Congressman Luis Gutierrez, as part of a seventeen-city, cross-country tour called United Families, which Gutierrez described as intending to put a human face on the immigration debate, Speaker Pelosi harshly criticized workplace raids by Immigration and Customs Enforcement (ICE):

"Who in this country would not want to change a policy of kicking in doors in the middle of the night and sending a parent away from their families? We have to have a change in policy and practice and again . . . I can't say enough, the raids must end. The raids must end."

The Speaker added, "It must be stopped. . . . What value system is that? I think it's un-American. I think it's un-American." She then joined Representative Gutierrez and the crowd at St. Anthony's chanting, "*Sí, Se Puede*,"—"Yes, It Can Be Done."

"We think that families are the cornerstone of our society and our nation, and an immigration system should preserve those families, not destroy them," Gutierrez told FOX News, making a point that, as you know, I ardently believe.

But hidden among the cheering crowd was Rick Oltman, an anti-immigration activist associated with a group calling itself Californians for Population Stabilization. Once the meeting was over, Oltman summed up the prevailing sentiment of about 60 percent of all non-Hispanic Americans (if the most recent polls are to be believed), saying, "I was embarrassed by what [Speaker Pelosi] said. Exhorting illegal aliens for taking responsibility for our country's future . . . In fact, sitting there in the audience I really resented that comment. I think it was pandering to the crowd but also insulting to American citizens who consider themselves to be patriotic, who obey the rule of law."

FOX News and several other media outlets adopted Mr. Oltman's outraged tone, treating the revelation of the content and tone of the Speaker's remarks as one more example of how out of touch she was with "ordinary" Americans.

I made a point of bringing up that hostile anti-Pelosi reaction when I spoke at the Border Issues Conference later in the week. My problem with the remarks, though I agree with and applaud her sincerity, is that she was preaching to a choir of immigrants, many of whom have been separated from their families by strict border enforcement, the crushed U.S. economy and the immigration mess. They are not the audience needed to either encourage reform or spur the president to act any faster.

At the conference, I spelled out an agenda for immigration advocates, which in the spring of 2009 was realistic and attainable, given the current realities.

First, we must recognize that Mexico's border violence is real, it is dangerous and it will color every aspect of the immigration debate until it is resolved. The more bilateral communication there is between the United States and Mexico the better, particularly at the presidential level. Mexico needs to feel that we view the country as more than just an exporter of undocumented immigrants and drugs. That we see Mexico as a partner, however troubled it is at the moment.

Speaking of the U.S. president's strong show of support for embattled President Calderón during the subsequent meeting in Mexico City, Dr. Juan Hernandez, former assistant to the Mexican president, cautioned me that, "President Obama finds a very different Mexico than the humble nation President Bush encountered. A Mexican people that on the one hand sees Obama as a rock star with incredible popularity. But Mr. Obama also encounters a Mexico that feels its institutions are stronger than ever, essentially solid and democratic, and one which wants to have equal status."

And while Dr. Hernandez's optimism may overstate Mexico's reality, it is clear at this point that our neighbor will not become a failed state, at least so long as its most revered institution, the Mexican army, prevails. Any reasonable assistance the nation's armed forces and federal law enforcement officials need in the fight against the drug cartels, overt or covert, must be provided, and the relationship between nations strengthened, augmented so it becomes more like the "special" relationship we have with Britain. Mexico is our new Ireland in terms of its vast contribution to the

American pie: the largest source of immigrants, and the nation destined in the twenty-first century therefore to play the biggest role in reshaping what America will look like.

Second, we must advocate quiet diplomacy with and within our own government on the immigration issue. This is not the time for street demonstrations or protests or waving "foreign" flags. This is the time passionately but quietly to support Homeland Security Secretary Janet Napolitano as she redirects ICE to its intended mission of fighting terrorists and criminal aliens, rather than raiding shops, fields and factories and destroying the lives of hardworking, law-abiding men and women who want only to provide a decent life for their families.

Secretary Napolitano knows the raids are foolish, wasteful and misdirected. They are a fraud against taxpayers who thought they were paying for elite cops to bust gangsters and terrorists, and instead watched as they were ordered to break into homes and workplaces and check identification to sort out the documented and the undocumented among the terrorized residents. We have to ask lawmakers on both sides of the aisle whether Phoenix would be the nation's kidnapping capital if ICE had not been diverted from the tough job of busting organized criminals and was instead directed to waste its time arresting meatpackers and chicken pluckers in Iowa, North Carolina and Mississippi.

This easy, no-cost change in recent federal policy does not require any new legislation, but its impact on the lives of American Hispanics is nevertheless profound. It will have the immediate practical effect of relieving the awful pressure on the 12 million undocumented workers and their families currently residing in this country. If the undocumented know the *Migra* is not going to be kicking in their doors at three a.m., then they can wait a reasonable period to have their status officially resolved. They will sleep better in the meantime knowing that ICE will not be victimizing them just because the agents have a quota of illegal workers to arrest by a certain date. (I was heartened that Secretary Napolitano has redirected hundreds of ICE agents to supplement other agencies now properly targeting the drug bandits.)

Following that reorganization of ICE, by using RICO and other federal criminal conspiracy statutes designed to fight organized crime, ICE and related law enforcement agencies can target criminal syndicates like the Aztecas, the Zetas, MS-13 and the 18th Street Gang, the way they went after the Italian Mafia and the Russian mob. Instead of wasting their time and our money ruining Juan's or Selena's life in Postville, Iowa, they can investigate, harass, arrest and convict real criminals and actual terrorist aliens.

Moreover, redirecting ICE will not only help the Mexicans in the fight for their nation's life against the drug cartels, it will also tremendously enhance law enforcement vis-à-vis the cartels' criminal operations here in the United States. And by so doing they can also redirect the Justice Department to its sworn mission. Instead of using eager young U.S. attorneys to prosecute workers who happen to hold a fake Social Security card, we can use those budding Eliot Nesses to prosecute killers, kidnappers, drug traffickers and creeps.

None of this requires debate. None of this should stir the ire of either proponents or opponents of immigration reform; yet the impact will be felt immediately in our community in the four corners of the United States.

The other part of this is the recognition that for the American Latino community as a whole, regardless of original nationality, be it Spanish, Mexican, Central or South American, Caribbean, Nuyorican or Chicano, the most important issue today is education. Our woeful performance on standardized tests, our dropout rate, our devaluing of education must end. *¡Despiértate!* Wake up! The education siesta is over. Every government program designed to help must be geared to encouraging education, motivating children and, importantly, providing tangible incentives to their parents to get involved. We must provide whatever is reasonable and appropriate to give our kids the chance to succeed.

In that regard, Latino leaders, as I said to the packed audience at the Border Issues Conference at the Rayburn House Office Building in March 2009, should use their newfound clout to push for passage of the DREAM Act. Let us put the omnibus issue of immigration reform on the shelf for now; it will keep until the next round of domestic initiatives. In the meantime, we must seek to improve opportunity for our youngsters, citizen, legal resident, visitor and immigrant alike. Nothing is more important than the economy and education right now, not even amnesty for undocumented workers.

If the DREAM Act is made the law of the land, the children of those migrant workers will have access to public schools and universities and to the military. Their lives will be regularized and their path into adulthood and citizenship made more promising.

Even as those youngsters are given a better shot at personal success in their worthwhile pursuit of the American dream, the governments of Mexico, the nations of Central America, the Dominican Republic and Puerto Rico, who are sending us their children, must do their part by making English-language training mandatory for all their children in their schools. Those governments know and want their youngsters to emigrate to the United States, at least for a time. Many of their economies depend on remittances from those children and their parents back to relatives who never left.

Why not provide those school-age youngsters before they leave home with a skill that will definitely give them more positive options and outcomes in their lives? The skills they need to do more, do better and get paid for it. I have little patience for those who criticize gringos and *yanquis* at the same time they have their hand out looking for what America can uniquely provide. Mandatory English-language training in all Latin American public schools is not a political statement. It has nothing to do with sovereignty, nationalism, chauvinism or hometown pride. It is a pragmatic recognition of twenty-first-century transnational reality. It is about giving the children a shot at a better life for themselves and their children.

Retaining our special identity as we continue to evolve into Americans first and foremost, we must assimilate and become part of the mosaic, melting pot or whatever metaphor suits you. In that regard, the special language needs of Hispanic children must be addressed. They must be given the resources they need to speak, read and write English. More generally, they must go to school, because absent that commitment to education, they risk becoming a permanent Hispanic underclass, with disturbing echoes of feudal society and serfdom. The primary responsibility for making that happen lies squarely on the shoulders of parents, not truant officers.

From Georgia to Arkansas to North Carolina to Nevada, from coast to coast and across the land, the category of students who are deficient in English is the fastest-growing segment of the public education population. That is an unavoidable fact, as, in a historic heartbeat, the surging Latino population has remade entire communities. Thirty-nine percent of Hispanic youngsters in the United States today are foreign-born. Like it or not they are here. However you feel about the inevitable Latinizing of America, it is now part of our national heritage that must be recognized and adjustments made.

Like every other big wave of immigrants going back to the middle of the eighteenth century, newly arrived Latinos are reenergizing some tired communities and causing increased friction and social problems in others. In the long term, whether immigration is popular or unpopular or even good or bad for the nation matters little. Even if not a single additional migrant arrived at our door, the demographic reality is that, going forward, the United States will be increasingly Latino, until by the end of this century the United States of America is majority Latino. Clearly, it is therefore in everyone's best interest that Hispanic Americans progress and, ultimately, prosper.

And even as Puerto Rican citizens of the United States from our new governor Luis Fortuño to me stand firmly by the side of Mexicans and other immigrants in advocating their rights, we also need those communities support to help us end Puerto Rico's 111 years in political purgatory. President Obama and the Congress must recognize the corrosive nature of Puerto Rico's colonial relationship with the United States and help *la Isla del Encanto* finally to choose between statehood and independence.

It is time for us also to put up or shut up when it comes to family responsibility. Aid to Dependent Children and similar federal programs can be helpful on a transitory basis, but long-term they are corrosive of ambition and self-esteem; they rot souls. Our community leaders must stop demanding extraordinary assistance, or that historic wrongs be righted and follow the lead of people like comedian, actor and social activist Bill Cosby who defies the race politicians and encourages personal responsibility in the African-American community. Programs should be crafted with goals larger than mere subsistence. *Sí, se puede*—"yes, it can be done"—is more than a political rallying cry. It is a noble goal and aspiration.

In some ways my life is odd and adventurous; in most others it is middle-class and, hopefully, reassuring. I'm like Oprah or Lassie, on a first-name basis with America. But aside from my colorful past and my unpredictable and improvisational workweek, like you, most of what I think about is my wife and kids, family, job, friends, pals, pets and how much is still in my 401(k). I go down that personal checklist first, knowing that at any moment the world fire alarm could go off and I could be sent somewhere I never expected next Tuesday. So I'm ready to roll for job and country anywhere, anytime. But in almost every other way I'm an ordinary, tax-paying, law-abiding, mid-brow American.

After a forty-year public career, being in many ways one of the nation's familiar and comfortable old shoes, I note with considerable chagrin that many, if not most, of my regular FOX News audience disagrees with me on immigration reform, this great issue of the day. Even though I promised myself this book would not be about immigration, that issue is central to this one big disagreement with people I otherwise like and who, more important, pay my bills. Working at FOX News gives a person an appreciation of the other guy's arguments on issues like gay marriage and abortion rights and, yes, even immigration. My positions on those issues have not changed— I still passionately support personal freedom, fairness and a path to normalcy for the undocumented—but I understand the sincerity and potency of the other point of worldview.

That is why I have tried to spell out a compromise position on immigration that I believe to be in the nation's best interest. Latinos are part of America's Great Progression, the next wave. As with those who came before, the nation will change us more than we change the nation. Given the chance we will help lead the United States to a new era of prosperity. Just call off ICE. Recognize that the federal program known as 287 (g) that deputizes local cops to enforce immigration laws has only deflected them from their mission of protecting and serving their communities. As Maricopa County Sheriff Joe Arpaio parades undocumented workers around in pink underwear, Phoenix, his principal city, has become a viper's nest of kidnappers and killers. Lower the temperature on the immigration debate. Celebrate the new union movement; they are far more reasonable than they have ever been, and their inclusiveness is unprecedented. Work with Mexico, Cuba, Venezuela and the rest of Central and South America. Remember the Monroe Doctrine. Don't cede the region to the neo-Communists. Be a good neighbor. Iron out a legal way that the transborder workforce can operate to garner the fruits of its labors and increase the bottom line for American farms and businesses.

And recognize that our nation stands on the frontier of monumental changes that will leave the United States unalterably changed, yet still the same, a beacon of liberty, enterprise and opportunity for the world. We are truly in this together.

Pass the salsa.